REIMAGINING

BRAZILIAN

TELEVISION

LATINO AND LATIN AMERICAN PROFILES

FREDERICK LUIS ALDAMA, EDITOR

REIMAGINING BRAZILIAN TELEVISION

LUIZ FERNANDO CARVALHO'S CONTEMPORARY VISION

ELI LEE CARTER

UNIVERSITY OF PITTSBURGH PRESS

Published by the University of Pittsburgh Press, Pittsburgh, Pa., 15260
Copyright © 2018, University of Pittsburgh Press
All rights reserved
Manufactured in the United States of America
Printed on acid-free paper
10 9 8 7 6 5 4 3 2 1

Cataloging-in-Publication data is available from the Library of Congress

ISBN 13: 978-0-8229-6498-8
ISBN 10: 0-8229-6498-8

Cover art: Makeup from *Capitu* (2008). Right to reproduce granted by TV Globo.
Cover design by Melissa Dias-Mandoly

To the villages in California and Rio de Janeiro that raised me /
Às aldeias na Califórnia e no Rio de Janeiro que me criaram

CONTENTS

ACKNOWLEDGMENTS

Although the seeds that gave life to this book were first planted during under-graduate study abroad trips to São Paulo and Rio de Janeiro, I began formally working on early versions while a PhD student at the University of California, Los Angeles. While in its present form the book has changed significantly from my time at UCLA, the final version owes much to the Eugene V. Cota-Robles Fellowship, the Graduate Research Mentorship Fellowship, the Dissertation Year Fellowship, the Graduate Summer Research Mentorship Award, and the Tinker Field Research Grant, which I received from the Department of Spanish and Portuguese, the Graduate Division, and the Latin American Institute. I am also thankful to the University of Virginia for having awarded me a number of grants (Excellence in Diversity Fellowship, Summer Stipend Award, and the AHSS/VPR), all of which allowed me to spend time in Rio de Janeiro to conduct research and write.

Over the years, a number of people have contributed to the completion of this project. In terms of my scholarship and intellectual development three deserve special recognition: Randal Johnson for teaching me new ways to think about Brazilian cultural production, for pushing me to refine and complete my work, and for modeling how to be a professional academic; José Luiz Passos for teaching stimulating graduate courses and expanding my knowledge of Brazilian literature; and David Haberly for so kindly reading numerous drafts of the manuscript and providing feedback that was essential in bringing the project to a close. At the University of Virginia, in addition to the Department of Spanish, Italian, and Portuguese as a whole, Hector Amaya, Daniel Chavez, Michael Gerli, Nitya Kallivayalil, Tom Klubock, Ricardo Padrón, Deborah Parker, Gustavo Pellón, and Simone Polillo all contributed to the project in their own unique ways. In Brazil, among many others, Ilana Feldman, Carlos Minchillo, and Alba Zaluar each helped as well. Last, I would like to thank the Projeto Portinari and TV Globo—specifically Mariana Panza, Rita Marques, and Thiago Lima Silva—for making available the images featured in this book.

A heartfelt thank you goes to the following family members and close friends for loving, teaching, and empowering me to be the best version of myself: Mom, Andrew, Sarah, Diane, Don, Peg, Chris, Jen, Kels, Dr. Mardini, Haifa, Tameem, Jamie, Jimmy, Joey, McG, Diego, Pedro, Vitor, Vó Marysa, Fernando, Regina, Fred, and Bisin. This is in no way sufficient recognition of your impact on my life, but know that each of you has played a central role in shaping my work and the person I am today.

REIMAGINING
BRAZILIAN
TELEVISION

Introduction

Over the past fifty years, TV Globo has dominated Brazilian television to such an extent that it has become difficult to distinguish the television network from the medium itself. Since the early 1980s, no Brazilian television director has achieved greater commercial *and* critical success than one TV Globo employee, Luiz Fernando Carvalho. This book is about the Global South's largest and most successful television network and its greatest director. More precisely, it is about the singular aesthetic and mode of production that characterizes Carvalho's work and the ways in which his work functions as both a counterpoint to and a reflection of Brazilian television fiction's past and present, and its transition into the future.

AN EMERGING POSTNETWORK ERA AND THE RISE OF THE TELEVISION DIRECTOR AND AESTHETIC INQUIRY

From the early 1950s through the mid-1980s, production and consumption of television programming in the United States were largely limited to ABC, CBS, and NBC. Media scholar Amanda Lotz contends that from the 1980s to the mid-2000s American television transitioned away from the network-centric model of production and consumption to one characterized by a proliferation of viewing options.[1] The "multichannel transition" phase, as Lotz refers to it, arose out of the confluence of technological innovations, government regulations weakening networks' control over program creation, and the emergence of "nascent cable channels and new broadcast networks," all of which expanded consumers' access to content (7–10).

By the time the multichannel transition phase had come to a close around 2005, the postnetwork era had begun to take root slowly. The characteristics of this new era are not yet fully defined, and, as Lotz herself notes, though its eventual dominance seems inevitable, even in 2014 "it remained impossible to assert that the majority of the audience had entered the post-network era or that all industrial processes had 'completed' the transition" (10). Nonetheless, it is apparent that, among other factors, incipient cable networks and Internet companies, time-shifting technologies, Video on Demand, tablets, and Internet TVs with applications like Amazon Prime, HBO Go, Hulu, and Netflix have provided spectators with more autonomy over what, when, where, and how they watch television content. Clearly, the days are now long gone when a television spectator had no option other than to sit down on a sofa in a living room at 8 p.m. to watch one of three prime time television series or sitcoms aired by the major broadcast networks.

Media executives and producers alike, particularly in the United States, but also elsewhere, understand that in response to the current audiovisual and more broadly popular culture landscape they must find innovative ways to capture increasingly diffuse and diverse audiences. While such a task is complicated relative to the network-era reality, it potentially expands opportunities for production, distribution, and reception. In a progressively more competitive marketplace, these opportunities have helped to spur the emergence of audiovisually rich and narratively complex series such as *Buffy the Vampire Slayer* (WB, 1997–2001 and UPN, 2001–2003), *The Sopranos* (HBO, 1999–2007), *The Wire* (HBO, 2001–2008), *Lost* (ABC, 2004–2010), *Life on Mars* (BBC One, 2006–2007), *Breaking Bad* (AMC, 2008–2013), *Mad Men* (AMC, 2007–2015), *Downton Abbey* (ITV, PBS, 2010–2015), *Game of Thrones* (HBO, 2011–), *House of Cards* (Netflix, 2012–), and Atlanta (FX, 2017-), to name a few of the most well known and critically acclaimed. Though these series are primarily writer-driven, there has also recently been an influx of well-known filmmakers taking on television projects.

Famously, in 1990 film auteur David Lynch created and directed the pilot for what would become the television cult hit *Twin Peaks* (ABC, 1990–1991). At the time, relative to the possibilities in film, American television was largely an artistic wasteland for a critically acclaimed filmmaker like Lynch. By 2010, however, the "small screen" had become a viable creative space for directors to develop complex and rich aesthetic narratives. Just in the past five years, for example, celebrated filmmakers Lena Dunham (*Girls*), Gus Van Sant (*Boss*), David Fincher (*House of Cards*), Martin Scorsese (*Boardwalk Empire*), Steven Soderbergh (*The Knick*), and Guillermo del Toro (*The Strain*) have all worked at least as both directors and executive producers for different television series. In his year-end writeup on the "Best Stuff from 2014" for his blog *Just TV*, media scholar Jason Mittell astutely notes the rise of television directors:

> This seems to have been the year when television direction began to eclipse (or at least match) its writing. There have always been series whose style and tone help distinguish them, but so many of my favorite series this year (*Fargo, Transparent, Hannibal, Girls, The Leftovers, Olive Kitteredge*) were notable for their innovative and striking visual and sonic sensibilities. Even series that I didn't love this year,

like *True Detective*, *Louie*, *Game of Thrones*, *Gracepoint*, and *The Missing* (and some I haven't watched yet, like *The Knick* and *The Honorable Woman*), stood out more for their excellent direction more [sic] than writing (at least this year). It will be interesting to see how this plays out going forward, as TV's production model still privileges writers over directors, but perhaps this is shifting, as per *The Knick*. ("Best Stuff")

While television directors, even those more famous ones, still largely remain hired hands, brought in to direct a few episodes, there have been a number of pieces discussing filmmakers newfound interest in working in television. A recent article in *The Guardian* hyperbolically declares "film directors are taking over TV" (Helmore, "Silver Screen"). Other examples include "Film Directors Are Embracing TV" (Maerz, *LA Times*); "Why Are Top Movie Directors Defecting to TV?" (Susman, *Moviefone*); "10 Best TV Shows Created by Filmmakers" (Travers, *IndieWire*); "Television Is Being Taken Over by Filmmakers, and That's a Beautiful Thing" (Epstein, *Quartz*); and "Filmmakers Moving Where the Money Is: Digital TV Series" (Setoodeh and Spangler, *Variety*). One obvious reason why the developing role of filmmakers in television has been announced in this way has to do with the enormous amount of content being produced to satisfy both the existing and emerging distribution channels. Such channels, whether the original three (ABC, CBS, NBC), incipient cable networks, or streaming sites like Netflix, which has dubbed itself as Internet Television, are in search of ways to differentiate themselves and stand out among the ever-growing and competitive crowd. Signing consecrated filmmakers, then, is a means to market and qualitatively distinguish a particular program and by extension, the network itself. To this end, there has been a heightened attempt on the part of producers and distributors to appropriate and align themselves with the accumulated symbolic capital of celebrated filmmakers. In turn and in theory, the director receives a substantial budget, creative freedom, and a potentially long-term revenue stream.

Not surprisingly, during this transformative period there has been a surge in the number of scholars undertaking aesthetic analyses of television programs. Steven Peacock and Jason Jacobs's 2013 edited volume *Television Aesthetics and Style* is a clear example of this interest. With the objective of establishing the emerging field of television aesthetics, the four-part compilation deals with the conceptual debate surrounding television aesthetics while also including essays that exemplify the practical application of aesthetic analyses of programs from different television genres (e.g., comedy, drama, nonfiction, and history). Central to both the theorization and application of the aesthetic assessment of television is the question of how to evaluate a particular program's artistic worth.

In Media and Television Studies, such an endeavor is a sensitive one insofar as it evokes Cultural Studies' ideological reservations regarding value judgments (Jacobs, "Issues of Judgement and Value" 428). Sarah Cardwell argues that these reservations have resulted in a paucity of aesthetic analyses of television programs for two primary, interconnected reasons: "First, the development of television studies out of sociology and cultural studies has led to a focus on television's import in political, ideological, and socio-cultural terms, rather than in artistic or cultural terms. Second, television is still regarded as artistically impoverished in comparison with other arts" (180). However, it is precisely television's artistically marginalized position that these scholars call into question. For example, Jacobs argues, "the continued sense that the television text is mostly inferior to the film text and cannot withstand concentrated critical pressure . . . has to be revised in the light of contemporary television" ("Issues of Judgement and Value" 433). In other words, to borrow freely from the title of Jason Mittell's most recent book, contemporary television storytelling is a "complex" endeavor. More often than not, and in addition to questions of production, political economy, and representation, a central aspect of contemporary television fiction's complexity is an audiovisual richness that deserves the full attention of the scholar.

In the late 1980s, David Thorburn already understood the importance of analyzing television's form. Whether its focus is political, ideological, or socioeconomic, Thorburn argued that an examination of television that does not account for a work's aesthetic characteristics is an incomplete analysis (163–64, 170). According to Thorburn, who was admittedly reluctant to go so far as to distinguish television as art, a scholar "must be able to read [television's] aesthetic artifacts [to fully understand the] historical and ideological dimensions" (165, 170). Nonetheless, traditionally "Little attention has been paid to what one may call the aesthetics of television: the analysis of thematic, formal, and stylistic qualities; the exploration of questions which arise from a thinker's interest in beauty and in art; and the consequent evaluation of an individual programme's achievements in these terms" (Cardwell 180). As Mittell points out, this is in large part due to an "explicitly antievaluative approach" that "dominates American television scholarship" and maintains "that questions of value should not be on the disciplinary agenda" (*Complex TV* 212).

Despite such reservations, building on Thorburn and beginning with Charlotte Brundson's work throughout the 1990s, television and media scholars have increasingly confronted issues of judgment, evaluation, art, and aesthetics in their assessments of television fiction (Cardwell, "Television Aesthetics" 72). In doing so, they call for a reexamination of select television programming and a repositioning of its place within the broader field of cultural production. At the heart of this call to arms is a belief that some television fiction embodies an audiovisual construction that demands to be engaged critically, and that television scholars are best prepared both to locate these examples and to take on the heavy intellectual lifting. Although much of the discussion surrounding television aesthetics in general centers on American and British television, it is also directly applicable to television production in Brazil.

AESTHETICS AND THE TELEVISION DIRECTOR IN BRAZIL'S MULTICHANNEL TRANSITION PHASE

As in the United States, albeit to a significantly lesser degree, since the late 1990s, early 2000s Brazilian television has slowly undergone a shift away from the monolithic network model toward one characterized largely by an influx of viewing options and distribution platforms (Borelli and Priolli 33–41). Of particular importance is the Lei 12.485/11 (Law 12.485/11), more commonly referred to as the Lei da TV Paga (The Pay Television Law). Following a nearly five-year contentious dispute that began as an effort to update the 1995 Lei do Cabo (Cable Television Law), President Dilma Rousseff signed Lei 12.485/11 into law on September 12, 2011. Designed to increase domestic production and competition in the audiovisual market, the law establishes quotas that require international pay television channels to broadcast a minimum of three and a half hours of content created by Brazilian production companies each week. One and a half hours of that total must come from independent Brazilian production companies. In addition to the content requirement, the law also stipulates that there must be one Brazilian channel for every three non-Brazilian pay television channels.

Due to the development of an increasingly competitive marketplace that has seen an emergence of new national and global players, TV Globo's grip over its historically faithful audiences has weakened. At the same time, there has been an uptick in demand for national content to fill the many emerging distribution channels. Moreover, Lei 12.485/11 has played a role in lowering pay television subscription prices. Consequently, during the first fifteen years of the twenty-first century, consumers' augmented access to pay television and the Internet and the financing and production stipulations of Lei 12.485/11 have all combined to encourage more frequent partnerships between networks (broadcast and cable, national and transnational) and independent production companies. In turn, these partnerships have produced some of the most aesthetically rich Brazilian television of the past decade and a half, including: *Cidade dos Homens* (*City of Men* 2002–2005) and *Som e Fúria* (a 2009 adaptation of the Canadian series *Slings and Arrows*)—both TV Globo and

O2 Filmes coproductions; *Mandrake* (2005 and 2007), an HBO and Conspiração Filmes coproduction; *Alice* (2008), an HBO and Gullane Filmes coproduction; *9mm: São Paulo* (2008–2009, 2011), a Fox and Moonshot Pictures coproduction; and *Sessão de Terapia*, a Moonshot Filmes and GNT coproduction (2012–2014). Though such partnerships have become an increasingly important aspect of networks' efforts to diversify their content and to attract and compete with pay television's growing audience, Brazil's most innovative television continues to come from Luiz Fernando Carvalho, a director employed by TV Globo.

Outside of Brazil, Carvalho is best known for his lone feature-length film, *Lavoura Arcaica* (*To the Left of the Father*), which, in addition to being widely considered a masterpiece of Brazilian cinema, was screened and won awards at a number of international film festivals. Nevertheless, nearly the director's entire professional career has been in television. Carvalho's artistic trajectory is quite interesting as it is in many ways the exact opposite of those followed by the consecrated North American filmmakers mentioned above, who first established themselves in film, moving into television only once the medium had become a viable artistic option. Spanning more than thirty years, Carvalho's time in television has seen him direct *Renascer* (1993) and *O Rei do Gado* (1996), two of the most commercially successful and critically acclaimed Brazilian telenovelas. Additionally, he has adapted works by canonical Lusophone authors such as Eça de Queirós, Ariano Suassuna, Machado de Assis, Clarice Lispector, Graciliano Ramos, and Milton Hatoum into short films, year-end specials, miniseries, and microseries (for the definition of a microseries and the other formats mentioned here, see the discussion at the end of this introduction). For all his success working in a number of different television formats, it has been in the microseries that Carvalho has set himself apart. Indeed, the cannibalistic hybridization of elements from disparate artistic fields and dialogic references to erudite, folkloric, and contemporary national and global popular cultures that characterize Carvalho's microseries *Hoje é Dia de Maria—A Primeira e A Segunda Jornada* (*Today Is Maria's Day—First and Second Journey* 2005), *A Pedra do Reino* (*The Stone of the Kingdom* 2007), *Capitu* (2008), *Afinal, o que Querem as Mulheres?* (*After All, What Do Women Want?* 2010), and *Subúrbia* (*Periphery* 2012)[2] have distinguished Carvalho as one of the most creative directors working in Brazil today, whether in film or television.

Despite the uniqueness of Carvalho's microseries, the recent emergence of other audiovisually complex television series, and Brazilian television fiction's overwhelming reach and socioeconomic impact both inside and outside Brazil, academic discourse in Brazil has tended to privilege film over television, often seeing the two as diametrically opposed. As a result, little scholarly research has examined the aesthetics of Brazilian television fiction. Media Studies scholar Roberto Moreira contends that Brazilian intellectuals view television as being an "ignorant, bastard, ignoble mass medium, whose primary function is to serve power structures" (50). In practice, such a perspective marginalizes the medium's artistic production in favor of that of film, a genre which, in Brazil, has traditionally been created by the elite for the elite (Moreira 50). Thus, the disconnect between the elitist social space occupied by the intellectual and the popular social space occupied by television helps to reproduce the type of research present in the Brazilian academy (Moreira 50).

Moreira's comments underscore two common ideological positions among Brazilian academics writing about the relationship between film and television. First, adhering to an Adornian mode of thinking, academics widely perceive television as an ideological tool used to control the masses. That is, television is "meaning in the service of power," churning out programs via a culture industry conceived of as being homologous to traditional industry and its methodical, streamlined production of consumable goods (Thompson, *Ideology* 7). By grouping individuals into an all-encompassing mass and equating the creation of symbolic goods with the Fordian mode of production of consumable goods, this perspective implies a passive creator and spectator. Consequently, it negates individual dispositions, quantities of symbolic capital, cultural competence, spatiotemporal settings, and specific modes and contexts of creation and reception.

Directly related to this first position, the second ideological position further marginalizes television by excluding it altogether from the realm of culture. As a result, this position inherently suggests a preconceived notion of what culture is and who determines and defines it as such. Both of these positions are implicit manifestations of a struggle in which different agents—critics, journalists, academics, filmmakers, to name a few of the most active participants—attempt to establish what they understand to be an appropriate intellectual discourse surrounding the field of audiovisual production. This struggle is made clear in practice within the academic realm insofar as scholarly inquiries into Brazilian audiovisual production disproportionately favor film over television.

Moreira's comments also highlight an important structural distinction between the ways in which individuals produce Brazilian film and television. Whereas a significant portion of current funding for film production derives from national or local state financing mechanisms such as those outlined in the 1993 Lei Federal 8.685/93, better known as the Lei do Audiovisual (Audiovisual Law), Brazilian television production is largely private and driven by revenue from advertising (Caparelli 22; Johnson, *The Film Industry* 64). Within the latter model, content producers and networks have an economic stake in attracting the largest possible audiences, characteristic of a type of creation that occurs in what Pierre Bourdieu calls the subfield of large-scale production (*The Field* 113–15). The competition for state funding among film producers as the primary means for financing a film, however, reduces the economic stakes, often resulting in a mode of production created by a few for a few—what Bourdieu refers to as the subfield of restricted production (*The Field* 113–15). Thus, because it is less subject to those market motivations that drive and ultimately support television's advertisement-driven economic model, much of Brazilian cinema has been less concerned with larger audience preferences than with producing art for those individuals possessing the cultural competence needed to understand a particular work.[3]

Broadly speaking, such a model has traditionally allowed filmmakers greater freedom to engage in more frequent and more explicit artistic experimentation. In contrast, since the late 1960s when the medium was becoming increasingly commercialized, Brazilian television has favored less experimental aesthetic modes of production—particularly focusing on those methods that have proven successful in the past. As is the case when determining what is and is not worthy of aesthetic inquiry, film and television's different financing models also affect how scholars approach the two fields, leading frequently to a dichotomous perspective that situates the best of film as art, while television is generally seen as passive entertainment. However, the diversification and amplification of television offerings and the emergence of narrowcasting, the result of Brazilian television's slow movement away from the network model, has increased articulations between television and film. Less rigid, medium-specific barriers have resulted in the more occasional experimental televisual work whose very existence complicates the all-too-common simplistic distinctions between film and television in Brazil. Conversely, further complicating such simplistic, dichotomous distinctions, Globo Filmes, TV Globo's film division, has coproduced a number of films in the past fifteen years that appropriate both the network's televisual aesthetic and creative talent.

Nonetheless, despite the ongoing transformation of Brazilian television, most television scholarship in Brazil—unlike film scholarship—continues to exclude aesthetic analyses, preferring to study televisual programming as merely a vehicle for mass communication. In general terms, studies of Brazilian television can be reduced to three primary areas: (1) the genealogy of the medium; (2) the formation and development of programming genres; and (3) the archaeology of reception (Freire, "Por Uma Nova Agenda" 206–07). Similarly, media scholar Sérgio Mattos organizes the academic bibliography surrounding television studies into five categories: (1) historical aspects; (2) social aspects; (3) political aspects; (4) economic aspects; and (5) complementary information (*Um Perfil* 38–61). Glaringly absent from both lists is aesthetic analysis as a possibility of scholarly pursuit. Despite this absence, a handful of Brazilian scholars have recently argued, either explicitly or implicitly, in favor of including aesthetic analyses as a viable area for television research.[4]

As Moreira's earlier comments suggest and as João Freire Filho confirms, widespread engagement in aesthetic analysis requires that Brazilian scholars first overcome the existing generalized disbelief in any meaningful approximation between television and culture ("TV de Qualidade" 92). Rather than perpetuate a circular logic that further marginalizes television because of its already marginalized position relative to more artistically consecrated fields such as film, literature, music, and painting, Freire argues that beyond a mere appropriation and mediation of other art forms that are traditionally considered to be superior to television, the medium is capable of producing "quality television," whose own technological and intellectual merits are worthy of praise and study ("TV de Qualidade" 94). Though in line with Freire's view, Arlindo Machado takes issue with the term "quality television." Despite the fact that his book *Televisão Levada a Sério* (*Television Taken Seriously*) (2000) was the first in Brazil to offer an explicit evaluative approach to Brazilian and global television, Machado does not undertake aesthetic analyses of the thirty programs he elects as being the "most important in the history of television" (31). Nonetheless, Machado is clear that his objective is to move beyond the more traditional technological or economic approaches to the medium (31). In doing so, Machado argues that the qualifier "quality television" is a misconception and is unjustly placed at the feet of television as a whole. No one, he correctly contends, speaks broadly of "quality literature" or "quality film" because the terms "literature" and "film" automatically imply a quality worthy of aesthetic examination (13). Moreover, by separating certain television programs and labeling them as "quality," Machado argues, the implication is that they represent an exception to the rule (13). Thus, rather than creating an isolated "ghetto of quality television," Machado argues in favor of a practice of production and critical reception that is "contaminated by quality" so that qualifiers are no longer necessary (13).

FROM THE FIELD TO THE WORK TO THE AUTEUR AND BACK AGAIN

Any movement toward aesthetic analyses of televisual programming requires the scholar to determine an effective theoretical and methodological model. Including aesthetics, some recent Anglophone work on television has made a concerted effort to examine works from all possible angles. The way in which

Ethan Thompson and Jason Mittell organize their book *How to Watch Tele-vision* (2013) exemplifies these and other television scholars' increased inte-rest in moving beyond the field's initial intellectual framework. Thompson and Mittell divide the book's numerous essays into five sections: (1) TV Form: Aesthetics and Style; (2) TV Representations: Social Identity and Cultural Politics; (3) TV Politics: Democracy, Nation, and the Public Interest; (4) TV Industry: Industrial Practices and Structures; and (5) TV Practices: Medium, Technology, and Everyday Life. The objective is, according to the two media scholars, to conduct close watchings that "make a broader argument about te-levision and its relation to other cultural forces, ranging from representations of particular identities to economic conditions of production and distribu-tion" (4).

Similarly, in *Television Studies: The Basics* (2009), Toby Miller proposes Television Studies 3.0—an analytical approach that brings the different cat-egories separated out in *How to Watch Television* under the same umbrella. For Miller, contemporary television studies should move beyond the field's traditional barriers to incorporate, among others, policy documents, debates, budgets, laws, geographical locations, genres, scripts, and reception (148–49). Miller argues: "To understand a program or genre we require an amalgam of interviewing people involved in production and circulation, from writers and editors to critics and audiences; content and textual analyses of shows over time, and of especially significant episodes; interpretations of knowledge about the social issues touched on; and an account of [sic] program's national and international political economy" (148).

From a slightly different perspective and with an eye toward dealing with what they understand to be political economy's methodological limitations, Timothy Havens, Amanda D. Lotz, and Serra Tinic have also proposed a more holistic research methodology that includes aesthetics among its points of in-quiry. In what they refer to as critical media industry studies, Havens et al. argue in favor of a framework that "emphasizes midlevel fieldwork in indus-try analyses, which accounts for the complex interactions among cultural and economic forces, and is drawn from our review of media industry scholar-ship as well as our own research" (237). Unlike in more traditional political economy approaches, Havens et al. include culture in two ways: "First, in an anthropological sense, critical media industry studies examines the business culture of the media industries; how knowledge about texts, audiences, and the industry form, circulate, and change; and how they influence textual and industrial practices. Second, in an aesthetic sense, critical media industry studies seeks to understand how particular media texts arise from and re-shape midlevel industrial practices" (237).

Thus, it is clear from Thompson and Mittell, Miller, Havens et al., and the previously mentioned work edited by Peacock and Jacobs that an increasing number of contemporary television scholars in the Global North are concerned with thinking about televisual texts in a comprehensive manner, one that necessarily includes aesthetic analysis. Though not written by a media scholar, Pierre Bourdieu's *The Field of Cultural Production* (1993) offers a useful model for a holistic examination and understanding of a text and its production and reception.[5] In this work, Bourdieu outlines a conceptual framework for analyzing the complex process for the creation of symbolic goods. According to Bourdieu, the field of cultural production is an elaborate, structured social space comprised of unequal relationships between myriad agents who occupy distinct positions in a constant struggle for diverse forms of capital. Inseparable from these positions are what he calls *prises-de-position* (position-takings), which equate to the works or the concrete manifestations of those agents who occupy positions within a particular field (*The Field* 131–37). By considering positions inseparable from position-takings and by situating both of these within the larger field of cultural production, Bourdieu's analytical model eliminates the reductive and subjective analysis that attempts to explain a work of art in and of itself. Additionally, it excludes those analyses that rely solely on a specific sociohistorical moment or a political economy as a means of defining or explaining a specific work. Instead, following this model, a complete explanation of a symbolic good or work of art involves a break from the objective/subjective dichotomy via a thorough analysis of the entire field, which, in addition to a sociohistorical and sociopolitical contextualization, includes an examination of the relationships between other possible positions and position-takings, modes of production, distribution, consumption, and critical research and commentary.

As an intricate relational structure comprising television networks, executives, directors, producers, actors, critics, and consumers, the Brazilian audiovisual field lends itself well to Bourdieu's model. However, while Bourdieu's framework aids in establishing a sociology of cultural production by analyzing the many elements that determine the creation of a work, it does not provide a model for aesthetic analysis. Because one of this book's primary objectives is to analyze the field in which Carvalho's microseries were produced as well as to examine the aesthetics that characterize them, an in-depth investigation into Carvalho's own unique mode of production within the broader field of audiovisual production *and* the resulting artistic elements that distinguish the works in question must be undertaken. To this end, in addition to engaging in a form of what John B. Thompson calls depth hermeneutics, in an attempt to construct a "radical contextualization" of Carvalho's *oeuvre* along the lines of Bourdieu, Miller, and the other scholars already mentioned, the analysis herein will borrow freely from literary, television, and theater criticism, while also building off of select aspects of auteur theory (Grossberg 20; Thompson, *Ideology* 277–91).

Originally conceived of during the 1950s by *Cahiers du Cinéma* journalists and later Anglicized by Andrew Sarris and Peter Wollen, classical auteur theory was a rather loosely constructed tripartite approach to the study of films. It maintained that (1) films have a guiding intentionality; (2) such an intentionality produces a common pattern across an artist's work; and (3) the intentionality of both individual and sets of films is that of the director (Hogan, "Auteurs and Their Brains" 68). As has been argued widely, classical auteur theory's emphasis on intentionality is extremely difficult to determine with any certainty. What is more, the centrality of intentionality can problematically function to reduce what are complex, collaborative creative processes to the work of a single individual.[6] Though Chapter Two deals with some of these issues in more detail, it is important to note here that this book's examination of Carvalho's position and his work borrows from auteur theory's broad attempt to determine the creative distinctiveness of a larger audiovisual corpus as well as the central agent(s) behind it through a comprehensive aesthetic analysis of the works in question.

As I attempt to show in the following chapters, despite working within the confines of TV Globo's media monopoly, Carvalho has maintained an uncharacteristically high level of production and artistic control over the works he has directed since at least 2005. Indeed, as works of television, Carvalho's microseries are intimate, artisanal productions, and his creative mark is visible in nearly every one of their aspects—from the lighting and framing of shots to the lace on a dress worn by even the most peripheral of characters. Nonetheless, no matter how much creative control Carvalho has, all of his works—as is the case with nearly all audiovisual production—embody a collaborative effort. With this in mind, I consider Carvalho's *oeuvre* through the framework of Bourdieu's theoretical model, which recognizes the interactive, sociohistorical reality that foregrounds and characterizes production. At the same time, however, my analysis appropriates—while working to justify this choice—the centrality of the director as a starting point for examining the singular aesthetic that distinguishes Carvalho's work and is so strongly associated with his name. In short, when combined with Bourdieu's model— strengthened further by the inclusion of the cited methodologies—auteur theory can serve as a bridge that uniquely links a primary creative agent and her broader sociohistorical context of production to questions of aesthetics. This type of analysis allows us, then, to examine Carvalho's work as a reaction to the broader field of Brazilian television production, resulting in a deeper understanding of both the director's experimental aesthetic and the contemporary state of Brazilian television fiction.

A ROAD MAP FOR THE PATH FORWARD

This book has two primary objectives. First, it seeks to engage in the emerging scholarship that examines select examples of television as works of art. While there are a number of scholars doing this type of research in the United States and Europe, this book aims to offer an example of experimental and innovative television fiction from the Global South—namely from the Brazilian entertainment market, one of the largest and commercially most successful in the world. Second, through the analysis of Luiz Fernando Carvalho's many works, his artistic trajectory, and his position as a director at TV Globo, this book also sheds light on the broader reality of contemporary Brazilian television fiction. To these ends, the first chapter's examination of Carvalho's 2010 microseries *Afinal, o que Querem as Mulheres?* shows the extent to which Carvalho is consciously aware of both his own artistic inclinations and a director's generally marginalized creative role in Brazilian television fiction. By starting with one of Carvalho's later works, the first chapter establishes the ongoing tensions between standardized and experimental television as well as between the television writer and the television director. Additionally, by reading the microseries as a metacritique of contemporary Brazilian television fiction, the first chapter offers examples of the ways in which Carvalho actively seeks to challenge the industry status quo, asserting himself as the primary creative agent and his work as an artistic counterpoint to everyday Brazilian television fare.

The second chapter takes a step back to establish the structural basis from which Carvalho works: namely his unique preproduction process. In analyzing this process, the chapter establishes how Carvalho, despite working in an overly commercial and standardized structure, assures himself a significant degree of creative control by repeatedly working with the same individuals and by putting his cast and crew through elaborate workshops and seminars before production begins.

Chapter Three focuses on Carvalho's decision since 2005 to move away from the telenovela, so as to work primarily with microseries. I situate this shorter format and the theatrical aesthetic that broadly defines Carvalho's works within Brazilian television's long tradition of the teleteatro. Additionally, this chapter connects the theoretical underpinnings of the defamiliarized *mise-en-scène* that characterizes Carvalho's work to Antonin Artaud's writings on early-twentieth-century realist theater in Europe.

A selection of the opening scenes from Carvalho's *oeuvre* over the past twenty-five years is examined in Chapter Four. This provides a deeper understanding of the ways in which they function to establish an ideological and artistic professional identity for Carvalho that characterizes his position in the field of television production. More specifically, I analyze how the director uses the opening scene as a foundational reinforcement to his other means of reimagining contemporary Brazilian television fiction: his singular preproduction process (discussed in Chapter Two) and his emphasis on the theater (Chapter Three). Together, the characteristic opening scenes and key repeated motifs—namely the color red and the self-referential theater—reveal the interrelated formal and narrative concerns that lie at the heart of the director's work.

Chapter Five examines Carvalho's concern with constructing a televisual language unique to Brazil. In this chapter, I examine the director's interest in nationalism by employing Anthony D. Smith's concept of ethno-symbolism. In doing so, I place Carvalho and his work within the context of the political and artistic legacy left by Brazilian modernism in the 1920s. I also question Carvalho's interest in constructing an ethical aesthetic, showing how in some ways it problematically mirrors TV Globo's attempts to construct, represent, and didactically communicate what it means to be Brazilian to its enormous audiences.

Focusing on Carvalho's *Projeto Quadrante* (*Quadrant Project*), Chapter Six continues with the examination of the director's attempt to construct a uniquely Brazilian televisual language. In *Projeto Quadrante*, the director takes his show on the road in what I define as Carvalho's televisual version of *mambembe*, or low-budget, makeshift traveling theater. With the *Projeto Quadrante*, Carvalho not only expands his production process beyond the confines of TV Globo's studios; he also moves beyond the historically dominant production and cultural axis of Rio-São Paulo, providing the spectator with possibilities for national engagement that transcend traditional television-viewing practice. Along these lines, this chapter briefly examines the *Projeto Quadrante* as an early example of convergence media in Brazil. It also pays particular attention to the project's decentralized production model and its use of canonical Brazilian literature as the narrative starting point for both representing and uniting the nation's dispersed and diverse television audience.

Chapter Seven analyzes one of Carvalho's most recent microseries, *Subúrbia* (*Periphery*) (2012). The analysis of this work serves two objectives. First, it further reinforces the established aesthetic and motifs that characterize Carvalho's television production by showing how he continues to develop these even into the present. Second, it provides insight into the ways in which a more competitive marketplace, one altered by increased access to the Internet and pay television, informs TV Globo's interest in experimenting with its programming. More specifically, I show how *Subúrbia* exemplifies the changing landscape of Brazilian television insofar as it is an example of TV Globo's efforts to reach the emerging lower-middle class, referred to as the *Classe C* (C-Class).

To conclude, I demonstrate how Carvalho's aesthetic project of reimagining Brazilian television fiction has come full-circle with his return to the telenovela in 2014. The argument here is that this work, *Meu Pedacinho de Chão,* is a (anti) telenovela insofar as it is the result of Carvalho's unique mode of production developed over his long career; is decidedly shorter than the traditional telenovela; and embodies and expands on Carvalho's characteristic theatrical aesthetic accumulation.

Because the chapters are thematic and not necessarily chronological, as needed, the reader is encouraged to use the outline of Carvalho's artistic trajectory at the end of this introduction. The outline serves as a reference for each of Carvalho's works, including Portuguese titles, air-dates and times, number of chapters, the network that produced the work, whether the work was an original or adapted screenplay, and a summary of Carvalho's various roles in the works' creation. While this book does not specifically engage each of the works mentioned, the outline does include all of Carvalho's works in both film and television. Those works that serve as the object of analysis are in bold print for easier access. The analysis of Carvalho's works focuses primarily on those where he was the lead, if not the only, director. Moreover, particular importance will be given to the shorter format works in which the traditional television author was not present as a creative force. In such works, Carvalho exerts the greatest degree of control over the artistic process and final outcome. Not surprisingly, these are the director's most experimental and artistic productions.

The outline also categorizes the works by their format, and it is important to understand how those formats are different. This book frequently refers to the microseries, telenovela, and special (e.g., teleteatro) genres. In doing so, it adheres to the following definitions of each: a microseries is a fictional narrative, shot in its entirety prior to airing, and comprises four to eight chapters. Similar to a miniseries, which includes anywhere from nine to fifty-five chapters, contemporary Brazilian microseries are, more often than not, adaptations of canonical literary texts. Although microseries sometimes air daily, they tend to be shown weekly during the 11:00 PM time slot.

A Brazilian telenovela, on the other hand, is melodramatic, realist fictional narrative typically made up of 150 to 220 chapters. Unlike the microseries, telenovela production occurs continuously while airing. As a result, telenovelas are dynamic and flexible by nature, and their narratives may be altered during filming, depending upon audience reception or other factors. Telenovelas, almost without exception, air Monday through Saturday in the prime-time slots between approximately 6:00 and 10:00 PM. Last, a special is typically a single, hour-long program, airing in a post-prime-time slot—after 10 PM. As discussed in detail in Chapter Two, Carvalho's specials were originally part of TV Globo's series *Caso Especial* (*Special Case*). The works presented in this series were generally adaptations of canonical literary texts, whether Brazilian or foreign.

Table 1. Luz Fernando Carvalho's Artistic Trajectory

Title and Network	Date, Time, and Number of Chapters	Format	Adaptation	Director	Screenwriter
A Espera	1986	Short film	A Lover's Discourse: Fragments (1977) by Roland Barthes	Yes	Yes
Helena, Rede Manchete	Jan. 9–Jul. 15, 1987 19:30, 161	Telenovela	Helena (1876) by Machado de Assis	Yes, with Denise Sarraceni	No; Mário Prata and Dagomar Marquezi
Carmem, Rede Manchete	Oct. 9, 1987– May 14, 1988 21:30, 180	Telenovela	Carmem (1845) by Prosper Mérimée	Yes, with José Wilker	No; Glória Perez
Vida Nova, Rede Globo	Nov. 21, 1988– May 5, 1989 18:00, 143	Telenovela	No	Yes	No; Benedito Ruy Barbosa
Tieta, Rede Globo	Aug. 14, 1989– Mar. 31, 1990 20:00, 196	Telenovela	Tieta do Agreste (1977) by Jorge Amado	Yes, with Reynaldo Boury, Ricardo Waddington, and Paulo Ubiratan	No; Aguinaldo Silva and others
Riacho Doce, Rede Globo	Jul. 31–Oct. 5, 1990 22:30, 40	Miniseries	Riacho Doce (1939) by José Lins do Rego	Yes, with Reynaldo Boury and Paulo Ubiratan	No; Aguinaldo Silva and others
Pedra sobre Pedra, Rede Globo	Jan. 6–Aug. 1, 1992 20:30, 178	Telenovela	No	Yes, with Gonzaga Bloth Paulo Ubiratan	No; Aguinaldo Silva and others
Renascer, Rede Globo	**Mar. 8–Nov. 14, 1993 20:30, 213**	**Telenovela**	**No**	**Yes**	**No; Benedito Ruy Barbosa**
Uma Mulher Vestida de Sol, Rede Globo	**Jul. 12, 1994 Post–prime time**	**Special**	**Uma Mulher Vestida de Sol (1947) by Ariano Suassuna**	**Yes**	**Yes, with Ariano Suassuna**
Irmãos Coragem, Rede Globo	Jan. 2–Jul. 1, 1995 18:00, 155	Telenovela	No, though it was a remake of the 1970 Dias Gomes's telenovela of the same name	Yes, with Ary Coslov, Reynaldo Boury, and Carlos Araújo [The latter two substituted Carvalho after the 55th chapter]	No; Dias Gomes and Marcílio Moraes
Farsa da Boa Preguiça, Rede Globo	**May 12, 1995 Post–prime time**	**Special**	**Farsa da Boa Preguiça (1960) by Ariano Suassuna**	**Yes**	**Yes, with Ariano Suassuna**
O Rei do Gado, Rede Globo	Jun. 17, 1996– Feb. 14, 1997 20:30, 209	Telenovela	No	Yes	No; Benedito Ruy Barbosa
Que seus Olhos Sejam Atendidos, GNT, Globo Sat	Dec. 14–15, 1997 23:00, 2	Documentary	No; research in Lebanon for Lavoura Arcaica	Yes	Yes
Lavoura Arcaica, VideoFilmes	**Oct. 29, 2001**	**Film**	**Lavoura Arcaica (1975) by Raduan Nassar**	**Yes**	**Yes, with Raduan Nassar**
Os Maias, Rede Globo	Jan. 1–Mar. 24, 2001 23:00, 44	Miniseries	Os Maias (1888) by Eça de Queirós	Yes	No; Maria Adelaide Amaral

Title and Network	Date, Time, and Number of Chapters	Format	Adaptation	Director	Screenwriter
Esperança, Rede Globo	Jun. 17, 2002–Feb. 15, 2003 20:00, 209	Telenovela	No	Yes	No; Benedito Ruy Barbosa
Hoje é Dia de Maria: Primeira e Segunda Jornadas, Rede Globo	First: Jan. 11–21, 2005 23:00, 8 Second: Oct. 11–15, 2005 23:00, 5	Microseries	No, though it was inspired by playwright Carlos Alberto Soffredini's work	Yes	Yes, with Luís Alberto de Abreu
A Pedra do Reino, Rede Globo	Jun. 12–16, 2007 23:00, 5	Microseries Part of the Projeto Quadrante	*Romance d'A Pedra do Reino e o Príncipe do Sangue do Vai-e-Volta* (1970) by Ariano Suassuna	Yes	Yes, with Luís Alberto de Abreu and Bráulio Tavares
Capitu, Rede Globo	Dec. 9–13, 2008 23:00, 5	Microseries Part of the Projeto Quadrante	*Dom Casmurro* (1899) by Machado de Assis	Yes	Yes, with Euclydes Marinho
Afinal, o que Querem as Mulheres?, Rede Globo	Nov. 11–Dec. 16, 2010 23:00, 6	Microseries	No	Yes	Yes, with João Paulo Cuenca, Cecília Gianetti, and Michel Melamed
Subúrbia, Rede Globo	Nov. 1–Dec. 20, 2012 23:30, 8	Microseries	No	Yes	Yes, with Paulo Lins
Correio Feminino, Rede Globo	Oct. 27, 2013 21:00 Aired as a part of the weekly TV Magazine, *Fantástico*	Special	Adapted from texts written by Clarice Lispector (under the pseudonym Helen Palmer) during the 1950s for the newspaper *Correio da Manhã*	Yes	Yes, with Maria Camargo
Alexandre e Outros Heróis, Rede Globo	Dec. 1, 2013 Post–prime time	Special	*Alexandre e Outros Heróis* (1962) by Graciliano Ramos	Yes	Yes, with Luís Alberto de Abreu
Meu Pedacinho de Chão, Rede Globo	Apr. 7–Aug. 1, 2014 18:00, 96	Telenovela	No, though it was a remake of the Benedito Ruy Barbosa and Teixeira Filho penned 1971 telenovela of the same name	Yes	No; Benedito Ruy Barbosa
Velho Chico, Rede Globo	Mar. 14–Sep. 30, 2016 21:00, 172	Telenovela	No	Yes, with Carlos Araújo, Gustavo Fernandez, Antônio Karnewale, and Philipe Barcinski	No; Benedito Ruy Barbosa and Bruno Luperi in collaboration wtih Luís Alberto de Abreu
Dois Irmãos, Rede Globo	Jan. 9 – Jan. 20, 2017 23:00, 10	Microseries Part of the Projeto Quadrante	*Dois Irmãos* (2000) by Milton Hatoum	Yes	Yes, with Maria Camargo

Chapter One

ASSERTING THE CREATIVE ROLE OF THE TELEVISION DIRECTOR IN A WRITER'S WORLD

Throughout nearly his entire career in film and television, Luiz Fernando Carvalho has either directed telenovelas or adaptations of canonical Brazilian plays or novels. However, in 2010, after a quarter-century directing television fiction, Carvalho cowrote and directed his first original screenplay, the six-part microseries *Afinal, o que Querem as Mulheres?* It is perhaps not surprising that Carvalho has described that microseries as his most authorial production in television to date.[1] With *Afinal, o que Querem as Mulheres?* Carvalho lays bare his assessment of Brazilian television by constructing a work of meta-fiction that is simultaneously a critique of television fiction's production and aesthetics and an example of an artistically engaged alternative. Just as important, the metacritique and its aesthetic framing also represent an attempt on Carvalho's part to assert the figure of the director as the primary creative agent behind the artistic construction.

THE BRAZILIAN FIELD OF AUDIOVISUAL PRODUCTION

In order to understand Carvalho's position in *Afinal, o que Querem as Mulheres?*, it is necessary to first situate his thirty-five-year professional trajectory as a film and television director within the broader field of Brazilian audiovisual production. Though scholars in Brazil tend to separate film and television fiction, creating and perpetuating an overly simple dichotomy that defines the former as art and the latter as mass entertainment, Carvalho's career has transcended these false boundaries, exemplifying the historical exchange that in part characterizes the field as a whole. Indeed, in his pioneering study *Televisão, publicidade e cultura de massa*, José Mário Ortiz Ramos argues that the solidification of the Brazilian audiovisual field was the result of the emergence of television and television advertising within the context of film's fragile industrial structure (14). Whereas the interdependent television and advertising industries have both prospered in commercial terms, Brazilian cinema has historically struggled to take off. Instead, with regard to production and audience reception, as in other Latin American film industries, Brazilian cinema has found itself stuck in a series of cyclical highs and lows.

Most film historians mark the beginning of Brazilian film production as June 19, 1898. It was on that day that the Italian immigrant Afonso Segretto used his recently acquired camera to film Rio de Janeiro's Baía de Guanabara as he returned to the city from Europe.[2] Not long after Segretto's first filming, Brazilian cinema experienced its Golden Age (*Bela Época*)—a brief period between 1908 and 1911 marked by a harmony between production, exhibition, and public reception.[3] Nonetheless, the arrival in 1911 of a group of Hollywood businessmen interested in the South American market signaled both the end of the Golden Age and the beginning of a local field of production largely structured by foreign interests. The emergence of the industrialized and highly technical Hollywood and, to a lesser extent, European films led early Brazilian filmgoers to reject local production as inferior (Johnson, *Film Industry* 20). As Brazilians became accustomed to the superior technical quality of North American films, the belief that these were the "'proper' or preferred form of cinematic discourse" became normalized (Johnson, *Film Industry* 11). Consequently, over the years audiences became "reluctant to accept alternative forms, even if produced locally" (11).

Along these lines, Brazilian film production after 1911 can be understood as a broad reaction to Hollywood's hegemonic position in the country. Put differently, historically, local-content producers either sought to *assimilate* to Hollywood or to *reject* the North American power. In the first instance, Brazilian filmmakers or businessmen adapted the Hollywood studio model to local film production. Hoping to compete in the international market, studios such as Cinédia in the 1930s, Atlântida in the 1940s, and Vera Cruz in the late 1940s and early 1950s all represented concerted efforts to implement and nationalize the preeminent foreign model of film production and the technical quality of foreign films. In direct contrast to the attempts at assimilation, some filmmakers explicitly reacted against the dominant presence of the North American film industry as well as against the studios' domestic attempts at imitation. Specifically, following Vera Cruz's financial failure in the early 1950s, an important group of young filmmakers, including future Cinema Novo figureheads Nelson Pereira dos Santos and Glauber Rocha, recognized that they did not have the necessary means to equal the technical level of most foreign films. Furthermore, these filmmakers positioned themselves politically, deciding that even if they could match foreign production quality, the results would certainly not be representative of Brazil's then current social reality. So, as Randal Johnson notes, "rather than imitate dominant cinema, which would make their work merely symptomatic of underdevelopment, they chose to resist by turning, in Ismail Xavier's words, 'scarcity into a signifier'" (*Brazilian Cinema* 379).

Cinema Novo, then, was the most obvious example of this reactionary camp of production. In its first phase (1960–1964), as implied by the movement's motto—"uma câmera na mão e uma ideia na cabeça" ("a camera in the hand and an idea in the head")—Cinema Novo filmmakers created works that explicitly contradicted the commercial, star-driven, high-budget, and high-quality studio films by producing nonindustrial, small-budget, ideologically driven films. Drawing on Italian Neo-Realism and the French New Wave, Cinema Novo films contained political messages and were formally characterized by what Glauber Rocha referred to as an *estética da fome* (aesthetics of hunger)—that is, a formal construction that was as precarious as the object (marginalized sectors of Brazilian society) it was representing. In these films, particularly toward the end of the decade, Brazil's underdevelopment, as represented by the northeastern *sertão* and urban *favela,* gained symbolic importance as the signifiers of an ongoing incompleteness or lack (Xavier, *Alegorias* 30). Nonetheless, however much Rocha and his colleagues sought to distinguish their work from the derivative Brazilian studio films by drawing attention to social ills, both faced a common reality: local audiences did not purchase tickets to see them. Thus, despite the studios' attempts to attract large audiences accustomed to Hollywood films and despite Cinema Novo's artistic achievements and resulting symbolic capital, locally produced films were never able to capture the hearts and minds of Brazilians in the way television eventually would in the late 1960s and early 1970s.

On September 18, 1950, Brazilian media mogul Assis Chateaubriand celebrated the inaugural airing of his São Paulo-based TV Tupi, Brazil's first broadcast television channel. Though the medium would eventually become the country's dominant source of audiovisual and cultural production, trumping even those more traditional sources located in the Global North, Brazilian television's early years were more of a whimper than a bang. From 1950 to 1964—the period scholars refer to as the *fase elitista* (elitist phase)—the concentration of television sets in the homes of the São Paulo and Rio de Janeiro (and later Belo Horizonte) elites served as the defining characteristic of the incipient industry. As is often the case with emerging, cutting-edge technology, owning a television set was a status symbol for a small, economically privileged group of Brazilians. In fact, by 1960 a mere 4.6 percent of Brazilian homes had a television set (Hamburger, *O Brasil* 22). In contrast, roughly 90 percent of homes in the United States had a television set in 1960 (Hamburger, *O Brasil* 21).

Cristina Brandão notes that early producers, eager to cater to their exclusive audiences, made a concerted effort to establish the new medium as a means of disseminating elitist culture ("As primeiras" 39). The preeminent fictional product of this culture was the highbrow teleteatro (television theater). Initially, these were primarily live adaptations of European canonical plays directed at a relatively small audience of early adopters who possessed the still expensive television technology *and* the cultural competence to consume and "appreciate" them. The first teleteatros incorporated little to no experimentation, opting instead for a stationary camera to film the actors' performances on makeshift studio stages. However, as the creative participants became more comfortable with the new medium, they began to explore the possibilities for creating a language unique to television. In doing so, early pioneers found their narrative model in theater and literature. Lacking a visual paradigm, however, they turned to cinema for inspiration. Paradoxically, despite the elite audience and the exclusive nature of the teleteatro's literary sources, the early producers specifically chose commercial Hollywood cinema as a model for its high production and entertainment value. Consequently, they helped set the production of television fiction on a path defined by commercial appeal and, as Alexandre Bergamo notes, in direct contrast to the political engagement that characterized Cinema Novo (74). Most importantly, however, is that the groundwork had been laid for attracting enormous audiences, helping television to succeed precisely where the Brazilian film studios of the 1940s and 1950s failed.

After the military dictatorship came to power via a *coup d'état* in 1964, life was very difficult for many Brazilians. At the same time, however, the period marked a critical moment for the growth of Brazilian television. During the 1960s, television audiences expanded, as both individuals' access to television sets and the number of networks producing and distributing programming increased. While the military dictatorship helped reduce the cost of television sets and worked to implement microwave technology throughout the country, to meet the expectations of a growing audience and to turn out a more efficient, less costly product, networks like TV Excelsior (1960) and TV Globo (1965) began to transition away from the teleteatro as their principal product, replacing it with what were then the earliest Brazilian examples of the daily, standardized telenovela (Mattos 13–17). Additionally, lowbrow variety shows like those headlined by Chacrina, Flávio Calvacanti, and Jacinto Figueira became quite popular in the 1960s and occupied an important place in some of the networks' newly implemented vertical and horizontal programming grids. Such "*baixo-nível*" (lowbrow) content, however, went against the military dictatorship's conservative, patriotic, religious, and family-centered ideology (Mattos 17; Ribeiro and Sacramento 116). The military dictatorship saw television as the ideal vehicle for disseminating its ideologies throughout the country's vast territory (Hamburger, *O Brasil* 30). For this to happen, however, the regime would need to provide the necessary infrastructure to make national broadcasting possible, and the networks would need to "*hige-nizar*" (clean up) their programming, so that it would represent Brazil—that is, in line with the regime's conservative conceptualization of the country—to Brazilians (Ribeiro and Sacramento 116).

More than any other network, TV Globo led the way in adhering to the military dictatorship's wishes. By the early 1970s, with the infrastructure to broadcast nationally and to take advantage of its existing stations and affiliates, TV Globo implemented what became known as the *Padrão Globo de Qualidade* (Globo Standard of Quality) throughout its programming grid. Defined by TV Globo's autocensorship and its use of incipient technology such as videotape, color, and cutting-edge graphics, the *Padrão Globo de Qualidade* led to a higher-quality product characterized by less improvisation, less informality, and fewer unexpected errors (Borelli and Priolli 55–57; Ribeiro and Sacramento 116). In its increasingly national-themed, realist, and colloquial telenovelas and new nonfiction news and informative entertainment programs like the *Jornal Nacional* (1969–), *Fantástico* (1973–), and *Globo Repórter* (1973–), audiences saw the network's innovative production and aesthetic standard as superior to the competition. This resulted in an "upward spiral of market domination" in which TV Globo's large audiences helped the network capture more advertising dollars, which were in turn reinvested in technology, talent, and other production-related costs (Straubhaar, "The Decline" 233). Such investments further distinguished TV Globo's products from the competitions', thereby increasing both its audience sizes and its advertising revenue (233).

By the end of 1979, the Brazilian economy was in a deep economic recession. Around the same time, in reaction to the deteriorating economy, the military dictatorship had given in to a process that would lead to a return to democracy (*abertura*). Despite unprecedented success in the mid-1970s, the film industry—which was by then heavily reliant on government financing mechanisms—was nearly broken. Amid the economic chaos, however, television—that is, TV Globo—was thriving. Powered by administrative competence—exemplified by figures like Walter Clark, José Bonifácio de Oliveira Sobrinho, and the former Time Life executive and naturalized Brazilian Joe Wallach—and by the benefits reaped from its relationship with the military regime, TV Globo entered the 1980s as the country's preeminent media company.

FROM THE BIG TO THE SMALL SCREEN

Carvalho's professional trajectory begins precisely at this crucial moment in the history of Brazilian audiovisual production. What is more, the director's trajectory is representative of broader socioeconomic and sociopolitical issues that have structured the Brazilian film and television industries for more than fifty years. While still enrolled as an undergraduate student of architecture in Rio de Janeiro, in the late 1970s Carvalho interned in the film industry as an assistant editor and director. Although he later left architecture to study literature, Carvalho eventually dropped out of school due to an increased workload in the film industry. Around this time, such domestic films as *Dona Flor e seus Dois Maridos* (*Dona Flor and Her Two Husbands*) (1976)—a Bruno Barreto adaptation of Jorge Amado's 1966 novel of the same name—and Neville d'Almeida's *A Dama do Lotação* (*Lady on the Bus*) (1978) had experienced unprecedented commercial success. By the end of the decade, however, hyperinflation had devastated the country's economy and sent national cinema into a deep fiscal crisis. With the economic collapse in full swing, Carvalho's opportunities in film decreased and eventually almost vanished. Looking for work, the young professional found a position in TV Globo's prestigious Director's Nucleus (*Núcleo de Diretores*). Aimed at developing emerging directorial talent, in the Director's Nucleus Carvalho learned the trade, working initially as a director's assistant for miniseries and other special programming (Carvalho, *Luiz Fernando Carvalho* 16).

In many ways, Carvalho's move from the big to the small screen in the early 1980s was symptomatic of a more far-reaching phenomenon that saw film industry veterans migrating to television and advertising in order to pay their bills and a lack of film production funds, causing film studios to rent out their lots to thriving advertising and television companies. The migration from the cinematic medium to the televisual one—or from the big to the small screen—sheds light on Brazilian film's historically weak economic position relative to television. Indeed, a similar phenomenon had occurred in the 1960s and 1970s when, during economic downturns, Vera Cruz and Cinédia rented their studios to startup networks TV Excelsior and TV Globo (Ramos 25). In short, while Brazilian film repeatedly struggled in the face of economic recessions, the increasingly commercially powerful television industry continued to thrive while also, to a certain extent, supporting the existence of the film industry.

Carvalho's professional trajectory of moving from film to television also contradicts preconceived notions that perpetuate an ideological separation of film and television as it pertains to their capacity for creating art. While the impetus for professional crossover has predominately been the result of economic hardship, the possibility of creating symbolic value for a large audience was and still remains a factor for filmmakers (as well as other artists) desiring to disseminate their work on a grand scale. In his study of the seminal TV Globo documentary programs *Globo-Shell Especial* and *Globo Repórter* during the 1970s, Igor Sacramento sheds light on film professionals' wide-ranging activity in television. Contrary to what one might hypothesize, Sacramento contends that the filmmakers who migrated to television during this period were not necessarily those who were more commercially inclined, but instead those with artistic objectives and direct ties to Cinema Novo (55). In fact, important Cinema Novo filmmakers as well as left-leaning intellectuals and artists, including Eduardo Coutinho, João Batista de Andrade, Gustavo Dahl, Glauber Rocha, Nelson Pereira dos Santos, Alfredo Dias Gomes, Gianfrancesco Guarnieri, and Ferreira Gullar, all worked in television during the 1970s (Sacramento, "Depois da" 55 and "A renovação" 123).

Though many were influenced by the then difficult economic situation, as one might imagine, these individuals' broader objectives differed. As already mentioned, some filmmakers and writers sought work in television in order to pay the bills and to continue making films or plays (Bergamo 78; Sacramento, "Depois da" 56). Others, however, especially those from Cinema Novo's later generation (1968–1972), lacked the symbolic capital and access to the means of film production readily available to the movement's more consecrated filmmakers. As such, these individuals found television to be a space where they could practice their craft and communicate with large audiences (Sacramento, "Depois da" 56). Of particular importance here is how both economically challenged *and* politically and artistically inclined filmmakers ultimately found in television a space to make a living and continue to do the work they loved.

Commenting on why he did not finish his degree in architecture, Carvalho reveals that he experienced something similar to the artistic and politically inclined filmmakers mentioned by Sacramento. That is, like those from Cinema Novo's second generation who lacked the necessary economic and symbolic capital to make their films, the young, not yet established Carvalho was running out of options to work in film, due to the economic crisis. To survive financially, but to also be able to continue to work as a director and construct audiovisual narratives, he eventually found his way to television. Even a cursory examination of the contemporary field of Brazilian audiovisual production reveals that not much has changed regarding the professional crossover between film and television. For example, such critically acclaimed contemporary directors as Karim Ainouz, José Henrique Fonseca, Jorge Furtado, Cao Hamburger, Fernando Meirelles, José Padilha, João Moreira Salles, and Walter Salles have all directed or produced television documentaries, specials, or series, in addition to their well-known films.[4] However, unlike these filmmakers' *occasional* small-screen endeavors and those Cinema Novo directors that *appropriated* the medium for their immediate financial and professional needs, Carvalho has worked almost exclusively in television, establishing himself as the most creative director, in either film or television, working in Brazil today.

Despite starting in film in the late 1970s and directing *Lavoura Arcaica* in 2001, one of the most important Brazilian films of the past twenty-five years, Carvalho continues to concentrate his creative efforts in television, where he has access to TV Globo's elaborate infrastructure, funding, and extensive audience. Such self-positioning goes against the broader tendency of the socially constructed figure of the Brazilian director, who, left with Cinema Novo's politically charged artistic legacy and often supported by state-run financing mechanisms, adheres to an ideological discourse that in practice perpetuates a sweeping rejection of the commercial concerns in favor of a more artistic and sociopolitically engaged production. For Jean-Claude Bernardet this rejection was, and in many ways still is, one of the key issues behind Brazilian cinema's subordinate position in its own market. Evoking the philosophical question, "if a tree falls in a forest and no one is around to hear it, does it make a sound?" Bernardet maintains that a film only exists once it enters the consciousness of the public it targets. What is more, he argues that an auteur without a public to view his or her film is no auteur at all (*Brasil em tempo* 22).

As such, within the Brazilian context, Carvalho's decision to create works for television rather than film is recognition on his part of the audience's importance. This is because, for at least the past forty-five years, network television in Brazil has consistently attracted enormous audiences, while Brazilian film's restricted mode of production and elitism, as Carvalho has characterized it, has disconnected film from maintaining a meaningful dialogue with a broader, more diverse public ("Educação" 23). However, the director's focus on television production and its large audiences creates a problem for Carvalho, who, like a number of his Cinema Novo predecessors, views himself as an auteur. Unlike in cinema, the television director in Brazil has traditionally occupied a subordinate creative role to the television writer. But whether through his work or in his writings and interviews, Carvalho has long challenged this reality, advocating for the director as a central figure in the creative process. Thus, he seeks to do what no Brazilian director has done before: be an auteur whose work is consistently seen by tens of millions of Brazilians. That he attempts to do this as a television director results in a direct challenge to the long-established cultural hierarchy that places television in an inferior position to cinema in artistic terms. Nowhere is Carvalho's position more explicit than in *Afinal, o que Querem as Mulheres?*, which melds form and content into a critical commentary on the subordinate role of the director and on Brazilian television fiction as a whole.

A METAFICTIONAL RESPONSE TO STANDARDIZED
TELEVISION FICTION

Afinal, o que Querem as Mulheres? is set in contemporary Copacabana. However, as is characteristic of the director's work, the iconic neighborhood has been defamiliarized so as to evoke an anachronistic time-space resembling 1960s pop art aesthetics. The protagonist and first-person narrator is a thirty-something PhD student of psychology named André Newmann (Michel Melamed). At the beginning of the microseries, André works obsessively to complete his dissertation, which attempts to answer the question: Afinal, o que querem as mulheres? (After all, what do women want?). Ironically, due to his failure to understand his girlfriend Lívia (Paola Oliveira) and her desires, Andre's single-minded and incessant focus on answering this question leads to the dissolution of their relationship. And yet, despite the difficulties it causes in his personal life and its effect on his mental health, his completed dissertation is a huge success, instantly becoming a bestseller as well as serving as the source text for a television series featuring the world-famous Brazilian actor Rodrigo Santoro as André Newmann. The fictional television series within Carvalho's microseries functions both to parody standardized television production and to juxtapose it to the unique type of production and aesthetic that have characterized Carvalho's own work from as early as 1993.

In *Metafiction: The Theory and Practice of Self-Conscious Fiction*, Patricia Waugh examines modern literature's tendency to create a self-reflexive aesthetic. Defined as a type of "writing which self-consciously and systematically draws attention to its status as an artifact in order to pose questions about the relationship between fiction and reality," Waugh argues that metafiction results in artistic output that "explicitly lays bare the conventions of realism," reexamining these conditions in order "to discover—through its own self-reflection—a fictional form that is culturally relevant to contemporary readers" (2, 18). As I will show below, although not a work of literature, Waugh's definition of metafiction is applicable to *Afinal, o que Querem as Mulheres?*. Carvalho's figurative and literal references to cinema and his use of non-traditional television techniques in *Afinal, o que Querem as Mulheres?* all call attention to *his* role as creator as well as to the microseries itself as something very different from other television programs.

Informing the microseries' metacritique is the differing degree of control a director has in film versus television. Carvalho comments on his experience as a filmmaker and specifically as a telenovela director in a 2008 interview in which he compares the production for *Renascer*, his 1993 telenovela, to that of *Lavoura Arcaica*. He says, "If in television, between takes I have the feeling of being spied upon, in film, on the contrary, it is as if I was alone in my room working, talking with my secrets, revealing myself without anyone watching: free from the captivity of rigor that is television" ("Entrevistas: Luiz Fernando"). According to Carvalho's conceptualization, film is an intimate space that releases the director from the overwhelming commercial expectations that characterize most television production. Despite the limits of Carvalho's romanticized generalization, his words are revealing insofar as they are representative of the reasoning behind his more recent decision to avoid directing longer formats such as the telenovela and the miniseries. Instead, since 2005, Carvalho has almost exclusively worked with the microseries, which, as Brazilian television's version of a long film, allows the director a greater degree of artistic and narrative control. Carvalho's choice to focus on the shorter microseries format, then, provides him an opportunity to distinguish himself from other television directors. Moreover, the decision also productively distances Carvalho from the artistic control and economic and symbolic capital possessed by famous telenovela authors.

THE TELEVISION DIRECTOR VERSUS THE WRITER

From the beginning of *Afinal, o que Querem as Mulheres?*, Carvalho positions himself as the creative force behind the work. While the title page vignette is still on screen, the spectator can hear Carvalho, in voice-over, shouting out orders: "Vamos rodar, atenção. Câmera! Roda. Ação!" (Attention, let's start filming. Lights! Camera! Action!). A cut to a shot of André sitting at a desk with his back to the camera precedes three different shots of a second camera on wheels entering into the room where the protagonist sits. Despite the accelerated editing, filtered neon red or blue lighting—achieved by placing colored gels over the camera's lens—key the viewer to the three distinct shots. Immediately before André breaks the fourth wall to inform the spectator of who he is and what he is doing, a clapperboard appears directly in front of the camera. Again, the spectator can hear Carvalho's voice as he reads what is on the clapperboard: "*Afinal, o que Querem as Mulheres?* Capítulo 1. Cena 1a. Take 3" ("*After All, What do Women Want?* Chapter 1. Scene 1a. Take 3") (figures 1.1 and 1.2). The subtle implication here is that the three opening shots of the camera entering the room where André sits at his desk are the previous takes mentioned by the director as he marks the footage for the forthcoming editing process.

The frantic tone created by the overlap of frenetic editing, fast-paced jazz music, the visible presence of the camera and clapperboard, and the artificial lighting is mitigated by Carvalho's directorial voice: a declaration that the microseries begins ("Lights! Camera! Action!") and ends ("Cut!") with the

31

FIGURE 1.1. Camera, opening scene of *Afinal, o que Querem as Mulheres?* (2010). Right to reproduce granted by TV Globo.

FIGURE 1.2. Camera, opening scene of *Afinal, o que Querem as Mulheres?* (2010). Right to reproduce granted by TV Globo.

figure of the director. Contrary to Brazilian television fiction's general focus on plot and character-centered causality—narrative elements that arise from the writer's pen—the opening scene of *Afinal, o que Querem as Mulheres?* emphasizes the work's formal construction. In doing so, Carvalho positions himself against the creative power structure that informs the production of Brazilian television fiction. Traditionally, with the exception of a select few, television directors receive little attention or critical acclaim relative to the superstar television writers like Sílvio de Abreu, Manoel Carlos, Gilberto Braga, and Glória Perez, among others. Esther Hamburger notes the extent to which the television writer both possesses and is perceived as possessing creative control over a work: "Even when not physically present in the studio, writers are considered to be the absolute authority, and they are the center of telenovela production" (*O Brasil* 45). As I will discuss further in Chapter Two, the opposite is true in Carvalho's works; it is the director who is the authoritative creative force, overseeing and driving the production. Carvalho uses *Afinal, o que Querem as Mulheres?* to deconstruct the writer/director hierarchy and his own inferior position within it. Central to this task is the cinema and the director's privileged position in that field as point of reference for asserting Carvalho's own relevance as a television director.

Visual references to Woody Allen and Stanley Kubrick films in *Afinal, o que Querem as Mulheres?* reinforce Carvalho's assertion of control, by evoking the figure of the auteur and the implicit experimentalism and individuality of that figure. As he recalls the first time he and Lívia met, for example, André pauses near a poster for Allen's *Manhattan* (1979) on his apartment wall—a reference I will return to shortly. In this same scene, a nondiegetic insertion of a shot of a countdown of numbers, evoking that which preceded the beginning of a film shown in a movie theater, introduces the flashback of André's memories. While the countdown was traditionally a signal to the audience that the showcase event was about to start and that in moments they would embark on a journey into a fictional universe, as used in *Afinal, o que Querem as Mulheres?* the countdown is a transitional device that introduces André's flashback, which itself takes place at the cinema. Memories, Carvalho suggests, are like the movies: while they contain elements drawn from reality, they are mere representations constructed within the context of any number of past and present emotional and sociopsychological factors. This analogy is taken full circle after the countdown, when the audience, now fully immersed in Andre's act of remembering, learns that André and Lívia, as in the movies, romantically stumbled upon one another while waiting in line for a screening of Stanley Kubrick's *2001: A Space Odyssey* (1968) (figures 1.3 and 1.4).

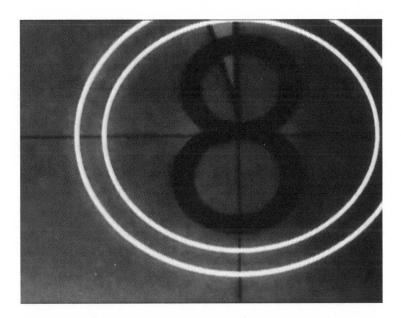

FIGURE 1.3. Cinema number countdown, *Afinal, o que Querem as Mulheres?* (2010). Right to reproduce granted by TV Globo.

FIGURE 1.4. 2001: A Space Odyssey, *Afinal, o que Querem as Mulheres?* (2010). Right to reproduce granted by TV Globo.

As the space where their love begins, the movie theater, and by extension art-house cinema as whole—as if to further emphasize its importance, the word "cinema" appears sixteen times on the marquee—symbolize the intimacy Carvalho uses to describe film production and to criticize its absence in standardized television. In contrast, André and Lívia's relationship becomes untenable due to the former's fame, which is directly linked to his new involvement with the telenovela adaptation of his best-selling book. To reinforce the suggestion that intimacy and standardized television are mutually exclusive, Carvalho includes a four-minute, lyrical sequence depicting André's rise to fame and his resulting separation from Lívia. The total lack of dialogue and the visual construction of this sequence, comprised by cross-cutting André and Lívia leading their separate lives, emphasizes the physical and emotional gap that now exists between the former lovers. Symbolically, the sequence culminates with Lívia turning off her television set when she sees André on *Altas Horas*, Sergio Groisman's late-night television talk show on TV Globo. As Lívia does so, she falls into the arms of Jonas, her new love. That André's love life is a metaphor for the disconnect between standardized television and intimate production is further emphasized by the fact that André's new fame makes it impossible for him to have a meaningful relationship, not just with Lívia, but with any woman.

After a number of promotional interviews on television and the success of the television adaptation of his book, André becomes a huge celebrity. His notoriety is such that, as he tells his mother, he cannot seem to find a woman who does not want to be with him because of who he is; that is, not the famous author, but the famous author whose work has been adapted to television. André himself further complicates the situation when, in moments of celebrity-induced confidence, he morphs into Rodrigo Santoro, his new alter ego. To remedy the situation, André's mother suggests that her son seek out a place where no one will know who he is. However, as André quickly learns, television's reach in Brazil has no limits. In search of anonymity, André ends up at a strip club in Copacabana. The sexually commoditized space, he hopes, will allow him to purchase the anonymous type of interaction he desires. Nonetheless, André's fame knows no limits, as is suggested by the exaggerated treatment he receives from all the females in the club. What is more, in the same way these women are interested in the idea of the famous André, the fact that the protagonist morphs into Santoro as a result of the intense attention he is receiving suggests that André is caught between himself—that is, nonfamous André—and a new idea of self, constructed and perpetuated through his celebrity. This psychological grappling between his id (Rodrigo Santoro) and his superego proves to be too much for André who, overcome by the female attention, passes out and is taken to a hospital, where he falls into a coma.

André's transformation into Santoro at the very moment that his fame and the resulting attention from women overwhelm him to the point of near-death, can be understood as a critical commentary on the broader relationship between standardized television fiction and a more meaningful form of artistic communication. Indeed, Carvalho emphasizes that this is the case by having André awaken from his comatose state determined to leave television behind and to focus on his next project, which attempts to answer a new question: "After all, what do men want?" Although that project is a commercial failure, during this period André is once again able to find love. In fact, in a symbolic restoration of normalcy, he meets Sophia, his new lover and the future mother of his daughter, at a movie theater where he has again gone to watch *2001: A Space Odyssey*. The broader implication is that while André no longer has a connection to commercial television, his recent experimental endeavor has led him back to a place where his own value system—and not one imposed by commercial demands—guides his decisions. André no longer transforms into Santoro because, once again outside of the structure of standardized television production, he knows who he is and what is important to him. In short, he does not need an artificial identity mediated by the public sphere.

Carvalho's own professional trajectory is somewhat similar to that of André. In 1997, following the commercially successful and critically acclaimed telenovela *O Rei do Gado*, the director decided to leave television to work exclusively on *Lavoura Arcaica*. At about this time, Carvalho recounts, he was burned out with television and at a creative impasse, no longer able to experiment within the excessively commercial structure (*Luiz Fernando Carvalho* 30). In *Afinal, o que Querem as Mulheres?* André has a similar epiphany. Immediately before coming out of his comatose state, while he is still in the indeterminate space between life and death, he cites Lacan: "What does it matter how many loves you have, if none of them gives you the universe?" For André, this is the realization that allows him to move away from the system that has coopted and transformed his identity and professional seriousness. Perhaps Carvalho would say, "what does it matter how large your audience numbers are, if they do not give you the universe?" To an extent, it was this realization that led Carvalho away from TV Globo in 1997. In one of his written texts the director actually makes a very similar declaration: "In all of these years, my audiovisual work has been nothing more than an attempt to express myself sincerely through sounds and images. Honestly, either I continue down this path, or absolutely nothing makes sense" ("Educação" 27). André's words about love can thus be interpreted as a metaphor for Carvalho's broader objective of experimenting with the televisual language to create works that are meaningful for him, beyond externally imposed commercial demands and even at the cost of losing his previously enormous audiences.

That this is the case is further suggested by the evocation of Isaac, the protagonist from Woody Allen's *Manhattan*, which is referenced by the poster hanging on André's apartment wall. Interestingly, as Carvalho has André do in the microseries, Woody Allen, the writer, director, and star of *Manhattan*, has the television writer Isaac leave the medium to focus on a more intimate project—writing his book. In one particular scene, Isaac, played by Allen, watches a taping of a television show for which he is a writer. The scene opens with a high-angle establishing shot of the television studio set where a program host interviews two guests. A subsequent cut to Isaac looking down on the set from an off-stage control room symbolizes his superiority over the televisual product he is watching. Isaac emphasizes his superior position by explicitly critiquing the program's lack of originality: "Jesus! This is embarrassing to me! I mean this is so antiseptic. . . . How do you see this [material] as chancy? It's empty! There is not any substance. . . . That's funny!? You are going by the audience's reaction? This is an audience that is raised on television. Their standards have been systematically lowered over the years" (Allen, *Manhattan* DVD). As simultaneously the creator and critic of the televisual product he is watching, Isaac's comments are contradictory. That is, he is ultimately criticizing himself, the position he maintains within the field, and the field as a whole, in comparison to "superior" forms of cultural production. In an elitist intellectual posturing, Isaac demeans a medium and an audience that pays his bills and that, eventually, will provide him with the financial security to pursue his book project. Like Isaac, Carvalho also criticizes television. However, unlike Isaac, Carvalho understands that the medium can offer a space in which artistic alternatives are plausible—alternatives he himself explores. Thus, rather than including himself or his position in his critique, as Isaac unconsciously does, Carvalho focuses his ire on criticizing what he views as the empty writing, acting, celebrity, and inconsequential directing of much of Brazilian television fiction.

To this end, *Afinal, o que Querem as Mulheres?*, like Allen's *Manhattan*, includes its own metafictional filming of a scene from the television adaptation of André's book. In this particular scene between Santoro and the actress who plays Lívia (Lavínia Vlasak), Carvalho parodies the actors' interpretations, calling attention to the pervasive use of an overly superficial and expository dialogue:

> Actress [standing next to a painting she is clearly not painting]: "You [Santoro]? How are you?"

FIGURE 1.5. Actress next to painting, *Afinal, o que Querem as Mulheres?* (2010). Right to reproduce granted by TV Globo.

FIGURE 1.6. Lívia next to her paintings, *Afinal, o que Querem as Mulheres?* (2010). Right to reproduce granted by TV Globo.

Santoro [sitting at a desk typing, although unconvincingly]: "I think I am getting there darling."

Actress [in a sweet, docile voice]: "André, this research is making you so . . . so pale! Is there something I can do for you?"

Santoro [overly pensive]: "Hmmm . . . maybe a . . . a cup of coffee."

Actress [smiling happily]: "Of course!" (*Afinal* DVD)

Within the context of the televisual adaptation of André's work, the point of this scene is to inform the spectator of the difficulties André is experiencing with his writing and research as well as Lívia's love for and devotion to the male protagonist. However, based on André and Lívia's heart-wrenching breakup, the spectator has already seen the source-text for this adaptation in the microseries' first chapter. In that scene, the spectator accompanies the dissolution of André and Lívia's relationship through the aforementioned montage of shots representing a back-and-forth between the present and temporally indeterminate flashbacks. While there is some dialogue in the scene, it is kept to a minimum. Instead, Carvalho communicates feelings of sadness and pain through a combination of music, dance, gestures and looks, skewed and obscured framing, expressionistic lighting, and a camera that sensually moves over and about the space and actors' bodies as they try, but are unable to grasp the complex reality of their dissolving relationship.

In contrast, the scene from the adaptation subordinates the audiovisual to a secondary role (figures 1.5 and 1.6). Captured in a traditional shot/counter-shot construction and characterized by high-key lighting, there is little that might be considered audiovisually uncharacteristic and might draw the spectator's attention away from what the actors are saying. As such, this type of construction emphasizes—first and foremost—the importance of the writer who creates the dialogue and the actors who bring it to life through the spoken word. However, by including trivial dialogue, the actor's caricatured interpretation of it, and the bland *mise-en-scène* in the televisual adaptation of André's book, Carvalho suggests that these are hollow creations that lack the ability to communicate beyond a merely superficial level.

In his parody of such creations, Carvalho depicts the televisual adaptation of André's book as essentially ridiculous. For example, in the aforementioned scene, Santoro interrupts the dialogue, informing the director that he cannot continue. The problem, it turns out, is that the liquid Santoro put in his eyes so as to be able to cry at the scene's obligatory emotional apex is preventing him from seeing who is standing in front of him. At this very moment, fusing reality and fiction, André, recalling his past interaction with Lívia, begins to speak with the actress as if she were in fact his former lover. Further highlighting the superficiality and emptiness present in her previous dialogue with Santoro, the actress who plays Lívia changes both her tone of voice and her facial expressions, resulting in a more genuine exchange. No longer confined by the shooting of the adapted scene, the actress begins to embody a form of expression closer to what the spectator saw with Lívia in the microseries' first chapter. Santoro, who is watching nearby and cannot bear to not have all the attention on him, interrupts the more genuine and sincere interaction between André and the actress, informing those present that he has just received his one-millionth Twitter follower. In a moment intended to play as critical and sarcastic, having replaced the brief instance of emotional depth present in the conversation between André and the actress, the scene ends with Santoro signing a painting of himself before looking into the camera to thank Brazil for his wonderful achievement. As it pertains to the broader comparative context of Carvalho's microseries, the oscillation between trivial or genuine interactions implies that superficial dialogue, hollow acting, and celebrity, all in the name of commercial demands and financial objectives, supplant more meaningful attempts to create a televisual language of consequence.

For this, Carvalho is clear about whom he blames. Indeed, in *Afinal, o que Querem as Mulheres?* Carvalho reserves his harshest critique for the director behind the adaptation of André's book. In perhaps one of the microseries' funniest moments, the unnamed director calls for makeup. Initially, it seems that he is asking for makeup to come and touch up one of the actors, which is also the understanding of the makeup artist as he approaches Santoro. However, the director stops him and quietly says, "No, it's for me." Here, through the use of humor, Carvalho suggests that the director, not unlike Santoro, is concerned with superficial elements, such as appearance and celebrity, more than with the creation of a meaningful work of art. Since a director works behind the scenes, the notion that she would privilege her image over the creative process seems absurd to Carvalho. For this reason, Carvalho makes it clear to the spectator that most television directors, like the one working on the adaptation of André's book, are not artists like himself, nor are they even really concerned with creating art. Along these same lines, in the scene described above, Santoro's inability to find a capital letter on the computer keyboard sends the crew into a frenzy. For the first time, the director raises his voice and asks someone to find the letter. In light of the "complexity" of the situation a production assistant yells for someone from the art department to come and help find the letter. The implication that the art department would be concerned with such a thing and that the director oversees such work only further emphasizes the lack of respect Carvalho has for his peers in television.

FIGURE 1.7. André clapperboard, *Afinal, o que Querem as Mulheres?* (2010). Right to reproduce granted by TV Globo.

FIGURE 1.8. Lívia clapperboard, *Afinal, o que Querem as Mulheres?* (2010). Right to reproduce granted by TV Globo.

FIGURE 1.9. Actress clapperboard, *Afinal, o que Querem as Mulheres?* (2010). Right to reproduce granted by TV Globo.

FIGURE 1.10. TV director clapperboard, *Afinal, o que Querem as Mulheres?* (2010). Right to reproduce granted by TV Globo.

FigurE 1.11. Rodrigo Santoro clapperboard, *Afinal, o que Querem as Mulheres?* (2010). Right to reproduce granted by TV Globo.

In *Afinal, o que Querem as Mulheres?*, then, Carvalho depicts the director and his crew as interchangeable mid-level employees who lack artistic sensibilities and are unable or unwilling to defy the commercially imposed rules. This artistic void leads them to focus to a greater degree on the superficial— that is, their own images and privileged professional positions. Indeed, during an interview Carvalho reveals his awareness that at least some of the "creative" employees in television are no more than paper-pushers: "I imagine that my rigor may bother contented *civil servants*, and I confess that I am *very hard* on them. Those who have been with me for some time know that the path is an *arduous* one; that we are fighting against many monsters and their technocratic formulas. This battle demands rigor on my part, and some are just not prepared for that" (emphasis added, "Uma Comédia"). Carvalho (re)states a similar position through Sônia, a peripheral character in *Afinal, o que Querem as Mulheres?* In response to André's question about what it is women want, she declares: "I want a man who takes care of me! . . . The solution is to bet on civil servants! Those state, federal, and global civil servants!" (*Afinal* DVD). Sônia's comments explicitly group *funcionários públicos* (civil servants), a denomination used in Brazil as an insult implying mediocrity, with the *globais*, TV Globo employees.[5] These individuals, Sônia's lines imply, are safe and comfortable in their positions. As such, one knows what to expect from them as they toe the company line.

Carvalho highlights this negative connotation by using a clapperboard to introduce both the characters from *Afinal, o que Querem as Mulheres?* and its parodical adaptation of André's book. The clapperboards that introduce the microseries' protagonists, André and Lívia, simply state their names. However, those that introduce the actress who plays a version of Lívia for the adaptation of André's book and the director of this series (Alexandre Schumacher) do not carry the individuals' names. Instead, they merely state their titles: *A Atriz* (The Actress) and *O Diretor de TV* (The Television Director). The clapperboard that introduces Santoro, however, uses his real name (figures 1.7, 1.8, 1.9, 1.10 and 1.11).

The assertion is that the creative contributions of the actors and directors are of very little importance in standardized television. Those actors, Santoro included, who have roles in the microseries outside of the adaptation of André's book maintain a heightened role relative to those who appear exclusively in the adapted series. That is, unlike "*A Atriz*" and "*O Diretor*," those who feature in Carvalho's microseries have clapperboards with their names on them. In contrast, whereas Carvalho asserts himself in the microseries' opening scene as the work's creative force, the director of the adapted series does not even deserve a name. Thus, in developing a defamiliarized aesthetic for his own microseries, Carvalho argues that he, unlike most directors, actively seeks out experimentation with the televisual language and that the television actors with whom he works, perhaps because of his artistic influence, are more capable than those with whom he does not work.

The combination, then, of Carvalho's artistic trajectory, his cultural competence, and his irritation with the state of contemporary Brazilian television fiction has placed him in direct opposition to the medium's dominant, commercially driven, and derivative aesthetics. In *Afinal, o que Querem as Mulheres?*, as in his interviews and writings, Carvalho parodies what he understands to be a disingenuous form of communication that is structured by market expectations rather than by the artists' need to create.

In the microseries, this belief is finally exemplified by André's decision to take on the new, already mentioned research project. In his first project, "After all, what do women want?," the subject matter is a popular, even sexy choice, easily marketable by the chauvinistic audiovisual machine, as André's newfound celebrity and the television adaptation of his finished book prove. However, his second intellectual project, trying to answer the question of what it is that men want, is far less interesting and commercially viable, as suggested by André's new job as a love doctor on an antiquated radio station in a run-down building on the outskirts of Rio de Janeiro. André's media marginalization evokes the inverse historical trajectory of the telenovela, which went from being highly successful on the radio to eventually dominating Brazilian television production and displacing the radio as the preeminent form of media. At the same time, André's new career in the economically inferior radio displaces the primacy of the superficial, commercialized image and allows him to engage in greater intellectual experimentation. Carvalho's point is clear; with regard to Brazilian television fiction: what matters first and foremost is capturing those large audiences sought by advertisers, not the artist's creative exploration and experimentation.

At the center of Carvalho's project for reimagining Brazilian television fiction is an attempt to subvert an aesthetic, production, and commercial reality that broadly functions to place the director in an inferior position relative to the television writer. To this end, the critique of standardized Brazilian television and its many creative agents, both through its form and content, that we see in *Afinal, o que Querem as Mulheres?* is a manifestation of Carvalho's position. To position himself in such a way and to gain more control over the creative process, Carvalho has consistently deconstructed TV Globo's standardized production models for television fiction. With this in mind, the next chapter examines Carvalho's long-standing collaboration with a consistent creative team and his implementation of an elaborate preproduction process as two means by which he exerts the greatest possible degree of control over his work within the TV Globo structure.

Chapter Two

CREATING THROUGH THE PREPRODUCTION PROCESS

In "Superávit" ("Surplus"), one of the comedy troupe and independent production company Porta dos Fundos's hundreds of extremely popular YouTube videos, Congressman Valdo tries to convince Congressman Laércio to participate in stealing public funds. Decidedly against such corruption, Laércio suggests that rather than stealing from the Brazilian people, Valdo and his colleagues should reinvest this money in art and culture for the good of the population. Incredulously, Valdo asks: "Do you want to watch more Brazilian films? Is that what you want? Do you want to go to the movies to watch *Avengers*, only to be forced to see a Brazilian film instead? If you tell me you want to watch more Brazilian films, I will take the money right now and set up a government-run competition to finance more films" ("Superávit").

Faced with Valdo's threat, Laércio's reaction reveals the horror of such a possibility. Consequently, at the deciding moment of his moral dilemma, Laércio concludes that it would be better to steal from the Brazilian people than to finance more Brazilian films. Though "Superávit" focuses primarily on the widespread political corruption in present-day Brazil, it also speaks to the historical disconnect between Brazilian films, the Brazilian filmgoing public, and the government's role in supporting the fledgling industry.[1] At issue is a generalized belief within the country's broader social imaginary that Brazilian films are not only inferior to those made in Hollywood and Europe, but are also mere vehicles for filmmakers to disseminate their political positions and highbrow artistic pretensions.

Within this context, then, Carvalho's intricate knowledge of and interest in cinema, as well as his conception of himself as an artist and an intellectual, are doubly complicated by his current position as a television director for the largest television network in Brazil ("Luiz Fernando Carvalho (não) está"). First, as in many parts of the world, although the tendency for a number of Brazilian artists and intellectuals has long been to reject the market, thereby adhering to and perpetuating the romantic conceptualization of the figure of the artist as operating on the margins of capitalism, in Carvalho's case such a stance would directly contradict his employer TV Globo's overarching mission: attracting the largest possible audience. At the same time, full acceptance of the market would run counter to the historical legacy of being a "true" artist in Brazil, placing Carvalho in an inferior position among like-minded producers. Second, as discussed in Chapter One, in Brazilian television the director has more often than not occupied a subordinate creative role to the all-powerful telenovela writer.

In short, Carvalho occupies a liminal space between the two discourses that characterize Brazilian cinema as an elitist form of art and Brazilian television as a vehicle for lowbrow commercialism. Consequently, the director's relationship with TV Globo must be understood as both contradictory and mutually beneficial. TV Globo provides Carvalho with funds, resources, and a general artistic license. What is more, TV Globo gives Carvalho access to an audience he would never have were he to only make films or work for one of the other Brazilian networks. Conversely, Carvalho provides the hegemonic TV Globo with a cultural cachet or symbolic capital it would not otherwise have as a monolithic large-scale producer. Thus, from his privileged position in the field of Brazilian audiovisual production where he holds a significant amount of symbolic capital while utilizing such capital within the confines of an economically dominant institution such as TV Globo, Carvalho's work represents a challenge to the preconceived, hierarchical notions of film and television, and the dichotomous labeling of lowbrow and highbrow culture in general. At the base of such a challenge is the unique preproduction process and creative team Carvalho has been developing and perfecting since as early as 1993.

WORKING AGAINST THE TRADITIONAL TELENOVELA

Whether working in another format and explicitly against the telenovela or directing a prime-time version of the immensely popular daily melodrama, Carvalho has long made the telenovela the point of departure for his unique mode of production and aesthetic. Beginning with the now-defunct TV Excelsior's daily airing of *2–5499 Ocupado* in 1963, the telenovela set out on a path to become Brazilian television fiction's commercially dominant format. By the early 1970s, under the direction of Walter Clark and José Bonifácio de Oliveira Sobrinho (Boni), the telenovela was synonymous with TV Globo, which, only five years after its inception, had transformed itself into the country's dominant network. Transitioning out of the period characterized in part by single airings of teleteatros, Clark and Boni sought an economically efficient format that would allow TV Globo to spread costs over a number of chapters while also producing local content that would appeal to the audience's cultural specificities (Clark and Barbosa Lima, "Um pouco de história" 34–36). Over the years that followed, TV Globo refined and perfected the production of its telenovelas, creating a process evocative of an assembly line or, as Hamburger has described it, "an organized routine, broken up into steps, recalling a Fordian mode of production" (*O Brasil* 43).

Indeed, today nearly all telenovelas employ more than 300 individuals who work 12 to 14 hours a day, 6 days a week, for 6 to 9 months, with the ultimate objective of bringing to life the 30 to 40 pages written each day by the telenovela author. The extremely fast pace and large scale of TV Globo's telenovela production process are such that anything outside a mode-of-production designed for maximum efficiency would simply not suffice to ensure that episodes were shot, edited, and finalized in time to go to air. Central to this efficiency is TV Globo's organizational structure as it pertains to television fiction. Like the Hollywood studio system of the 1940s, TV Globo promotes and is home to a vertical production model based on maintaining a number of the country's most famous television writers and actors on long-term contracts. Such contracts allow the media conglomerate to feature these individuals across its programming platform and in other media vehicles, from entertainment news magazines and websites to films and plays. The contracts also ensure that audiences strongly associate the most famous and sought-after talent with the Globo brand and not with rival networks. In this way, the telenovela is at the center of what is simultaneously TV Globo's concrete and discursive practice. As the commercial and narrative format most desired by Brazilian television advertisers, the telenovela—especially the *novela das nove* (the 9 p.m. telenovela, referred to previously as the *novela das oito* [8 p.m.], despite airing at 9 p.m.), the prime-time crown jewel—gives prominence to, and is often built around, the network's most celebrated writers and actors. Indeed, in narrative terms, the efficiency-based model begins with telenovela writers constructing formulaic scripts characterized by archetypal storylines that adhere to classical narrative's character-centered plot development.

While there are a number of ways in which one might stage such a narrative, the most common and efficient option used by television producers is to present famous actors who recite facile expository dialogue. Allowing actors to drive narration through the spoken word eliminates the need for more elaborate visual construction. Rather than intricate experimentation, medium or medium close-up shots, which unfold visually through shot/countershot editing, serve as the primary vehicle for capturing dialogue. For a Brazilian television director who aims to move beyond implementing preestablished rules and to put her imprint on a particular work, the telenovela's tendency to emphasize dialogue in this way undermines the director's capacity for audiovisual construction, ultimately marginalizing her artistic input in favor of that which comes from the writer or actors.

Though Carvalho has worked in television since the early 1980s, he has long been hostile to the industry's tendency toward factorylike production and the resulting emphasis on the spoken word and lack of audiovisual experimentation. Both in interviews and in his own writings about his work, Carvalho has frequently criticized television fiction as being repetitive and lacking in creativity. While his criticism almost always focuses on the telenovela, he also takes aim at naturalism more broadly.[2] For Carvalho, whether in television, film, or theater, naturalism has become so ubiquitous that it has lost its communicative power ("Educação" 25). By framing his critique in this way, Carvalho takes issue with nearly all Brazilian television fiction, independent of the specific format.

In 2002, for example, during a long interview with the online film magazine *ContraCampo*, the director highlights his understanding of two of the most prominent problems with Brazilian television fiction: (1) a general lack of experimentation; and (2) the networks' constant focus on refining formulas proven to capture the largest audiences sought by advertisers. Carvalho's concern is that decision makers' overwhelming preoccupation with audience share, production budgets, time constraints, and so forth has supplanted the possibilities for creative exploration, reducing television fiction to an overly conventional and industrialized symbolic good. In practice, this means that directors must work as efficiently as possible, eliminating the creative aesthetic and stylistic experimentation that could potentially threaten market-imposed expectations, if not received positively by the television audience ("Luiz Fernando Carvalho (não)"). Within the generally homogenous confines of television production, Carvalho concludes, individuals "substitute a search for creative expression with one for commercial success," resulting in "excessively descriptive works"—that is, those that leave little to no room for imagination ("Luiz Fernando Carvalho (não)").

Renascer, Carvalho's critically acclaimed and commercially successful telenovela from 1993, exemplifies the difficulties a television director encounters when the network's commercial demands limit creative exploration. The first ten chapters share a number of formal and narrative similarities with Carvalho's later microseries, albeit without the explicit theatricality and antinaturalism of those shorter-format works. As in his later works, in *Renascer* Carvalho initiated a practice of putting his cast and crew through an elaborate preproduction process, aimed at preparing them intellectually, emotionally, and aesthetically for the forthcoming creative endeavor ("Entrevistas: Luiz Fernando"). Within this production model, at the time a novelty but now fundamental to all of Carvalho's work, much of the experimentation and the establishment of the work's artistic contours occur during the preparatory period. It is during this period that Carvalho creates an environment focused on allowing the work's participants a great degree of freedom to explore and experiment with different communicative and artistic possibilities.

The fact that Carvalho had the time to implement his artistic laboratory and to prepare and complete *Renascer's* first ten chapters without any feedback from the audience provided him the necessary creative freedom to make an audiovisual product that was aesthetically unlike the majority of the telenovelas at the time. Not only are the first ten chapters of *Renascer* different from other telenovelas from the early 1990s, they are unlike the rest of the work itself.

Shortly after completing *Renascer,* Carvalho offered insight into why this was the case by recalling the difficulties he experienced while making the 1987 telenovela *Helena*: "Although my background is primarily in video, my theoretical training is film. When I started directing for television in 1987, I was very concerned with making a film on television. My first job was to adapt *Helena,* for TV Manchete, and at the time I would repeat to myself: 'I'm going to make a film!' I tried it for a few good chapters—studying the type of narrative, I elaborated scenes within certain concepts, worried about the camera position. . . . Soon, however, I began to set aside such concerns" (Almeida and Araújo, *As Perspectivas* 113–14). Why Carvalho eventually "set aside such concerns" exemplifies the reality surrounding the production of a typical telenovela. Generally, a telenovela goes to air with approximately twenty completed chapters or about three weeks of content. The problem, then, for a director interested in a slower creative process arises when the small backlog of preshot chapters runs out, and daily deadlines impose themselves as a driving force behind the production. Clearly, as was the case in *Helena,* the sheer vastness of *Renascer's* remaining 203 episodes and its accompanying economic imperatives (audience share, advertising, product and merchandising obligations, and so on) made it virtually impossible for Carvalho to maintain an intimate, purposeful, creative relationship with the actors, or to continue the carefully constructed, often unconventional shots that characterize the work's first ten episodes. Broadly speaking, commercial expectations for large-budget, prime-time programming make significant artistic experimentation almost unviable. Moreover, even when such experimentation is possible, executives and producers, in an attempt to ensure commercial success and their jobs, often revert to the proven model already in place. Excluding, for example, some of Guel Arraes's work,[3] one-off specials, and the rare TV Globo and O2 coproduction, this is true as well for the network's shorter fictional formats. For example, contemporary programming like *Grande Família* (2001–2014), *Os Normais* (2001–2003), *A Diarista* (2004–2007), *Toma Lá, Dá Cá* (2007–2009), *Tapas e Beijos* (2011–2015), *Pé na Cova* (2013–), and *Mister Brau* (2015–) follows the standard American situational comedy model.

In what reads as almost an invocation of Isaac from *Manhattan*, Carvalho argues that the narrative and aesthetic homogeneity of telenovelas and of these shorter works help to form an audience "reared on a standardized televisual language" ("Carvalho Invoca"). Implicit in Carvalho's critique is an Adornian conception of the medium as a culture industry. In his polemical and influential essay "How to Look at Television" (1954), Theodor Adorno highlights the standardization of television production, arguing that "the repetitiveness, the selfsameness, and the ubiquity of modern mass culture" tend to eliminate individuality in the works as well as in the audiences' reactions to those works (216). Indeed, like Adorno, Carvalho's concerns revolve around a field of production that has become a model of machinelike efficiency over the years. But while Adorno spurns the medium as a whole, Carvalho's work is an experimental response to the norm of naturalism. It represents an attempt to construct a language that communicates with the spectator beyond superficially reproducing models that attract audiences and promote consumption. In short, it is a reimagination of the initial steps to the production of Brazilian television fiction.

ARTISTIC CONTROL: THE CREATIVE TEAM

A reimagining of Brazilian television fiction first requires structural changes. For Carvalho, the most important of these has been the implementation of an elaborate, very intimate preproduction process that challenges the norm through experimentation. Before any audiovisual work goes to air, its producers must put time into structuring the concept and determining its accompanying aesthetic details. In *Art Worlds*, Howard Becker argues that "The way the work is produced bears no *necessary* relationship to its quality" (emphasis added, 2). While it might not be *necessary*, it is fairly evident that for nearly any endeavor, art included, the amount of effort invested in an initial process *can* serve as a deciding factor for a work's commercial or critical success, or lack thereof. Of course, not all producers place the same emphasis on preproduction, which might be predetermined by their target audience as well as economic and time constraints. For Carvalho, however, whether preparing for a one-hour special or for the beginning of a 200-chapter telenovela, the period prior to filming is of the utmost importance. It gives him time to establish what he desires to extract from each of his characters—their emotional, psychological, and physical states—and to specify the fictional world's atmosphere in the greatest detail possible (Almeida and Araújo, *As Perspectivas* 116). To this end, as the basis for the development of his singular televisual aesthetic, Carvalho employs a production model that is unique within the context of Brazilian television production. Indeed, the very existence of this model deconstructs what Carvalho understands to be contemporary standardized television fiction's flaws: its factorylike production; its superficial audiovisual constructions; its overemphasis of celebrity; and the marginalized creative role of the director, all of which, as discussed in Chapter One, Carvalho heavily criticizes in *Afinal, o que Querem as Mulheres?*

While the structural *and* aesthetic antecedents of Carvalho's microseries can be traced to his end-of-the-year TV Globo specials *Uma Mulher Vestida de Sol* (*A Woman Clothed in the Sun*) (1994) and *Farsa da Boa Preguiça* (*The Farce of Good Laziness*) (1995), the origins of this highly involved preproduction process can be found in the 1993 telenovela *Renascer*. Later, beginning around 1997, with the making of *Lavoura Arcaica*, as I discuss in greater detail toward the end of this chapter, Carvalho radicalized the artistic mode of operation and process for subverting the standardized television production initiated in *Renascer*. Because Carvalho's preproduction process is consistent throughout his microseries, in the sections that follow, to avoid being overly repetitive, I will focus primarily on his continuous and long-established professional relationships with the specific individuals that form his creative team and on examples from his implementation of workshops and seminars.

The selection of a group of trusted audiovisual professionals is Carvalho's first step toward challenging production norms and inserting creativity in his work. Although the director's creative team experiences slight changes depending on the individual's availability for a particular work, its members generally come from a small, select group chosen by Carvalho throughout his decades of experience. Carvalho is clear that for his work the formation of a good team is central to its success (Almeida and Araújo, *As Perspectivas* 116). But for Carvalho, the creative team is more than a group of individuals working together. Instead, they come together to form what the director refers to as his spiritual family (Kogut, "Luiz Fernando Carvalho mergulha"). By mentioning spirituality, Carvalho evokes the idea of an artistic religion, to which adherents must give themselves over entirely. To expand the metaphor further, Carvalho is the spiritual leader—a positioning that is determined in discourse and practice by Carvalho himself, through interviews, writings, and paratexts and by those very individuals who make up his creative team.

Considering Carvalho's difficult and demanding professional persona, such dedication on the part of his creative team is extremely important ("Uma Comédia"). Despite possessing the power and symbolic capital to be able to work on almost any TV Globo project, television star Antônio Fagundes is one of those devoted to Carvalho's process and vision. During an interview while in preproduction for the microseries *Dois Irmãos*, Fagundes revealed that when Carvalho invited him to take on one of the work's most rigorous roles, he not only accepted immediately, but that acceptance was based on the prospect of being able to work with the director on a future project.[4] Unlike Fagundes, Brazilian television and film star Cauã Reymond had never worked with Carvalho before *Dois Irmãos*. However, eager to be a part of the director's unique creative process, the Brazilian superstar approached Carvalho about a possible role in the adaptation of Milton Hatoum's novel. Regarding his subsequent work on that microseries, Reymond says: "I have never been a part of a work, not even in film, that included so much preparation. . . . Unlike normally when I have to do all my own research in preparation for a particular role, everything [when working with Carvalho] is so complete. I asked Luiz for this role. I very much wanted to work with him" (Kogut, "Luiz Fernando Carvalho Prepara"). Reymond's comments exemplify the space Carvalho's productions occupy in practice as an experimental enclave within the TV Globo structure and the interest some actors have in exploring the artistic possibilities inherent to the director's creative process.

While the above examples have to do with the acting talent, there are also a number of devoted key continuing members of Carvalho's production team. Some of these members include: Walter Carvalho (director of photography for *Renascer, O Rei do Gado,* and *Lavoura Arcaica*), Beth Filipecki (costume designer for *Capitu* and *Afinal*), Raquel Couto (assistant director), Lia Renha (art director for *Uma Mulher* and *Hoje é Dia*), Edna Palatanik (consultant), José Tadeu (director of photography for *Hoje é Dia* and *A Pedra*), Adrian Teijido (director of photography for *A Pedra, Capitu, Afinal,* and *Suburbia*), Yurika Yamasaki (art director for *Lavoura*, costume designer for *Rei do Gado*, and art producer for *Os Maias*), Luciana Buarque (costume designer for *Uma Mulher, Hoje é Dia, A Pedra, Suburbia,* and *Alexandre e Outros*), Thanara Schonardie (costume designer for *Meu Pedacinho de Chão, Velho Chico,* and *Dois Irmãos*), João Irênio (production designer for *Hoje é Dia, A Pedra,* and *Suburbia*), Marco Antônio Guimarães (composer for *Lavoura* and *A Pedra*), and Tim Rescala (composer for *Hoje é Dia de Maria, A Pedra's* opening, *Capitu,* and *Afinal*). As this list implies, "all artistic work, like all human activity, involves the joint activity of a number, often a large number, of people" (Becker 1). Along these lines, actress and longtime team member Eliane Giardini emphasizes what she refers to as a "creative confluence" that characterizes Carvalho's preproduction process. For her, working with the director is like working in the theater: "In TV," she says, "you work a lot, but there is little interaction.

Here with Carvalho, that is not the case. Instead, the preproduction process is a full immersion; twelve hours a day, sharing freely in the creative process with the other participants. As such, there is a ton of connection, exchange, and convergence. Everything is done with an eye toward the end result. It is from this cauldron of creative exchange that the work emerges" (Kogut, "Luiz Fernando Carvalho Prepara").

While what Giardini says of Carvalho's preproduction process is true, and while the actors and team members mentioned above could correctly be interpreted as constituting a multiplicity of creative voices guiding the production, independent of other participants, it must also be recognized that Carvalho himself is the one creative constant in each of his works. Carvalho, then, is like a composer directing an orchestra. In fact, during the wrap party for the as yet unreleased microseries, *Dois Irmãos,* Giardini told me that when she works with Carvalho she feels like a piano, one that is constantly being tuned by the maestro in order for him to play. When I asked her who the maestro was, she responded, "É o Luiz Fernando, claro!" ("It's Luiz Fernando, obviously!"). As such, the gathering and consistent use of familiar team members is best understood as an attempt on Carvalho's part to further control those elements that, due to different matters related to production, he must delegate to others.

Of course, this type of situation does not exclude artistic collaboration. Instead, it means that, especially within the unique context of Carvalho's tightly controlled microseries productions he chooses to work with individuals in whose creativity he has a greater degree of trust. As Patrick Colm Hogan notes regarding filmmaking, and the point I am making here, "there is a guiding creative force for a film in that there is someone who sets the general structures for the components of the film, assigns subordinates to work out the particulars, and then selects the instantiations of those structures" (70). Carvalho is precisely the individual and creative force that establishes—at the levels of both discourse and practice—the overall structures and accompanying aesthetic for his microseries, and he does this, more than at any other stage, during preproduction. Peter Schepelern further underscores the role of a guiding presence, defining artistic control as a structural distinction between an art film and a mainstream film. As he points out, with regard to the former, the director is often in complete control of the work, having the final say over even the smallest details. In the latter, however, the director is frequently subject to questions beyond her control, thus removing, in the very least, some of her artistic autonomy. Nevertheless, in both cases, independent of the degree of control, Schepelern notes that a creative force or an auteur can represent her "artistic vision through themes, style, or technique; they can also be represented by the steady use of the *same co-workers, cinematographer, editor, composer, or actors*" (emphasis added, 106).

In his very well-researched book on Steven Soderbergh's eclectic professional activity in Hollywood, Mark Gallagher employs production analysis to argue in favor of replacing what he refers to as the "inadequacies of the casual privileging of directors as the focal points of claims about film authorship" with "a model of collaborative authorship that recognizes the conditions of contemporary screen practice" (75, 77). What is more, Gallagher sets out to deconstruct the often-invoked studio versus independent film dichotomy in interpreting the importance of film authorship (76). Gallagher correctly points out that authorship is a complicated process that involves "diverse ways production teams perform, and viewing publics recognize, the art of filmmaking" (76). Indeed, though the concept of the auteur has rightly been deconstructed—or in the very least, problematized—in search of more holistic understandings of how complex audiovisual works are made and consumed, one needs to be careful not to apply a universal theoretical model. More often than not such a model is reduced to the Global North and how it elects to produce within that context or how it appropriates the Global South for its financial/creative needs. The point is simply that not all contexts are the same; and in the same way a scholar might make a concerted effort to take into account the numerous factors and agents participating in a particular production so as to demonstrate its ongoing complexities, she must do the same with the local context where the object of study was produced. Gallagher's analysis centers on a very specific production framework—Soderbergh's position in poststudio, contemporary, global Hollywood. While in general this is made clear, Gallagher frequently makes a rhetorical move from the specific—Soderbergh and contemporary Hollywood—to the macro— "contemporary screen practice"—thereby implying that what is true of contemporary Hollywood is universally true (77). Thus, though Gallagher's argument is quite convincing, it, and others like it, do not necessarily hold up in the vastly different reality experienced by Carvalho within the TV Globo structure.

Nonetheless, even as he advocates on behalf of a collaborative authorial understanding of filmmaking, Gallagher makes a concession to the possibility of individual authorship. He proposes that there are "four conditions under which single individuals merit the attribution of primary authorship of a screen text: (1) demonstrable evidence of supervision of production elements; (2) creative collaboration with the same individuals across a body of films; (3) multihyphenate activity, or demonstrated investment in multiple aspects of the production and postproduction processes; and (4) work within the art-cinema sector, in a small-scale production, or in another industrial formation allowing a high degree of creative autonomy" (77).

As I have already shown, Carvalho's microseries clearly meet each of Gallagher's first two conditions. Regarding the third: in addition to directing, Carvalho has also received screenwriter and producer credits for his microseries and has frequently worked as an uncredited editor. On the surface it might seem that because Carvalho works for the largest television network in Brazil he does not meet the fourth condition outlined by Gallagher. It is certainly true, as I have emphasized thus far, that more than anything TV Globo is a market-driven entity which seeks to capture the largest possible audiences to, in turn, sell to interested advertisers. As such, it necessarily imposes commercial limitations on Carvalho, expecting that he, like the other network's directors, will garner substantial audiences, will be productive, and will complete his work under or at budget.

That this is the case is made clear in a 2007 article from the São Paulo–based newspaper *Estadão*. In light of *A Pedra do Reino*'s poor audience shares, the piece highlights TV Globo's decision to keep a close eye on Carvalho's future work:

> The poor performance of *A Pedra do Reino* will not inhibit the production of the upcoming titles for Luiz Fernando Carvalho's *Projeto Quadrante*. But TV Globo's executives will follow more closely the project's forthcoming titles. *Dom Casmurro*, for example, the project's next production will take place in Rio, which already makes supervision more accessible than it was in the Paraiba backwoods, where filming for *A Pedra do Reino* took place. It is not that TV Globo has lost confidence in the director, but after *A Pedra do Reino*, the order is to keep a close watch on his vanguardist tendencies. ("Ibope de *A Pedra*")

One can sense in this statement a certain degree of credit given to Carvalho for his previous works. Indeed, immediately prior to *A Pedra do Reino*, Carvalho's *Hoje é Dia de Maria* was a huge success, both in terms of audience share and critical reception. Thus, prior to making any rash decisions, the executives mentioned in the article would seem to want to make sure that the 2007 microseries was an anomaly, rather than an indicator of a broader disconnect between Carvalho's work and the network's post–prime-time audience.

Whatever the case, the article echoes Carvalho's earlier comments on television production and his feelings of being "watched." Additionally, it points to the centrality of economics as the network's guiding force. Though the work might be a masterpiece of television—which I would argue it is—the immediate concern must be with the bottom line. In short, "vanguardist tendencies" are okay as long as the expected audience share tunes in. When this is not the case, supervision becomes a necessary measure. For another director, a similar situation would have almost certainly signaled the end of her creative freedom. However, over his long career, Carvalho's unique mixture of critical and commercial success, combined with the abundance of acclaim he received for *Lavoura Arcaica,* have all helped to carve out an unprecedented space for the director within TV Globo's commercial structure. Moreover, as the above quote implies, even while being more closely supervised, Carvalho has gained a significant degree of artistic freedom and less external input into his work by primarily making microseries, which are both less commercial and more experimental relative to the telenovela.

Over the years, once the dust has settled, TV Globo has come to understand that Carvalho offers it something beyond economic capital. That is, he offers the network prestige and critical acclaim for one of their products among an array of other spectacles that are more conventional and represent a lower risk. Nevertheless, it would be misleading to imply that TV Globo is only interested in Carvalho due to the symbolic capital he brings the network. The fact is that the network uses Carvalho's experimental work, in terms of both its production and form, to test out novelties it can potentially implement in its other programming.

All these factors allow Carvalho to reproduce for television a process that was central to the making of his lone feature-length film. For *Lavoura Arca-ica,* the director and the actors were at the film's rural Minas Gerais location for a total of three months prior to shooting the work's first scene. Counting a month for filming, they spent a total of four months on location *(Luiz Fernando Carvalho* 92). While three months is certainly a long time, what is most interesting about this preparatory period is the way in which the actors incorporated their roles: they developed their creative voices by studying and working. For example, Carvalho made it each individual's job to: read Raduan Nassar's 1975 homonymous novel, which served, unaltered, as the film's script; choose their own lines from the novel; and then make them come to life via their daily interaction with one another and the physical space in the Minas Gerais interior where filming took place. As reinforcement, Carvalho divided the day into different class periods. For example, the men worked daily in the nearby fields, plowing the land and milking the cows. Like the men, Carvalho also charged the women with embodying the traditional Arab-Brazilian women portrayed in Nassar's novel. Consequently, they tended to household duties such as cleaning and cooking. Later in the day, all the actors had Arabic, dance, and voice classes, as well as other activities directly related to the construction of the narrative universe *(Luiz Fernando Carvalho* 92).

Directly in line with the conditions outlined by Gallagher, the intimate, almost familial production process that characterized *Lavoura Arcaica* is, to an extent, made possible due to the overwhelming creative control Carvalho had in the construction of his film. In addition to being the director, he was the voice-over narrator, adaptor, screenwriter, and editor. This process represents an important mark in Carvalho's artistic trajectory, since he later adapted this mode of production for his microseries. He suggested that this was case in 2005, shortly before the premiere of *Hoje é Dia de Maria*:

> I had been preparing myself, maturing so as to be able conduct this type of creative training with the whole group. I always missed being with the whole group. I always missed creating along with the actors, with art direction.... As you can see here, there is a conglomerate of workshops and of artists. In short, our everyday life here consists of workshops in which people come out of one creative shed and enter into another. This blood flow permeates throughout. I need it to permeate; to permeate all departments." ("Carvalho Invoca")

In the comments above, Carvalho discusses his mode of production as a holistic artistic process having evolved over time. The creative control, wide-ranging attention to detail, and interaction across all artistic departments referred to by the director, while often not plausible for much of the fast-paced production of the telenovelas, let alone his own, is, however, central to all of his microseries.

In 2012, perhaps to keep an eye on the director or to reward him as a sort of artist-in-residence, TV Globo provided Carvalho with a large, permanent rehearsal warehouse and atelier at their Projac Studio grounds in western Rio de Janeiro. Carvalho recognizes that the warehouse is something he long desired and that it has been important for the interactive type of televisual production he aims to create (Kogut, "Luiz Fernando Carvalho Prepara"). The warehouse, which Carvalho refers to as "home," is known to those who work at Projac as Luizlândia (Luiz Land). It has a high-ceilinged open space that measures approximately 19 x 34 meters. Inside the warehouse, the walls of which feature Carvalho's paintwork, there is a piano, a film projection screen, and a stage. The space and its neighboring atelier have few barriers between them, resulting in osmosis of diverse activities such as costume and makeup, set design, dance rehearsals, among others. In short, the permanence and proximity of the two spaces produce the creative interaction or "blood flow" Carvalho so desires, ultimately providing him with the tools to explore his artistic interests and allowing him to conduct a preproduction process similar to that of his lone feature film, albeit within TV Globo's gigantic commercial structure. As such, over the years, Carvalho has been able to achieve a high degree of creative autonomy, thereby fulfilling Gallagher's fourth requirement for individual authorship.

PREPRODUCTION WORKSHOPS AND SEMINARS

Prior to having his permanent space at Projac, Carvalho went to great pains to create a centralized work environment in which he could freely interact with his creative team across all departments. In the early 1990s, Carvalho had experimented with an intimate mode of production for the stagings of Ariano Suassuna's plays, *Uma Mulher Vestida de Sol* and *A Farsa da Boa Preguiça*. In each of these year-end specials, which were shot entirely on Projac sound stages, Carvalho constructed theatrical narrative universes, inciting the spectator to engage in an imaginative interpretive process so as to fill in the numerous narrative gaps. As mentioned previously, in 1997, not long after these specials, Carvalho left television to work on his feature-length film. Not surprisingly, his experience with *Lavoura Arcaica* maintained the intimate production of the year-end specials while at the same time expanding the narrative world beyond their closed theatrical spaces. In 2004, when the director began preproduction for *Hoje é Dia de Maria* (2005), he was still figuring out how to transfer what he had learned from *Lavoura Arcaica* to his work in television. For *Hoje é Dia de Maria* and his subsequent microseries *A Pedra do Reino,* the answer was to take the production intimacy of the year-end specials and, in the manner of *Lavoura Arcaica,* move them away from Projac. In doing so, Carvalho not only created an independent narrative universe, but also an independent production hub, free of the executives' watchful eyes and the factorylike processes governing television production at the TV Globo studios.

With the desired structure in place, nearly five months before *Hoje é Dia de Maria* was set to air, Carvalho and his team began work on the aesthetic contours of Maria's fairytale. As is the case in all of Carvalho's microseries, discussions during this initial phase centered on the director's conceptualization of the *mise-en-scène*—that is, Carvalho's view of what the microseries' fictional world should look like and what it should evoke. The website for *Hoje é Dia de Maria* provides evidence of Carvalho's role as the primary creative source behind the work and his final say over nearly all aspects of its creation. At the same time, members of the creative team speak time and time again of Carvalho's decisive role as realized in practice. For example, in commenting on the creation of the appearance of the antagonist, Asmodeu, makeup artist Vavá Torres says that they tested a number of horns, wigs, and masks, and that Luiz Fernando ended up preferring the most simple of these ("Caracterização" *Hoje*). For her part, Luciana Buarque reveals that the director's orientation was the guide for her aesthetic choices, declaring that Luiz Fernando wanted clothes that embodied an inherited Brazilian-ness ("Figurino" *Hoje*).

For Carvalho, costume and makeup, as well as other elements of *mise-en-scène,* are essential aspects in the construction of the story he is trying to tell. That is, these are central considerations that give a particular work a communicative capacity that moves beyond the descriptive. Thus, as the observations above imply, it is Carvalho who has final say over the specificities of the characters' clothing and makeup. Carvalho says: "As for the costumes, I expect them to represent what I want from the character. On the day of dress rehearsal, there is improvisation in the dressing room. It is more than just the clothes having to have some characteristic. How will they aid me in expressing the actor's movement in the filmic space? How will the clothes dialogue with the musical form of the space? Wardrobe and costume design is a great concern to me, it can enrich the characters' body movements" ("A subversão"). Both Carvalho's remarks and those of Torres and Buarque regarding costume and makeup are just a few of the many examples that stress Carvalho's determinant artistic presence throughout his works. Indeed, during the summer of 2013, I myself witnessed firsthand just how much control Carvalho exerts over even the smallest aesthetic details. While spending nearly five hours at Carvalho's newly minted TV Globo rehearsal space, I watched as he conducted a dress, camera, and lighting rehearsal for his then forthcoming year-end special, *Alexandre e Outros Heróis.*[5] Late into the night, during a production meeting for the following day, Carvalho listened intently as costume designer Luciana Buarque explained and showed him detailed, computer-generated images of all the characters' costumes. Displeased with the work, Carvalho gave an extensive explanation about why he found these images to be disconnected from the fictional reality he sought to create and what he wanted done going forward. On numerous occasions during this interaction, Carvalho reiterated that he had already gone over exactly what he expected during previous meetings and that he was displeased that his instructions had not been followed.

This anecdote further illustrates that, despite working in such a commercially driven sector, Carvalho has found ways to react against and even subvert the system. As in the metacritique in *Afinal, o que Querem as Mulheres?,* in an ideal world the director would be more than a mere administrator. Instead, she would maintain a place at the forefront of a work's artistic creation. Unlike the fictional director in *Afinal, o que Querem as Mulheres?,* for example, Carvalho is concerned with makeup as it applies not to his image in the public sphere, but to its expressive qualities for the fictional narrative he is constructing. Carvalho's ubiquitous presence in these early phases of production, then, can be understood as the director positioning himself as both the fulcrum around which creation occurs and the motor that drives that creation. It is not that Carvalho is simply, to use a term employed by Jason Mittell, an author of "origination," but instead also one of both "responsibility" and "management," who has final say over what is and is not included in his works (*Complex TV* 87–88). As discussed in Chapter One, in the opening scene of *Afinal, o que Querem as Mulheres?* Carvalho asserts to the TV Globo audience the director's central role, at least as it pertains to his work. In his preproduction process, Carvalho asserts this same idea to his cast and crew by establishing a work environment that flows first from his own creative concerns. Rather than a simple top-down model, however, it is better to think of Carvalho's production as a tightly controlled collaborative effort wherein the director is the trunk of a tree whose many branches extend freely outward, but only exist insofar as they remain attached to the trunk.

In addition to the consistent use of a creative team, the other way Carvalho achieves his centrality is through a series of workshops and seminars conducted by experts from different fields. The workshops and seminars, which Carvalho first began using in television for the production *Uma Mulher Vestida de Sol*, serve to bring his cast and crew into contact with a number of variables Carvalho himself would be unable to provide. Nonetheless, these workshops and seminars are ultimately determined and controlled by the director. Around the second week of September, roughly a month and a half before shooting began on *Hoje é Dia de Maria*, Carvalho gathered his entire cast for a series of workshops and seminars centered around activating the participants' shared past ("*Hoje*" *Memória Globo*). Designed to emphasize different aspects of nonverbal communication, theatrical physicality, and a distinct aural milieu, the workshops focused on physical communication, dance, prosody, and singing. The microseries' juxtaposition of the fantastic and folkloric with the modern and urban played out in a theatrical narrative milieu directly contrasts TV Globo's more traditional audiovisual realism. Nonetheless, despite the work's lack of realism, the specific workshops were directed toward making the actors' movements, accents, and singing as natural as possible, resulting in a cohesive reality as it pertained to the fictional world Carvalho desired to create.

Paradoxically, then, Carvalho's workshops and the aesthetic they help to develop simultaneously work toward familiarizing to the cast the work's defamiliarized aesthetic. Thus, in order to add to the cohesiveness of *Hoje é Dia de Maria*'s visually distinct and purposefully artificial fictional world, the workshops are designed as a prerehearsal to ensure that the actors become acquainted with communicative elements that may be otherwise unfamiliar or appear unnatural. For example, one defining characteristic of *Hoje é Dia de*

preliminary, in-depth aesthetic investigations and a series of workshops and seminars. Unique to the preproduction for this 2007 adaptation of Ariano Suassuna's 1970 novel is the fact that it took place far from Rio de Janeiro, Brazil's film and television capital. During the last three months of 2006, Carvalho and his cast and crew relocated to Taperoá, Paraíba, to prepare for and film the microseries. The production took over the sleepy northeastern town of 14,000 inhabitants, transforming a part of its main street, Chá da Bala, into the story's scenic city. Inspired by the idea of a *cidade-lápide* (tombstone-city), a space honoring the memory of ancestors, Carvalho's crew remodeled and painted the exterior facades of local houses in painstaking detail. Moreover, in 25 days, Carvalho directed 80 local workers as they covered the 2,000-square meter area with 40 centimeters of dirt and enclosed it by constructing 35 alcoves, creating a large octagonal arena ("A Pedra" Memória Globo). The arena served as the microseries' primary setting and helped establish the visual reference to a northeastern Brazilian baroque aesthetic, defamiliarized by an atemporal influence stemming from a medieval aesthetic. In addition to the set construction, along the lines of the "creative confluence" referred to by Giardini and Carvalho's permanent space at Projac, the director's team transformed a number of existing edifices to allow for a back-and-forth between costume and design preparation, workshops, and seminars, resulting in a creative and cultural exchange, with the latter informed by the geographic specificities of the participants ("A Pedra" Memória Globo).

A Pedra do Reino's various workshops focused on cast preparation and included acting, dance, and body and voice expression classes. Carvalho invited the critically acclaimed Brazilian actor Ricardo Blat, who played one of the many Asmodeu derivations in *Hoje é Dia de Maria*, to serve as the cast's acting coach. Along with Carvalho, Blat worked daily with the cast, exploring the interconnectedness of body and spoken word. The objective, as with the *fala caipira* in *Hoje é Dia de Maria,* was to create a level of naturalness that transcended mere memorization of lines—to make the spoken lines not a step in the process, but the process itself. Tiche Vianna, who had formally studied the *linguagem das máscaras* (language of the masks) and the *commedia dell'arte* in Italy, further elaborated on Blat's work by a body expression workshop using masks. Vianna, who also worked with Carvalho on *Hoje é Dia de Maria* and *Capitu,* used the blank masks to develop the actors' imaginative, sensorial relationship to the characters they were preparing to interpret. For Vianna, the use of masks in the actors' preparation allows them to leave reality behind and enter into the realm of the imagination (*Diários* 15). Again, the work of both Blat and Vianna exemplifies the practical application of one of Carvalho's broader artistic objectives: to establish a level of naturalness and improvisation that supersedes a more rigid type of acting driven by the descriptive memorization of lines and physical placement within the narrative space.

Tay Lopez, who plays Adalberto Couro, a young, fervent intellectual revolutionary, notes Carvalho's desire for his actors to act as naturally as possible, despite the work's characteristic theatricality: "Luiz always told us that this scene did not have to be overly rehearsed; he said that when one begins to rationalize too much, one runs the risk of moving away from the real" (*Diários* 73). Juliana Paes, who worked with Carvalho on *Meu Pedacinho de Chão* and *Dois Irmãos,* observes how Carvalho encourages, yet directs improvisation: "Luiz likes the creative process and the actors, and he creates ideal conditions for our sensibilities to flourish. He believes in the body free of vices and habitual gestures. Our imagination and improvisation are guided by *his* hand" (Kogut, "Luiz Fernando Carvalho Prepara"). What the actors recognize in the above comments is that Carvalho seeks to reclaim the body and expression of the actor from the markers and vices of telenovela acting, which is highly dependent on spoken effects and overacted facial and body modulation. The mask and corporal workshops function to reset the dramatic capabilities of the actors. In essence, such workshops represent one of the earliest steps in Carvalho work toward ultimately relegating the spoken word to a subordinate position relative to the audiovisual construction (figure 2.1).

In addition to these workshops, *A Pedra do Reino* had three seminars. Iconic Brazilian actress Fernanda Montenegro, who worked with Carvalho on *Hoje é Dia de Maria,* gave the first seminar, on the craft of acting. Psychoanalyst Carlos Byington (as he had for *Hoje é Dia de Maria*) gave a seminar on Jungian archetypes and their correspondence to the characters in Suassuna's novel. Finally, Suassuna himself gave a seminar in which he discussed his novel and what inspired him to write it (figure 2.2).

Clearly, along with the type of interpretation described above, the seminars demand a significant amount of time, something that is generally not available in the fast-paced production that characterizes the majority of Brazilian television fiction. Nonetheless, the examples here of the seminars and workshops from Carvalho's preproduction process for *Lavoura Arcaica, Hoje é Dia de Maria,* and *A Pedra do Reino* apply to all the director's work since 2005. As we will see in the following chapter, this preparatory process and the centrality of theater as an aesthetic model are the defining characteristics of and base for Carvalho's project of reimagining contemporary Brazilian television fiction.

FIGURE 2.1. Carvalho guiding rehearsals for *A Pedra do Reino* (2007). Right to reproduce granted by TV Globo.

FIGURE 2.2. Ariano Suassuna lecture during preproduction of *A Pedra do Reino* (2007). Right to reproduce granted by TV Globo.

Chapter Three

SETTING THE STAGE

FROM THE TELETEATRO TO THE MICROSERIES

The discussion thus far has centered around two primary, interrelated elements in Carvalho's work. By emphasizing the medium's artifice, the first is the assertion of the director in place of the television writer as the primary creative figure in Brazilian television fiction. The second is that Carvalho has developed an intimate and multilayered preproduction process as a means of exerting directorial control over his work in Brazilian television. As illustrated in the analysis of *Afinal, o que Querem as Mulheres?*, these elements counter the medium's generalized marginalization of the director's creative role and the ubiquitous naturalism and factorylike productions common to standardized television in Brazil. Consequently, these two elements reveal as much about Carvalho's work as they do about the broader reality that structures a significant portion of contemporary Brazilian television fiction.

Throughout the years, Carvalho's generalized discontent with this reality has led him to seek a greater degree of autonomy over his work in television. As the previous chapter argues, the use of a consistent creative team and an extensive preproduction process has long served as a base from which Carvalho is able to exert a greater degree of artistic and administrative independence. In addition, two other important factors strongly influence the aesthetic and structural format of his reaction against conventional television. Finding inspiration in Antonin Artaud's writings from the early twentieth century, the first is the theater's role in Carvalho's works as a primary source for the deconstruction of naturalist aesthetics and narrative construction.[1] The second, directly related factor is Carvalho's determination, since 2005, to work almost exclusively in the smaller, more experimental microseries format. The root of that format lies in the Brazilian teleteatro (televised theater).

FROM THE TELETEATRO TO THE DIFFERENT STAGES:
MOVING TOWARD THE MICROSERIES

From January 11 to January 21, 2005, Carvalho's first microseries, *Hoje é Dia de Maria*, aired nightly as the showpiece of TV Globo's year-long fortieth anniversary celebration. Due to the work's surprising commercial success,[2] the network gave Carvalho the go-ahead for another five episodes, which came to be known as the *Segunda Jornada* (*Second Journey*) and aired over five consecutive days beginning on October 11, 2005. While *Hoje é Dia de Maria*'s precise date of inception is not known, one can be relatively certain that Carvalho first conceived of the idea in the early 1990s. Indeed, during an interview with Valmir Santos for the *Folha de São Paulo*, the director states that he conceptualized the microseries around 1990 ("Carvalho Invoca"). Memória Globo, a site dedicated to the construction and preservation of TV Globo's institutional culture and memory over the past fifty years, suggests that Carvalho began work on a form of *Hoje é Dia de Maria* around 1993. In his doctoral dissertation, "As minisséries no processo da TV: o Caso *Hoje é Dia de Maria*," Ronie Cardoso Filho notes that while the playwright Carlos Alberto Soffredini prepared the original version of the script in 1995, TV Globo elected not to produce what was then intended to be a one and a half hour special along the same lines of Carvalho's year-end specials from 1994 and 1995 (103).

Importantly, as noted by Cardoso, *Hoje é Dia de Maria* was initially supposed to be a year-end special, and the idea for the work first emerged around the same time Carvalho staged *Uma Mulher Vestida de Sol* (1994) and *A Farsa da Boa Preguiça* (1995), year-end special television adaptations of Ariano Suassuna's homonymous plays. Placed within the broader context of Carvalho's work, these facts point to a continuous artistic trajectory in terms of both aesthetics and format. In other words, *Uma Mulher Vestida de Sol* and *A Farsa da Boa Preguiça* should be understood as the earliest examples of Carvalho's interest in a more compact narrative format and an antinaturalist televisual composition. What is more, characterized by an aesthetically hybrid and theatrical *mise-en-scène*, these shorter-format works demonstrate Carvalho's first reactions against the ubiquitous and commercially dominant telenovelas.

Before the telenovela definitively took over Brazilian television in the late 1960s and early 1970s, the teleteatro was the medium's primary spectacle. In her important work on the history of the teleteatro at TV Tupi, Brazil's first television network, Cristina Brandão defines the teleteatro as a single airing of a dramatic representation of a play, short story, novel, or even a film that has been adapted for television (*TV Tupi* 53). Early on, Brandão contends, Brazilian teleteatro was the result of a type of television production guided largely by cultural rather than commercial objectives (*TV Tupi* 49). For the greater part of the 1950s, during Brazilian television's *período elitista* (elitist phase), the teleteatro was simply filmed theater.[3] More precisely, a stationary camera, from the perspective of an imaginary audience, filmed actors as they interpreted a dramatic piece—more often than not an adaptation of a canonical

European play. Throughout this period, television as an artistic vehicle in its own right was not necessarily important to teleteatro producers (Brandão, *TV Tupi* 37). That is, what was important was not the newly minted technology's potential for creating a unique audiovisual language; rather, television served to reproduce the theater that its still relatively few spectators were accustomed to seeing live on stage. Such an attitude was in part due to a general lack of understanding of the new technology and its communicative and creative capacity. But it was also the result of the cultural rather than commercial impetus behind early television production in Brazil, where very few, well-to-do individuals owned the expensive, incipient technology.

Nonetheless, as time passed and the medium began to be seen increasingly as a business, a struggle emerged between industry and culture, between marketing and artistry, and between the private sector and state omnipresence (Brandão, *TV Tupi* 49). With this new attitude came a greater push to create a distinguished product that could not be seen anywhere else, the uniqueness of which would encourage individuals to purchase television sets. As actors, directors, and producers began to better grasp the nature and potential of the new medium, they eventually turned to radio and cinema as models for the construction of a teleteatro that explored the artistic and technological possibilities afforded by the incipient vehicle. More precisely, teleteatro producers discovered in the radioteatro[4] the production, commercial, and dramatic precedent for which they had been searching (Brandão, *TV Tupi* 41). There was, however, still a need for a visual precedent. Ultimately, film, owing mostly to its primacy as an audiovisual medium, provided television with the visual reference it sought to complement radio's narrative model. Thus, filmic techniques, combined with literary and theatrical sources, supplied a potential answer to the television producer's desire to distinguish and bring prestige to the teleteatros and to capture larger audiences. Eventually, however, despite the genre's artistic sensibilities and its aesthetic development, the growing commercialization of television led networks to invest in more profitable formats, like the telenovela, not unlike what had occurred earlier with the radioteatro, which was replaced by the radionovela.

The increasing numbers of television sets throughout Brazil and the installation of the military dictatorship were arguably the two central, interrelated factors behind the eventual dominance of the telenovela. By 1970, when the transition from the teleteatro to the telenovela was in full swing, in large part due to government-backed infrastructure allowing for a truly national broadcast network and financing initiatives for purchasing television sets, 22.8 percent of homes in Brazil had a television set. In the following years of that decade, riding the coattails of what came to be known as the period's *milagre econômico* (economic miracle, 1968–1973), 56.1 percent of all Brazilian households had a television set (Hamburger 22). Importantly, in 1970, after continued persecution by the military regime, the progressive São Paulo network TV Excelsior closed its doors. Similarly, in 1980 TV Tupi had its government-issued license canceled by the military regime. Consequently, as had increasingly been the case since TV Globo's inception in 1965, aided by the repressive regime, the majority of the expanding number of Brazilian television sets was tuned to the TV Globo network, which now had a national reach.

With the country connected increasingly through the public's access to television, networks explored the most efficient ways to attract the largest possible audiences in exchange for revenues from the burgeoning advertising sector. Of all the possibilities, the telenovela proved to be the most economically viable. Unlike the teleteatro, whose production costs were wrapped up into a single presentation, the telenovela's serial narratives allowed networks to spread those costs over a number of chapters, resulting in a significantly less expensive and more profitable production. Additionally, in contrast with the teleteatro's close-ended narrative, the telenovela's open-ended storytelling structure could potentially be influenced by the audience, while also catering to their desires and expectations. Along these lines, in her seminal work on the *folhetim*, Marlyse Meyer conceives of the Brazilian telenovela as an extension of the nineteenth-century *feuilleton*. In what she describes as a contemporary audiovisual revitalization of the weekly stories previously printed in newspapers throughout Europe, Meyer notes that while the telenovela spectator encounters a shiny new technological shell, the *folhetim's* core persists: "the serial, the fragment, the suspended time that erases the linear time of a story fragmented into multiple plotlines, all of which are tied up into a main core, coming together to compose an 'exciting intrigue,' open to changes as determined by the audience's taste" (387).

In his seminal work *Communications, Culture, and Hegemony*, Jesus Martín-Barbero also sees the telenovela format as stemming from nineteenth-century serial narratives. For Martín-Barbero, the melodrama central to these narratives functions as a "drama of recognition . . . a struggle to make oneself recognized" (225). Like their literary predecessors, celebrated telenovela authors construct their massive narratives with an eye toward drawing the largest possible audience, which is then encouraged to participate in the creative process through focus groups, letters, emails, or other forms of communication. As Martín-Barbero notes, these means of communication comprise a public sphere through which one can "make oneself recognized" as her ideas are potentially implemented into or somehow affect the trajectory of the long-form narrative. From the perspective of the producers, one important result of this process is that it has great potential to raise the spectator's level of emotional and psychological investment in the cultural commodity. Moreover, the loyalty that accompanies this investment provides television executives and producers with a more predictable audience they can sell to advertisers. In fact, in many ways, this type of communicative interaction significantly predates the current and ongoing technological interaction—through Twitter, Facebook, and specialized blogs, for example—that many fans now experience with favorite television series.

By the late 1970s audiences had developed strong ties to the telenovela, which had cemented itself as an integral part of Brazilian daily life. Consequently, the respective networks relegated the relatively unprofitable teleteatro to rare special presentations. As an example of the programming transition, in 1979, not long before Carvalho left film to work in TV Globo's *Núcleo de Diretores*, the Rio de Janeiro network initiated a series of one-off specials that aired in a late time slot on Tuesday or Wednesday evenings. These specials, known as the *Terças* or *Quartas Nobres* (Noble Tuesdays or Wednesdays), "were heirs to the old teleteatros: modernized through an updated televisual language, the specials represented close-ended stories through a narrative repertoire that drew from adaptations of novels, short stories, plays, films, or even original screenplays" (Brandão, *TV Tupi* 64). All the specials were produced under the umbrella of TV Globo's *Caso Especial* (Special Case) series, which spanned the period from 1970 to 1995, totaling 170 programs. Notably, both *Uma Mulher Vestida de Sol* and *A Farsa da Boa Preguiça* were a part of the *Caso Especial* series, with the latter representing the series' 170th and last program (*Dicionário da TV Globo* 417).

The names used to describe the rebranded teleteatros—"noble" and "special case"—signal TV Globo's attempt to create a type of prestige programming that both harkened back to the medium's early years and served as its own counterpoint to the commercially driven telenovela. An early form of narrowcasting, these programs were aimed at a smaller and proportionally more educated audience relative to programming designed for earlier in the day when the greatest number of spectators was watching. Indeed, that the specials aired in a post-10:30 p.m. time slot is evidence that the network targeted a specific demographic—one that likely did not have to be at work early the next morning, suggesting an interest in attracting white-collar workers who had more autonomy over their time and the cultural competence to understand more complex adaptations. Moreover, the specials' infrequent airings and inconsistent promotion—often marketed only during the week of or even the night before airing—lends support to the view that they were less important in economic terms relative to the prime-time telenovelas (Brandão, *TV Tupi* 59).

TV Globo, however, is not and never has been in the business of losing money. Thus, while from 1970 to 1995 the specials occupied an economically inferior time slot relative to their previous prime-time programming throughout the 1950s and early- to mid-1960s, the network justified and maximized their existence by using them as a space for testing new romantic pairings, actors, authors, and directors (Brandão, *TV Tupi* 59, 64). A good example of this was the TV Globo produced *Aplauso* (1979), a series of teleteatros coordinated by three well-known and respected Brazilian artists: Paulo José, Ferreira Gullar, and Domingos de Oliveira. According to José, the *Aplauso* teleteatros purposefully positioned themselves as a singular, experimental televisual product whose very existence was in direct opposition to industrial production (Brandão, *TV Tupi* 58).

José's characterization of *Aplauso*, and the late teleteatro in general, as being an experimental product can be directly applied to Carvalho's *Uma Mulher Vestida de Sol* and *A Farsa da Boa Preguiça*, both of which, as already mentioned, like the *Aplauso* programming, also fell under the broader umbrella of the *Caso Especial* series. In contrast with his long, frenetically paced, and narratively dynamic telenovelas, the structure of the two specials is more akin to Carvalho's later microseries. Like the microseries, the specials employ a similar mode of production characterized by a shorter period of time for filming, a longer period of time for narrative preparation (aesthetic research, acting workshops, seminars, character studies, rehearsals, etc.), and larger budgets per episode. Additionally, unlike the telenovelas, whose narratives potentially change throughout their time on the air, like their teleteatro antecedents, the specials and microseries' narratives are fully set prior to airing. Last, whereas Carvalho's telenovelas have all aired in prime time (in either the 6, 7, or 9 p.m. time slots), his specials and microseries have always aired post–prime time.

The formats' respective time slots highlight their distinct commercial *and* aesthetic objectives. The microseries, like the teleteatros before them, air in a time slot dedicated to "innovative ideas and more sophisticated plots," while the telenovelas are shown during the period of the evening when the largest audiences are tuning in (*Guia Ilustrado TV Globo* 3). In short, while telenovelas' narratives and aesthetics attempt to please all viewers, thus limiting experimentation, aimed at a smaller, more sophisticated audience, specials and microseries enjoy greater creative liberties. Intent on taking advantage of such liberties, Carvalho has, whenever possible, opted to work in the shorter format of the special or microseries along with lesser-known actors and away from TV Globo's studios. Together, each of these tactics combine to cede a greater degree of control to the director.

RETHINKING AESTHETICS AND THE ROLE OF THE DIRECTOR

In addition to the structural, programming, and production similarities Carvalho's year-end specials and microseries share with Brazilian television's long tradition of the teleteatro, one can also extend the director's connection to theater by locating the theoretical underpinnings that inform his aesthetic in Antonin Artaud's *The Theater and Its Double* (1958). Though Carvalho eclectically draws from a number of aesthetic sources, perhaps more than anyone else, Artaud's ideas on theater have influenced the way he theorizes his own work (*Luiz Fernando Carvalho* 89). At first glance, it might seem odd that a Brazilian television director working in the twenty-first century would find inspiration in the writings of a French poet, actor, and director who worked in and wrote about early-twentieth-century theater. Nonetheless, Artaud's and Carvalho's respective dissatisfaction with the preeminence of the written and spoken word over a work's visual makeup and the dominant role of the author relative to that of the director serve as important commonalties in their individual searches for alternative artistic models.

Artaud's frustration with the Western theater of his time was largely based on what he viewed as the disproportionate and repressive presence of the written and spoken word:

> The theater as we conceive it in the Occident has declared its alliance with the text and finds itself limited by it. For the Occidental theater the Word is everything, and there is no possibility of expression without it; the theater is a branch of literature. . . . The idea of the supremacy of speech in the theater is so deeply rooted in us, and the theater seems to such a degree merely the material reflection of the text, that everything in the theater that exceeds this text, that is not kept within its limits and strictly conditioned by it, seems to us purely a matter of *mise-en-scène*, and quite inferior in comparison with the text. (68)

In affirming that such theater is a mere extension of literature and that its *mise-en-scène* is nothing more than ornamental support for the spoken word, Artaud in essence asserts that theater has lost possession of the very language that distinguishes it from other art forms. If the "word is everything," as Artaud argues it was at the time, how then is theater any different from literature? In response, Artaud maintains firmly that for a singular theatrical language to exist it must necessarily be constructed through the *mise-en-scène*. More precisely, for his purposes, *mise-en-scène* is the "visual and plastic materialization of speech" *and* "the language of everything that can be said and signified upon a stage *independently* of speech, everything that can be affected or disintegrated by it" (emphasis added, 69). If theater is to create a language that stands alone as distinct in the same way literary and musical languages do, Artaud contends that it must change course and move as far away from the written and spoken word as possible, "substituting for the spoken language a different language of nature, whose expressive possibilities will be equal to verbal language, but whose source will be tapped at a point still deeper, more remote from thought" (110).

The emphasis on *mise-en-scène* in Artaud's conceptualization of theater has two principal, interdependent consequences—one professional, the other communicative or artistic. In the first consequence, the director replaces the author as the principal creative figure because the director determines and has final say over the *mise-en-scène*, which substitutes the word as the art form's most important aspect (37–38, 107). Regarding this point Artaud is both clear and forceful in his formulation: "In my view, no one has the right to call himself author, that is to say creator, *except* the person who controls the direct handling of the stage" (emphasis added, 117). Returning the director to the place of artistic authority, he continues, "we shall *renounce* the theatrical superstition of the text and the *dictatorship* of the writer" (emphasis added, 124).

Artaud viewed the "realistic, social theater" of his time as being dominated by a spoken language derived directly from the literary source and, as such, overly psychological. Such theater, however, for Artaud, misses the mark insofar as "the domain of the theater is not psychological but plastic and physical" (50, 71). Consequently, rather than appealing to the audience's intellect through speech, which functions "as a completed stage of thought which is lost at the moment of its exteriorization," a theatrical piece should appeal first and foremost to the audience's senses, an act that begins with the director's own sensibilities (Artaud 70). With the director at the helm controlling and exploring the *mise-en-scène,* the second, communicative or artistic consequence of Artaud's theorization can now play out. That is, the director can and should engage the audience's senses through the total activation of the stage, which is "a concrete physical space," demanding to be "filled, and to be given its own concrete language to speak" (Artaud 37). Reducing the role of speech and supplanting its superiority, the concrete language of the stage "is intended for the senses and, independent of speech, has to first satisfy the senses . . . " (Artaud 37).

In 2008, Carvalho published a short essay titled "Educação pelos sentidos" ("Education through the Senses") in which he offers his thoughts on Brazilian film and television, commenting on *Hoje é Dia de Maria* and the *Projeto Quadrante* in particular. As the title suggests, the essay reveals clear affinities with Artaud's position as laid out above. Like the theorist's critique of the role of the author and spoken dialogue in the realist theater of his time, Carvalho's essays describe his work as a search for a language unique to his field—one that supplants both the dominant position of the screenwriter and the incessant focus on dialogue and naturalism, which, in his view, have combined to prevent television from meaningfully communicating with the audience (25). Consequently, like Artaud, Carvalho proposes a shift in creative control. Although not as explicit as the playwright, who argues provocatively and polemically that the preeminence of spoken language makes the director a "slave" to the author, Carvalho more subtly supports "true artists" taking control and developing a new mission for the medium (*The Theater* 119 and "Educação" 23). For Carvalho, in order for this mission to become a reality, those capable individuals have to push the limits of the televisual language beyond the control of the literary, realist, and dialogue driven narrative, emphasizing instead the magical, imaginative space of the Brazilian unconscious ("Educação" 24).

Here, in the same spirit as Artaud, Carvalho proposes a type of language that appeals first and foremost to the spectator's senses. It is a language that desires not to *describe, tell,* or *explain* to the audience what is going on, but instead to galvanize its senses through the activation of an eclectic mixture of aesthetic elements derived from what the director refers to as a "genetic patrimony" or Brazilian ancestrality ("Educação" 24). Though I will discuss the concept of ancestrality in greater detail in Chapter Five, it is important to note here that Carvalho defines ancestrality as an invisible yet omnipresent cultural past that persists through the continued existence of shared stories, language, lived experiences, sounds, images, and memories embodied by the creative participants and the spectators. The extrapolation beyond the spoken dialogue and the activation of shared ancestrality occurs through the prioritization of the *mise-en-scène*, which incorporates all of the artistic components at the director's disposal. These include all creative sources spread out almost infinitely to and through all lived experience. As an example of this idea in practice Carvalho affirms, "when you get the whole creative group together, the artistic language produced is a combination of everything one has heard, read, and experimented—it is a vast, amorphous combination of one's life experiences, guided by the necessity to express all that one has lived up until the moment the clapperboard signals for action" (*Luiz Fernando Carvalho* 89).

By summoning these commonalities in an imaginative and experimental manner, Carvalho creates an aesthetic that aims to challenge the overly familiar audiovisual language to which the audience is accustomed. The objective is not unlike Viktor Shklovsky's conceptualization of defamilarization wherein "The technique of art is to make objects 'unfamiliar,' to make forms difficult, to increase the difficulty and length of perception. . . . After we see an object several times, we begin to recognize it. The object is in front of us and we know about it, but we do not see it—hence we cannot say anything significant about it. Art removes objects from the automatism of perception in several ways" ("Art as Technique" 16). Regarding Shklovsky's point, Carvalho's work invites the audience to participate in an interpretive exercise for which senses become the principal guide to understanding a work whose primary objective it is to "increase the difficulty and length of perception" through the radical activation of a seemingly limitless—albeit highly theatrical—*mise-en-scène*.

THE DEFAMILIARIZED THEATRICAL *MISE-EN-SCÈNE*

The type of television that aesthetically characterizes a significant portion of Carvalho's work, particularly those shorter-format works, is at its very core fundamentally theatrical. Specifically, in the director's specials and microseries, theatricality informs everything from the setting and space to the lighting and acting. Within the broader context of Carvalho's artistic trajectory in television, theatricality first became the organizing aesthetic principle for one of his works in 1994 when he directed *Uma Mulher Vestida de Sol*. This particular special represents a key moment in Carvalho's career, not only because in it he explores a theatrical *mise-en-scène*, but also because it contains the first hints of the experimental aesthetic accumulation that characterizes his later works *Hoje é Dia de Maria, A Pedra do Reino, Capitu, Afinal, o que Querem as Mulheres, Subúrbia,* and *Meu Pedacinho de Chão.*

Uma Mulher Vestida de Sol is a domestic Shakespearean tragedy that tells the story of an unattainable love set against the backdrop of a familial land dispute in the northeastern Brazilian *sertão,* or outback.[5] There, the heroine, Rosa, lives a melancholic and repressed life with her grandmother, Donana, and her widowed father, Joaquim. Joaquim is an extension of the harsh *sertão* he continuously tries to control, but that, in actuality, seemingly controls his behavior. Though the *sertão* serves as the setting and landscape that organizes the special's narrative, its representation does very little to create a depiction of the real place. It is not, for example, Euclides da Cunha's naturalist depiction in *Os Sertões* (1902), Nelson Pereira dos Santos's neorealist representation in *Vidas Secas* (1964), or Walter Salles's romantic-realist portrayal in *Central do Brasil* (1998). Here, instead, the spectator is presented with a deconstructed version of the Brazilian backlands; one that eschews realism and is both poetic and expressive.

Because traditional representations of the *sertão,* like those cited above, are strongly rooted in the Brazilian social imaginary, the very idea of the *sertão* partially loses its capacity to communicate beyond seemingly fixed characteristics, transmitted through widely disseminated literary and audiovisual representations. To this end, the setting in *Uma Mulher Vestida de Sol* has less to do with the *sertão* as an actual physical place and the numerous preconceived ideas and images the *sertão* conjures in the minds of Brazilians, and far more to do with the sensory and psychoemotional responses the *sertão* as an imagined universe has the possibility to evoke. The same is also true for the whimsical and fantastical representation of Brazil in *Hoje é Dia de Maria*; the chaotic, violent, and oneiric portrayal of the northeastern village of Taperoá in *A Pedra do Reino;* the *tenebroso* El Greco– and Caravaggio-inspired operatic depiction of Rio de Janeiro in *Capitu*; the kitsch, Andy Warhol–inspired 1960s pop-culture representation of Copacabana in *Afinal, o que Querem as Mulheres?*; the colorful, sensual, yet raw "Blaxploitation" representation of the periphery in *Suburbia*; and the ludic, neo-baroque, and cartoonish representation of the village of Santa Fé in *Meu Pedacinho de Chão*. Instead, in *Uma Mulher Vestida de Sol*, rather than Cunha's, Santos's, or Salles's respective realist representations of the *sertão*, Carvalho's vision is closer to João Guimarães Rosa's mythic representation of the Brazilian backlands.

In each of these works directed by Carvalho, but beginning with *Uma Mulher Vestida de Sol*, the mechanism for moving the spectator beyond a merely logical understanding of what he or she is seeing and toward a sensorial experience is always the physical space in which the narrative plays out. If in broad terms we understand space in contemporary Brazilian television as being a mix between relatively limited shooting on location and, more commonly, shooting in fabricated yet realistic studio sets, then nearly all of Carvalho's specials and microseries undermine standardized television's spatial paradigm either through the use of nontraditional spaces and/or through an overtly artificial transformation that defamilarizes those spaces.

In the tradition of teleteatro, Carvalho's minimalistic staging of *Uma Mulher Vestida de Sol* takes place on a large sound stage, sparsely decorated to evoke the arid *sertão* of Brazil's northeast. Though the sound stage itself is not a "nontraditional" space for television production—many fictional living and working environments are shot on sound stages—its theatrical appropriation distinguishes it from the way this space is normally utilized in contemporary Brazilian television. That is, rather than, for example, constructing or filling the stage with elaborate and realistic props to mask the presence of the physical space itself, *Uma Mulher Vestida de Sol* embraces the emptiness of the sound stage to call attention to its artificiality.

Despite the special's minimalistic treatment of the sound stage, there are a total of twelve on-screen spaces. In addition to these, in broad terms, there is the off-screen space of the expansive territory of the *sertão*, alluded to at

FIGURE 3.1. Crane shot, *Uma Mulher Vestida de Sol* (1994). Right to reproduce granted by TV Globo.

FIGURE 3.2. Crane shot, *Hoje é Dia de Maria* (2005). Right to reproduce granted by TV Globo.

different moments through dialogue and sounds that are implied to be indigenous to the land. Encouraging the spectator to fill the narrative gaps, props are used sparsely. The most prominent of these is a twisted and thorny fence that traverses the sound stage from front to back. The fence divides the disputed land and separates the conflicting sides of the family, while at the same time serving as a meeting point, a line of defense, and a means of passage from one side to the other. To the right is Joaquim's domain; to the left is that of Antônio, the brother-in-law he so despises. Framed passageways to unseen backstage and off-screen spaces represent the characters' respective homes, although in two instances a bedroom in Joaquim's house is formed by the projection of an illuminated rectangle onto the sound stage floor.

The floor, which is covered in sand, and the sound stage walls, which evoke the rural northeast's characteristic *pau-a-pique* (wattle and daub) construction, are the color of the land, giving the drama a telluric quality. Because these two distinct components of the sound stage share the same color, they seemingly flow into one another, evoking the boundless extent of the *sertão*. Nonetheless, Carvalho frequently problematizes any fixed idea of space. For example, as is also the case in *Hoje é Dia de Maria*, throughout the program, numerous crane shots pull out to reveal what are actually the limited confines of Rosa's life in the *sertão* (figures 3.1 and 3.2).

Thus, visually suggesting that the space is limitless by matching the color of the walls to that of the floor, and then undoing that suggestion by revealing the actual physical limits of the space, Carvalho simultaneously invites the spectator to believe in the reality of the represented space without ever forgetting that is in fact an artificial creation. The real/artificial dialectic that in part characterizes the narrative space is not specific to this special or the special as a medium. Instead, in the same way, space both characterizes and reveals the artificiality of each of Carvalho's microseries and the telenovela *Meu Pedacinho de Chão*.

Of all of Carvalho's microseries, *Capitu* utilizes a space closest to that of *Uma Mulher Vestida de Sol*. Set in late-nineteenth-century Rio de Janeiro, the work is staged within the limited confines of the historic Automobile Club building in downtown Rio de Janeiro. Although not shot on a sound stage per se, and while its *mise-en-scène* is more luxurious and detailed, corresponding with the Bento Santiago's family's wealth, the microseries carries over the minimalism and theatrical staging of *Uma Mulher Vestida de Sol*. In both instances, there is abnegation of the actual place of each of the works' respective settings. There are a few moments when we see external shots of Dom Casmurro riding a modern-day train in Rio de Janeiro, or Capitu, dressed in an elaborate nineteenth-century dress, strolling with Bentinho through pre-

FIGURE 3.3. Automobile Club narrative space, *Capitu* (2008). Right to reproduce granted by TV Globo.

FIGURE 3.4. Automobile Club narrative space, *Capitu* (2008). Right to reproduce granted by TV Globo.

sent-day Rio de Janeiro's bustling downtown area, or Escobar going for a swim in the ocean. Otherwise, however, the narrative is confined to the expressive spaces constructed inside the Automobile Club. As is the case in the special, props such as columns, elevated stages, furniture, or even chalk drawn on the floor characterize *Capitu*'s on-screen space. Additionally, shadows and framed passageways suggest the existence of a number of off-screen spaces in the microseries.

Although the physical space of the Automobile Club is larger than the sound stage of *Uma Mulher Vestida de Sol*, the number of different settings in *Capitu* is similar to that of *Uma Mulher Vestida de Sol*. Nonetheless, the increased space of the open-plan, multistory building allows Carvalho to show greater visual depth than in the special. Since Carvalho more frequently shoots in-depth in *Capitu*, the spectator might see two or even three fairly large settings in the same shot, something not possible in the more limited physical space of *Uma Mulher Vestida de Sol*. However, the Automobile Club is a preexisting structure not designed for filming, which creates difficulties not encountered on the sound stage. In *Capitu*, existing walls or columns from inside the historic building had to be worked around or appropriated into the narrative space. For example, by adding a dining table and chairs, Carvalho repurposes the existing elevated foyer to serve as the family's dining room. At another moment during the narrative, this same space—shot head on, revealing its greater depth—becomes a sort of family room through the simple subtraction of the dining table and the addition of a sitting area (figures 3.3 and 3.4).

In both instances, the building's beautiful stained glass windows serve as a source of natural light. They also reveal the grandeur of the space by drawing the spectator's attention upward. In narrative terms, this particular space is featured during moments when the family is discussing and searching for clarity regarding Bentinho's future as a priest in the Catholic church. Thus, the natural, bright lighting, the stained glass, and the upward expansiveness of the space captured in depth symbolize the struggle of Bentinho's mother, Dona Gloria, to decide whether to satisfy her maternal desire to keep her son by her side or to fulfill her religious obligation to place him in a seminary.

Bentinho's eventual matriculation in the seminary and the strain this causes on his budding relationship with Capitu are the focus of the first three and a half chapters of the microseries, nearly 70 percent of the work. In contrast, the novel focuses on this theme for less than 30 percent of Dom Casmurro's narration. Throughout this first and the latter part of the microseries, Dom Casmurro directs the spectator to the narrative moments of interest through voice-over narration or in-scene commentaries on his adolescence, early adult-

FIGURE 3.5. Dome, *Hoje é Dia de Maria* (2005). Right to reproduce granted by TV Globo.

hood, and marriage to Capitu. In this way, the microseries plays as a single long flashback of the protagonist's life, covering everything from Bentinho's birth to the death of his own son, Ezequiel. However, space and time in the microseries are complicated by the fact that Dom Casmurro explores his past by actually physically appearing in it. The same type of construction appears in *A Pedra do Reino* as well. Thus, the representation of space and time is actually more than a mere flashback to Dom Casmurro's past. What the spectator sees is not what *necessarily* happened, but instead a version of what happened as remembered by Dom Casmurro. Past and present, then, conflate into a subjective act of remembering so that what the audience experiences is Dom Casmurro's memories of a past that has led to his present circumstances.

Within the trajectory of Carvalho's work, the space of *Capitu* lies somewhere between that of *Uma Mulher Vestida de Sol*'s limited sound stage and the expansive, seemingly limitless, space of the 2005 microseries *Hoje é Dia de Maria*. Set in a large steel dome, *Hoje é Dia de Maria* began a trend in Carvalho's work of shooting in reappropriated spaces outside the confines of TV Globo's Projac Studios. The dome had been constructed in the western Rio de Janeiro neighborhood of Recreio, where it was used four years earlier for the third edition of the 2001 *Rock in Rio* music festival. Composed of 48 tons of steel and draped with a canvas cover measuring over 5,700 square meters, the dome's diameter measures approximately 54 meters, while the ceiling at its highest point is nearly 26 meters—nearly the equivalent of a nine-story build-

ing ("*Hoje*" *Memória Globo*). The dome's interior base was composed largely
of the locale's natural soil and existing vegetation, including trees, bushes,
weeds, and dirt. As such, unlike *Uma Mulher Vestida de Sol*'s and *Capitu*'s exclusively closed and darker spaces, *Hoje é Dia de Maria* provides the sensation
of being simultaneously both inside and outside the enclosed space.

In order to create the illusion of an expansive or even unlimited space
consistent with the unrestricted realm of Maria's fantastical world, Carvalho
called upon artist and set designer Clécio Regis and his crew to paint the
dome's interior walls. Using the theatrical technique known as the cyclorama,
the interior's painted background extends approximately 167 meters in cir-
cumference and over 9 meters in height (figure 3.5).

The lower third of the curved wall is painted so as to represent an extension of the landscape. Depending on the scene—that is, depending on where
Maria or the other characters are in their respective journeys—the lower third
of the wall might be a painted extension of the foreground's arid *sertão* or
distant mountains or hilly pastures. The upper two-thirds of the wall portray
distinct versions of the sky at different spatiotemporal moments in the narrative—the morning, afternoon, or night. Again, depending on the scene, the
wall might be painted a clear sun-drenched sky-blue or a combination of soft
pastels to distinguish one space from another. Intricate lighting further differentiates spatiotemporal changes. For example, reflectors were used to soften
the illumination, making the blue painting appear more like the sky. Additionally, while a harsher and more direct lighting characterizes the desert area, the
lighting in the somber forest area was diffused through panels composed of
leaves ("*Hoje*" *Memória Globo*).

In essence, the dome's undefined interior functions as a metaphorical
blank canvas, or perhaps more aptly, a white board, allowing the scenery to be
altered or erased in accordance with aesthetic or narrative need. In this sense,
the dome possesses the spatial flexibility of the sound stage. However, its vast
size gives Carvalho the freedom to experiment with different elements on a
scale that would not be possible in a smaller, more restricted space, like the
one that characterizes *Uma Mulher Vestida de Sol*. Thus, while *Hoje é Dia de
Maria* has fewer settings (seven) than *Uma Mulher Vestida de Sol,* their on-
screen presence is far more elaborate than in the special. The settings, appearing according to the narrative's nonchronological development, are: *a casa
do sítio* (Maria's home), *o País do Sol a Pino* (the Land of the Burning Sun), *o
agreste* (the wild), *o vilarejo* (the village), *o despenhadeiro* (the crag), *a fazenda
e os casebres* (the plantation house and slave quarters), and *o bosque* (the forest). There is also an eighth setting, *o mar* (the sea), which is shot outside the
dome, on location at a beach outside Rio de Janeiro.

FIGURE 3.6. Taperoá village, *A Pedra do Reino* (2007). Right to reproduce granted by TV Globo.

Despite their many visual commonalities, the individual settings function to drive Maria's journey onward. In terms of the narrative, the spaces may be classified in four broad groups—home, journey, rejuvenation, and love. What is more, Carvalho constructs each of the spaces in *Hoje é Dia de Maria* so as to be physical manifestations of Maria's imagination and emotional state. For both the young, innocent child and the later sweet and naïve adult, space is fantastical and without limits. The *casa do sítio* and *fazenda* represent Maria's homes, with the first corresponding to her childhood home and the second to her dwelling as an adult. In both instances, the spaces are comparatively fixed; that is, Maria does not advance through these two spaces so as to get to another place, instead lingering for a period of time and leaving only after a specific incident impels her to do so. Unlike the *casa do sítio* and *fazenda*, the *País do Sol a Pino* and the *vilarejo* settings are physical mediums through which Maria passes to get somewhere else. These two settings appear to be the most open or limitless as well as the most threatening to Maria. The *agreste* and the *despenhadeiro* settings, however, fall somewhere between the first two groups as they are relatively closed spaces through which Maria moves, although at a slower pace. At the same time, the *agreste* for Maria and the *despenhadeiro* for Pai are spaces of rejuvenation, insofar as the child and father both find in these settings a motive to push forward on their journeys. Meanwhile, the *bosque* setting symbolizes love, as it is in this space that Maria reunites and reconciles with her father and begins an amorous relationship with Amado. Along with her newfound friendship with Quirino and

FIGURE 3.7. Inside village home, *A Pedra do Reino* (2007). Right to reproduce granted by TV Globo.

FIGURE 3.8. Northeastern sky, *A Pedra do Reino* (2007). Right to reproduce granted by TV Globo.

Rosa, these relationships cause Maria to linger in the space longer than she does in others.

Like *Hoje é Dia de Maria*, the space in *A Pedra do Reino* is an audiovisual representation of the character Quaderna's internal state of being. From the space of the town square, Quaderna frenetically summons his memories of his epic, familial tale. Because, as Quaderna informs us, the tale is both "enigmatic and bloody," what we see and hear, insofar as it represents the actualization of his memories, is also enigmatic and bloody. While the physical and narrative spaces in *Uma Mulher Vestida de Sol*, *Capitu*, and *Hoje é Dia de Maria* differ in their size and scope, they are all set in closed spaces. In comparison to these, it would seem that *A Pedra do Reino* would be an outlier as it was shot and produced far from the entertainment centers in southeastern Brazil, on location near the northeastern village of Taperoá, Paraíba. There, inspired by medieval and baroque visual references, Carvalho and his team refashioned the preexisting village homes to form an enclosed circle around a large dirt area (figure 3.6).

Separated from off-screen spaces by a large gate that provides access to the village, the communal dirt area serves the same function as the spatially limited, theatrical spaces of Carvalho's other works. Like the sound stage, dome, or Automobile Club, the village circle's *mise-en-scène* is flexible and narra-

tively dynamic, changing according to the given spatial and temporal point
in the narrative.

Unlike in his other works, however, Carvalho does not transform the dirt-
floored theatrical space with props to suggest living or working spaces. Consequently, we do not see, for example, the suggested spaces of Rosa's bedroom
in *Uma Mulher Vestida de Sol* or of Bentinho's family's living room in *Capitu*.
Instead, *A Pedra do Reino* is similar to *Hoje é Dia de Maria* in that the larger
physical space in which the narrative takes place allows for more substantial and therefore more realistic props, primarily as they relate to characters'
homes or places of work. More specifically, *A Pedra do Reino* takes advantage
of the internal spaces of the village's preexisting homes. As a result, more than
any of the other mentioned works, *A Pedra do Reino* juxtaposes an overtly artificial space, the village circle, with others that are more realistic, the existing
homes.

Moreover, the very presence of the expansive northeastern sky above the
village square differentiates *A Pedra do Reino*'s space from Carvalho's other
works because it situates the artificial within a broader, realist milieu (figures
3.7 and 3.8).

This is not to suggest, however, that in extrapolating beyond the confines
of the closed space of the village circle, the microseries' *mise-en-scène* is no
longer theatrical. Instead, as is the case in those few moments in *Capitu* when
Carvalho shoots outside the Automobile Club, the theatrical acting, chronologically incongruous costumes, and artificial props that are present in the
mythical space of the village circle continue outside of that space in *A Pedra
do Reino*. In doing so, they highlight the work's theatricality, emphasizing further the artificial in the work's, and more broadly, Carvalho's *oeuvre*'s ongoing
realist/artificial dialectic.

Each of Carvalho's specials and microseries discussed thus far take place
in folkloric, mythical, or dreamlike spaces. This is also the case with the physical and narrative spaces of *Meu Pedacinho de Chão* (discussed further in the
conclusion to this book), which strongly evoke those of *Hoje é Dia de Maria*.
As physical, nonverbal representations of their protagonists' psychological and
emotional states, the explicit antinatural settings in these works make perfect
sense within the context of their fictional worlds. Carvalho's repeated attempts
to challenge the ubiquitous naturalism of Brazilian television fiction through
the creation of an artificial aesthetic based in an eclectic theatrical *mise-
en-scène* have become a familiar characteristic of his television production.
However, the more audiences associate a specific type of aesthetic with Carvalho's work, the more he runs the risk of losing the communicative power he
seeks to instill in his defamiliarized audiovisual construction. Paradoxically,

then, it is entirely possible that in his attempt to offer a defamiliarized model of Brazilian television, the repetition of a blatantly artificial construction could very well culminate in its familiarization, creating the opposite of the desired effect. Therefore, Carvalho's broad reimagination of contemporary Brazilian television fiction requires the director to also reimagine his own fiction as he continues to push the boundaries. Thus, in *Afinal, o que Querem as Mulheres?* and later in *Suburbia* (2013), which is analyzed in greater detail in Chapter Seven, Carvalho takes a step toward defamiliarizing not just standardized Brazilian television, but his own work as well.

Set in present-day Rio de Janeiro, *Afinal, o que Querem as Mulheres?* is both Carvalho's first original screenplay and the first of his specials or microseries that does not take place in an obviously fabricated space. Throughout the work's six chapters, there are a number of scenes that are shot on location in Rio de Janeiro's Zona Sul (South Zone): André and a friend enjoying a day at Ipanema beach, for example; André dining with his girlfriend, Tatiana at Guima's in Gávea; and Lívia and Jonas spending an afternoon at the city's picturesque Lagoa (Lagoon). While these and similar scenes might imply a heightened sense of realism, thereby distinguishing this from Carvalho's other overtly artificial works, they actually function to emphasize the presence of the artificial. In *A Pedra do Reino* and *Capitu*, for example, whereas at different moments characters venture outside of their fabricated fictional universes into nonfabricated spaces such as the *sertão* or downtown Rio de Janeiro, in *Afinal, o que Querem as Mulheres?* the inverse is actually true. These spaces, as with those in *Uma Mulher Vestida de Sol* and *Hoje é Dia de Maria*, evoke real spaces, but are at their very core imagined and indeterminate.

On the other hand, André's world in *Afinal, o que Querem as Mulheres?* is very clearly contemporary Rio de Janeiro, a version of a place that is quite familiar to the spectator through its constant portrayal in television and, therefore, its presence in the Brazilian social imaginary. André's existence, then, is always situated in actual spaces in Rio de Janeiro. However, as is the case in Carvalho's other works, what the spectator sees is slightly skewed from the realist expectations the setting evokes because the narrative space is an extension of the protagonist's psychological and emotional state. Consequently, despite the minimally aestheticized external, on-location scenes in *Afinal, o que Querem as Mulheres?*, the majority of the narrative takes place in highly aestheticized internal spaces like offices, apartments, or beauty salons. By using Brazil's best-known city as the setting for André's story, Carvalho further challenges the expectations of an audience familiar with his work by moving from an audiovisual construction whose fictional worlds are consistent in their antinaturalism toward one that prioritizes a realist setting only to

FIGURE 3.9. Lagoon, *Afinal o que Querem as Mulheres?* (2010). Right to reproduce granted by TV Globo.

FIGURE 3.10. André's mom's apartment, *Afinal o que Querem as Mulheres?* (2010). Right to reproduce granted by TV Globo.

FIGURE 3.11. Animated Freud, *Afinal o que Querem as Mulheres?* (2010). Right to reproduce granted by TV Globo.

undercut it through a series of highly artificial aesthetic interruptions. For example, André's professor and psychiatrist morphs into an animated version of Sigmund Freud, or André, when overwhelmed with all that is going on in his life, experiences his hair transforming into octopus tentacles (figures 3.9, 3.10, and 3.11).

As should be clear by now, the narrative spaces in Carvalho's works can be broadly defined by their artificiality. Moreover, both the content of these spaces, or their *mise-en-scène*, and the means to capture all of this—the cinematography—are also highly artificial. Of particular importance is that the generalized artificiality of Carvalho's work—whether in terms of the space, the *mise-en-scène*, or the cinematography—is simultaneously a means for combating the ubiquitous naturalism of Brazilian television and a way to challenge the importance of the written word and to assert the director as the central creative figure. Of equal importance is that the artificial, aesthetically hybrid audiovisual constructions that distinguish Carvalho's later works can be traced back to—as is similarly the case with the narrative spaces discussed above—*Uma Mulher Vestida de Sol*. That this is the case should be understood as a demonstration of Carvalho's long-running concern with the field of television fiction, as well as a symptom of his desire to differentiate himself and his work from the industry's existing possibilities.

Though *Uma Mulher Vestida de Sol* does not possess the same degree of aesthetic accumulation found in Carvalho's later microseries, it does mark the beginning of an experimental televisual language, which the director develops further starting with *Hoje é Dia de Maria*. To be clear, it is not as if Carvalho was not experimenting with narrative and aesthetic possibilities prior to the 1994 special. In fact, there are many moments in *Renascer*, particularly in the telenovela's first ten chapters, where he tests the limits of prime-time television. Nonetheless, the point here is that before 1994, experimentation was limited to isolated moments within the broader context of the long-form, fast-paced telenovela. The 1994 special, however, is the first time Carvalho creates a work that is in its entirety an experimentation—from the setting to the *mise-en-scène* to the editing and cinematography. Directly related to its experimental ethos, at the center of which—in theoretical, structural, and practical terms—is a characteristic theatricality, this special serves as the earliest example of Carvalho's use of different artistic elements to explore the sensorial as a means for transcending dialogue-driven narrative construction. With this in mind, the next chapter analyzes *Uma Mulher Vestida de Sol*'s opening scene, locating in it the most important of these elements before drawing attention to their presence in the director's later microseries. Moving forward in this way situates Carvalho's individual works within a broader artistic trajectory while also establishing the aesthetic contours that have come to distinguish Carvalho as the most creative director working in Brazil today.

Chapter Four

ESTABLISHING THE AESTHETIC TONE

THE OPENING SCENE AND MOTIFS

Television fiction in Brazil is synonymous with the telenovela format. What is more, the primary source from which the realist, melodramatic narratives derive is the telenovela writer who sits at the top of the format's creative hierarchy. Thus, the opening scene of most television fiction in Brazil is one of the few instances in which a director can assert those audiovisual elements that are distinctive to her creative style. As Jason Mittell notes, "The beginning of a narrative is an essential moment, establishing much of what will follow" (*Complex TV* 55). Despite the obviousness of the claim, something he himself recognizes, Mittell correctly contends that a deeper understanding of beginnings (and endings) helps the scholar uncover the "complex poetics involved in television storytelling, both at the beginnings and in ongoing episodes" (*Complex TV* 85). Carvalho's work differs on a number of levels from the type of "complex" television referred to by Mittell. Nonetheless, an examination of a selection of the opening scenes from Carvalho's *oeuvre* over the past twenty-five years is useful for understanding the ways in which the director has used these scenes to establish an ideological and artistic professional identity that characterizes his unique position in the field of television production. Though I will discuss the specifics of this positioning in further detail in Chapter Five, for the purposes of this chapter I examine how Carvalho employs the opening scene as a foundational reinforcement to his other means of reimagining contemporary Brazilian television fiction: his singular preproduction process (discussed in Chapter Two) and his emphasis on the theater (discussed in Chapter Three).

To varying degrees and in accordance with their individual styles, the openings of Carvalho's different works eclectically hybridize music, dance, theatrical acting, computer-generated images, and other elements of *mise-en-scène*, like lighting, costumes, and props. In turn, all these elements are uniquely brought together by the transformative presence of Carvalho's unconventional framing and use of the camera. At their core, each of these scenes prioritizes the audiovisual composition over the development of the plot. What is more, as I alluded to briefly in Chapter Three, they establish their respective fictional worlds as not grounded in realism, but as psychological and emotional extensions of their protagonists. In this way, the opening scenes not only stress Carvalho's creative presence, they also establish the aesthetically hybrid, anthropophagic model he develops and intensifies in all of his future microseries.

Ilana Feldman has argued that the audiovisual makeup that characterizes Carvalho's work in *Hoje é Dia de Maria* and *A Pedra do Reino* is essentially baroque. Feldman states that "In Luiz Fernando Carvalho's opera mundi, both in *Hoje é dia de Maria* and, more radically, in *A Pedra do Reino*, the staging includes, incorporates, and devours, aiming to bring together all forms of artistic expression, *à la* baroque, whose literal meaning is 'accumulation,' by uniting and mixing cinema, theater, poetry, painting, circus, opera, literature, romance, odyssey, satire, tragedy, Picardias, *cordel*, *maracatu*, *papangus*, and chivalric novels" (4). Of course, one could augment Feldman's "opera mundi" with *Capitu*, which is more operatic in both its formal and narrative structure than any of Carvalho's works. To Feldman's understanding of the baroque as characterized by excess, contrasts, and accumulation and its application to Carvalho's work, one can productively add Angela Ndalianis's specification of the keys to what she calls the neo-baroque logic: (1) a self-reflexive relationship to the illusion created; (2) playful engagement with a spectator who acknowledges the status of performance; and (3) a tendency toward virtuoso display and spectacle (266). Ndalianis argues that "the neo-baroque combines the visual, the auditory and the textual in ways that parallel the dynamism of seventeenth-century baroque form, but that dynamism is expressed in technologically and culturally different ways" (267). In his microseries, Carvalho accumulates all of the elements mentioned by Feldman in order to playfully engage with a spectator who cannot help but acknowledge the ongoing performance. As suggested by Ndalianis's definition of the neo-baroque, Carvalho does this through the interplay between "all the means of expression utilizable on the stage" (Artaud 39), which results in a cannibalization of disparate artistic elements evocative of Oswald de Andrade's provocative literary call to arms via his *Manifesto Antropófago* (1928).

THE BEGINNING OF THE BEGINNING: ROSA'S TRAGIC *SERTÃO*

As I have argued thus far, Carvalho's work in television is directly linked to theater at multiple levels: historically and structurally by the development of the microseries from the teleteatro; theoretically and ideologically by way of the director's interest in and implementation of Artaud's writings on early twentieth-century European theater; aesthetically through the construction of overtly antinatural and artistically hybrid fictional universes that emphasize theatrical staging and acting; and symbolically through explicit references to the theater itself, which along with the color red serves as one of a number of central motifs that run throughout the director's body of work. As discussed in Chapter Three, *Uma Mulher Vestida de Sol* is the first of Carvalho's works to embody these multiple linkages to theater. Additionally, this special represents one of the earliest attempts by Carvalho to explore the opening scene to establish the work's narrative world as a psychological and emotional extension of its protagonist. In what follows, I conduct a close reading of *Uma Mulher Vestida de Sol*'s opening scene, before briefly discussing the opening scenes of some of Carvalho's other works. Finally, I identify and analyze two key motifs that run throughout all of Carvalho's audiovisual production— namely, the color red and the physical presence of an actual or evoked theatrical stage.[1] Together, the characteristic opening scenes and the repeated motifs reveal the interrelated formal and narrative concerns that lie at the heart of the director's work.

Though *Uma Mulher Vestida de Sol*'s opening scene does not contain the same degree of aesthetic hybridity that characterizes Carvalho's later works, it does serve as a landmark in the director's artistic trajectory, paving the way for more substantial experimentation, beginning with *Hoje é Dia de Maria*. As is the case with those works following *Hoje é Dia de Maria*, *Uma Mulher Vestida de Sol* is set in an overtly theatrical space. Within this space, the special's opening scene eschews a realist aesthetic, combining dance, music, and unconventional cinematography as a means for expressing the protagonist Rosa's psychological and emotional state. In doing so, the subsequent unfolding of the narrative plays as an audiovisual manifestation of Rosa's internal and familial struggles. That is, everything the spectator sees or hears exists somewhere in a time-space just beyond reality. For Carvalho, opening the narrative in this way serves two primary functions. First, it helps orient the expectations of a television audience reared on naturalism and therefore unaccustomed to explicit variations from the norm. Second, it liberates the director from having to create within the limiting conventions of realism. Consequently, the possibilities for experimentation, both formal and narrative, are endless, and the spectator is invited to play along.

Accompanied by the sound of a fife flute playing faint Mediterranean music, the first image in *Uma Mulher Vestida de Sol* is that of a fragmented body twirling gently about in a closed, dark space. Quick hits of black that mimic a voyeuristic blinking eye come into focus to reveal a dancing female dressed in a grayish-white and red spotted dress—colors nearly identical to those that compose the letters of the special's title page (Uma Mulher Vestida de Sol in grey) and a rose dripping blood (red). The subtle conveyance of the grey and red, previously separated in the title page, to the dancing woman's dress and therefore her body, combines with the peaceful music and the woman's care-free presence to introduce the protagonist in a harmonious, balanced state. In this indeterminate time-space, Rosa has yet to be tilted to one side or the other. Rather, she simultaneously embodies the connotations of both the figure of the *mulher vestida de sol* and the red rose of her name. Nonetheless, within the broader narrative context, Rosa's initial harmonious state foreshadows the inevitable rupture of that harmony, as suggested by the sudden, unex-plained appearance of red rose petals, which pierce the darkness and begin falling gently to the floor around her.

As the opening scene continues, the spectator follows from the perspec-tive of the unveiled blinking eye, which watches while Rosa dances before the camera. The fact that this eye first focuses on the young woman's bare legs presents a moral conflict, since when the cinematic gaze moves to a more ob-jective, omniscient viewpoint, the spectator realizes that the blinking eye is actually Joaquim, voyeuristically watching his daughter. While Joaquim gazes upon his daughter, the voice-over narrator poetically and dramatically defines the dark space where the characters congregate: "[the] poor, hunger-stricken *sertão*, where men struggle for land, goats, and sheep; where there is love and blood; land and death; all that is nourished in man is present in this lost land" (*Uma Mulher Vestida* DVD). In Suassuna's 1947 play, rather than an omni-scient narrator, the *Juiz* (Judge) speaks these words at two different moments during a conversation with the *Delegado* (Deputy). Neither of these charac-ters, each of whom provides a certain comic relief in the original play, appears in Carvalho's melodramatic tragedy. Moreover, by displacing this passage to an unknown, omniscient narrator and juxtaposing it with images of Rosa dancing while Joaquim watches her, Carvalho turns the humor of Suassuna's play into a foreshadowing of Rosa's tragic death while also hinting at the pos-sibility of incest, a theme the director explores in his future works *Lavoura Arcaica, Os Maias,* and *Hoje é Dia de Maria.*

However, prior to the voice-over narrator speaking these first words, the audiovisual construction emphasizes music, dance, fragmented shots, sen-suous camera movements, and lighting that is at times evocative of German Expressionism or tenebrous, evoking Caravaggio. Such an emphasis situates the spectator's focus primarily on the preverbal—that is, on the psychology and emotions that underlie the space and characters. The focus on the nonver-bal runs counter to the overwhelming majority of Brazilian television fiction, which, as Chapter Three argues, centers on narrative constructs that place characters in situations so as to allow them to partake in some form of spoken

FIGURE 4.1. Vignette, *Uma Mulher Vestida de Sol* (1994). Right to reproduce granted by TV Globo.

FIGURE 4.2. Rosa dancing, *Uma Mulher Vestida de Sol* (1994). Right to reproduce granted by TV Globo.

FIGURE 4.3. Projection of two shadows, *Uma Mulher Vestida de Sol* (1994). Right to reproduce granted by TV Globo.

communication. In contrast, Carvalho makes an effort in this opening scene and in nearly all his future work to let the audiovisual construction, not the spoken word, do the communicative heavy lifting. In this example, separated from the image, the words spoken by the narrator conjure up notions of a harsh, Darwinesque land where individuals engage daily with other humans and with nature in a struggle for survival. Nonetheless, when juxtaposed with Carvalho's beautifully constructed, lyrical images, the result is an audiovisual poem that problematizes the centrality of the spoken word, creating a complex subtext that evokes a depth of human emotion at the center of Rosa's story.

These emotions, which include joy, conflict, serenity, jealousy, desire, and loss, are further emphasized and symbolized through the introduction of three different female characters, each of whom appears in isolation from the others. First, delicately lit against a nearly blacked-out floor, the spectator sees the same fragmented female from the first shots, but now in her entirety. She continues to dance in the foreground: her liberated smile and movements, combined with the soft lighting, represent her feelings of harmony, joy, and peace. However, at the same time, Rosa's body very clearly projects two shadows, not just one, onto the backlit wall directly behind her (figures 4.1, 4.2, and 4.3).

In contrast to the harmonious confluence of the aforementioned vignette's colors in Rosa's dress, the shadows suggest that Rosa's apparent harmony and happiness are merely fleeting and superficial, and that, at least in this life, she cannot be both the *mulher vestida de sol* and the bleeding rose. The metaphysical division represented by the shadows is physically embodied, and thus taken a step further, through the brief introduction of the second and third females.

The second woman, who we later learn is Donana, Rosa's maternal grandmother, appears standing in a nearly blacked-out space wearing a beige dress.[2] In one of the instances of the tenebrous lighting Carvalho repeats frequently in *Lavoura Arcaica, Os Maias, A Pedra do Reino*, and *Capitu*, Donana is frontally lit with soft lighting like that of a candle. Although Donana smiles, her smile is not innocent and hopeful like that of Rosa from the previous shot. Rather, it is distorted by years spent in the harsh *sertanejo* reality marked by "pobreza, fome, seca, fadiga," (poverty, hunger, drought, and fatigue). These words, each of which is feminine in gender, are narrated in voice-over as the spectator observes Donana standing nearly motionless close to the black background. Donana's smile appears to be that of a woman who has gone mad; an individual removed from childhood innocence and damaged by past experiences, as yet unknown to the spectator. Furthermore, the positioning of Donana's appearance between the appearance of Rosa and that of a young girl, both of whom are happily dancing, implies that Donana's smile is a remembrance of better days. Indeed, such better days are evoked in the next shot when the image of Donana fades to black before introducing the young girl who appears only in this opening scene.

Unlike the earlier shot of Rosa dancing and the bifurcation of her body into two distinct shadows projected onto the backlit wall, the young girl is still one harmonious being, evidenced by the projection onto the ground of her single shadow. In this way—although it is never made clear, and therefore left to the spectator to determine—the girl is in all probability a flashback to Rosa's innocent childhood, a reading supported by the fact that her movements are picked up in the following shot of Rosa dancing in exactly the same way. Further support for such an interpretation is the accompanying voice-over narration, which suggests the moment and cause of Rosa's lost innocence. As the young girl smiles and looks directly up at the camera, the spectator hears the narrator say, "A luta pela terra, cabras e carneiros" ("The struggle for land, goats, and sheep") (*Uma Mulher Vestida* DVD). The narration of these words over a shot of the young girl suggests that the struggle for land, goats, and sheep is actually a metaphor for Joaquim's personal struggle to conquer his terrestrial domain, of which Rosa is a part. Whether this is a matter of incest or merely Joaquim's overly protective desire to exert control over Rosa's life is again left to the spectator to decide.

By constructing a visual flow that moves from Rosa to the two shadows and then to the second and third females, Carvalho subtly alerts the spectator to the possibility that Rosa herself, as she exists at the beginning of the narrative, is a liminal space upon which past, present, and future psychoemotional states converge. In fact, the grey and red colors of her dress, representing Rosa's two distinct existences, are another indication of her ambiguous emotional state. Toward the end of this sequence, all three women reappear. Gone are their smiles. All of them, in each of their representative diachronic time-spaces, are summoned to the body of young Rosa who, dressed in a grayish-white sundress, shamefully or fearfully hides her face from the subjective camera that moves across her body and throughout the space. Rosa's feelings of shame or fear are in part the result of the *terra* (land). Using a theatrical metaphor, the land—in this case the enigmatic Brazilian *sertão*—is the stage upon which the characters not only interact with one another, but also through which they come into existence. While the spectator can only identify fully the centrality of the land as the narrative develops further, the narrator again foreshadows its importance, affirming that "tudo que é alimentado no homem está presente nesta terra perdida" ("all that is nourished in man is present in this lost land") (*Uma Mulher Vestida* DVD). The idea that what is nourished in man is also present in a fallen land suggests an amalgam of the two, spatializing both the land and its inhabitant as sites of an interconnected, flawed, desolate reality wherein the harshness of one is transposed onto the other and vice-versa.

The analysis of *Uma Mulher Vestida de Sol*'s opening scene is meant to point to how Carvalho uses this introductory space to establish the audiovisual construction of his work as a means for expressing, never describing, the protagonist's psychological and emotional state. The degree to which an opening's expressiveness trumps plot-related elements depends on the individual work. For example, *A Pedra do Reino*'s opening scene, much of which runs for three minutes without spoken words, is conspicuously aggressive in eschewing plot development for an expressive audiovisual construction. The opening scenes in *Hoje é Dia de Maria, Capitu, Afinal, o que Querem as Mulheres?, Subúrbia,* and most recently, *Meu Pedacinho de Chão,* however, all contain some expository narration. Nonetheless, as is the case in *Uma Mulher Vestida de Sol,* such narration is accompanied by an audiovisual construction that, in its direct contradiction of almost all other fiction on Brazilian television, calls attention to itself above any present exposition.

FROM *MARIA'S* FOLKLORIC UNIVERSE TO QUADERNA'S EPIC AND BLOODY *CIDADE LÁPIDE*

As is evident in the preceding analysis, the artificiality that characterizes both Carvalho's individual works and his *oeuvre* as a whole is the result of different combinations of artistic elements. These range from expressive dancing and gestures, anachronistic costumes, and computer-generated images to archival visual insertions and disparate forms of diegetic and nondiegetic music—all framed by the use of a camera that moves through the space, both caressing and fragmenting the characters, but very rarely presenting them in a straight-forward manner. The combination of such artistic elements and the emphasis on the artificiality of their construction is Carvalho's attempt to draw the spectator's attention to an alternative televisual language, one that stands against that of the conventional telenovela. Moreover, and of equal importance, these techniques serve as means for expressing the characters' emotions, rather describing them or having the characters merely talk about them.

As in *Uma Mulher Vestida de Sol*, Carvalho uses the opening of *Hoje é Dia de Maria* as a space to prioritize the formal aspects of his work and their existence as an audiovisual manifestation of Maria's understanding of her encounters with the world she discovers during her journey. The microseries begins like a fairytale, with the omniscient third-person narrator's (Laura Cardoso) voice-over: "Far away, in a land still without a name, there lived a poor, broken family. Once upon a time, there was girl named Maria" (*Hoje é Dia* DVD). To different ends and varying degrees, Carvalho employs a narrator in every one of his shorter-format works as well as in his most recent telenovela, *Meu Pedacinho de Chão*. Depending on the work, as is the case with *Os Maias, A Pedra do Reino,* and *Capitu*, even when not physically in a scene, the narrator might serve as one of the main characters. The presence of the narrator in these particular works is largely due to the narrator's centrality in the novels upon which they are based. In Carvalho's other works, the narrator occupies a more marginal role, serving as a means to initiate, move forward, and sometimes even conclude the story. This is the case in *Hoje é Dia de Maria*, where we learn in one of the last scenes that the opening voice-over narration mentioned above is actually Maria's grandmother telling her a bedtime story.

Thus, in *Hoje é Dia de Maria*'s opening scene, the narrator's words emphasize the fanciful and folkloric nature of Maria's story, while also alerting the spectator to the story's indeterminable time-space (a far-off, nameless place), the problem or cause of Maria's journey (a poor family undone by some unknown incident), and finally, to Maria herself (once upon a time, there was a

FIGURE 4.4. Opening scene from *Hoje é Dia de Maria* (2005). Right to reproduce granted by TV Globo.

girl named Maria).[3] In a more explicit manner than is the case with *Uma Mulher Vestida de Sol,* this opening scene's references to the fairytale genre prepares the spectators to expect a work that is in not grounded in realism. Indeed, Carvalho wastes little time emphasizing the narrative's artificiality. During Cardoso's narration, a whimsical adaptation of the *ciranda* (round) "Que Lindos Olhos" ("What Beautiful Eyes") plays while a tracking shot speeds up to reveal an animated version of Maria giggling and swinging from a large tree. This is the first time—though he has often repeated it since—Carvalho introduces the use of computer-generated images into his work. What is more, as discussed in greater detail in Chapter Two (and again in Chapter Five), the computer-generated images are strikingly similar to Candido Portinari's series of paintings depicting rural *paulista* children playing and flying kites in open fields, among other adolescent activities, which served as visual inspiration for the construction of Maria's world (figures 4.4 and 4.5).

The spectator first sees Maria from the perspective of her future stepmother, Madrasta (which means stepmother). While scanning the farmhouse and its surroundings, Madrasta fixes her eyes on the protagonist, who is off in the distance, partially obscured behind some barren tree branches. Not unlike Rosa's movements in the opening of *Uma Mulher Vestida de Sol,* Maria lightly skips away from the house toward the tranquil countryside. As she comes into focus, we see her white linen dress and her hair tied in braids with red bows. Those familiar with Carvalho's work will notice Maria's strong resemblance

FIGURE 4.5. Candido Portinari, *Brodowski* (1942), 46 × 55.5 cm. Right to reproduce granted by João Candido Portinari / Fundação Portinari / Projecto Portinari.

to the heroines from *Renascer, Uma Mulher Vestida de Sol, A Farsa da Boa Preguiça, Capitu,* and *Suburbia,* all of whom serves as examples of the ongoing intertextuality in Carvalho's work, insofar as they themselves are multiplied citations whose root is Portinari's *Menina com Tranças* (1955) (figures 4.6, 4.7, 4.8, 4.9, 4.10, and 4.11).

In short, in the microseries' opening scene, Carvalho presents the audience with an elaborate artistic accumulation, freely combining oral storytelling, animation, obscured framing, attention-grabbing body movements with references to Portinari's paintings to Brazilian folk music and to Brazilian modernism—the latter represented by the inclusion of updated versions of Villa-Lobos's piano reappropriation of the folk *cirandas.* Together, these distinct elements function as an external representation of both Maria's imaginative understanding of her grandmother's story and her own internal emotional state as she creates the fictional universe in her mind. To reinforce Maria as the narrative fulcrum, every shot of her in the opening scene is taken from

Figure 4.6. Rosa's dress, *Uma Mulher Vestida de Sol* (1994). Right to reproduce granted by TV Globo.

Figure 4.7. Nevinha's dress, *A Farsa de Boa Preguiça* (1995). Right to reproduce granted by TV Globo.

FIGURE 4.8. Maria's dress, *Hoje é Dia de Maria* (2005). Right to reproduce granted by TV Globo.

104

FIGURE 4.9. Candido Portinari, *Menina com Tranças e Laços* (1955), 34.5 × 20 cm. Right to reproduce granted by João Candido Portinari / Fundação Portinari / Projecto Portinari.

FIGURE 4.10. Capitu's dress, *Capitu* (2008). Right to reproduce granted by TV Globo.

FIGURE 4.11. Conceição's dress, *Subúrbia* (2012). Right to reproduce granted by TV Globo.

an angle that falls somewhere between her eye level and ground level. Such angles establish the gaze or perspective of a child, highlighting the expansiveness and wonder with which she sees her surroundings. Similarly, Maria's white dress is representative of her purity and innocence just as her skipping to the nondiegetic sound of the *ciranda* represents an internal playfulness and carefree state. Moreover, Maria's innocence, playfulness, and purity appear linked to the rural location of her home. In turn, that home—presented first through computer-generated images—is itself a child's utopia, as well as the center of and the point of departure for Maria's imagined, folkloric universe.

If the audiovisual construction of *Hoje é Dia de Maria*'s opening scene functions to establish Maria's vision of the world as, for the most part, innocent and light-hearted, that of Dinis Quaderna (Irandhir Santos), the protagonist and first-person narrator from *A Pedra do Reino,* is calculated and violent. In direct contrast to the computer-generated images present in the first scene of *Hoje é Dia de Maria, A Pedra do Reino* opens with an aerial shot of the expansive *sertão*, accompanied by a rising crescendo of drumbeats, interrupted by a descending pitch of a Galician *gaita* (bagpipe). The juxtaposition of the sounds of the two instruments provokes the sensation of something rising high into the sky before falling to the ground. Sure enough, out of nowhere Quaderna seemingly falls from the sky down into the village square. There, with absolutely no explanation, like his female protagonist predecessors, Rosa and Maria, both of whom open their respective works by dancing, Quaderna leads the miscroseries' entire cast in an approximately four-minute choreographed dance. Immediately following the dance, he narrates Ariano Suassuna's novel's prologue nearly verbatim from atop a traveling stage. Like the cited opening scenes from *Uma Mulher Vestida de Sol* and *Hoje é Dia de Maria*, here the noticeable fusion of cinematography, music, *mise-en-scène*, dance, and theatricality establishes an ambiguous, mythical space, alluding to Quaderna's quixotic psychological state and to the microseries' circular storytelling.

As with *Hoje é Dia de Maria*'s use of computer-generated images and other artificial elements—and later with *Capitu*'s intermixing of distinct time periods—the fact that Quaderna has magically fallen from the sky into this indeterminate location establishes the space as one that does not abide by conventional rules. Upon hitting the ground, Quaderna rolls to his feet and begins to move about to the sounds of the *gaita, caixixi* (a maraca-type instrument probably originating in Africa), and the *zabumba* (a type of drum often used in *Forró*). Although subtle, the combination of these culturally disparate instruments references northeastern Brazilian culture's Iberian and African influences. Accordingly, the music establishes the region's connection to the

FIGURE 4.12. Candido Portinari, *Cangaceiro Sentado* (1958), 129 × 96 cm. Right to reproduce granted by João Candido Portinari / Fundação Portinari / Projecto Portinari.

FIGURE 4.13. Cangaceiro, *Uma Mulher Vestida de Sol* (1994). Right to reproduce granted by TV Globo.

FIGURE 4.14. Homem do Olhar Triste, *Hoje é Dia de Maria* (2005). Right to reproduce granted by TV Globo.

FIGURE 4.15. Dinis Quaderna posture, *A Pedra do Reino* (2007). Right to reproduce granted by TV Globo.

diverse geographical sources embodied in the instruments while also further obscuring any one definitive geographic identity—that is, the setting is Quaderna's imagined version of the *sertão*.

Like the music, the *mise-en-scène* references the region's diverse cultural heritage, although also in an ambiguous manner. Quaderna's clothing, for example, is a nod to Portinari's and Glauber Rocha's artistic representations of the *cangaceiro*, the northeastern Brazilian bandit or outlaw, previously represented in a similar fashion in *Uma Mulher Vestida de Sol, A Farsa da Boa Preguiça,* and *Hoje é Dia de Maria* (figures 4.12, 4.13, 4.14, and 4.15).

Carvalho's version of the costume, however, crosses the realistic and popular figure of the *cangaceiro* with the figure of an idealistic, mythical, and aristocratic knight, signaling the protagonist's apparent family ties to Dom Sebastião and Portuguese royalty. Quaderna's appearance becomes even more convoluted through the addition of visual elements evocative of a clown. While also mirroring the enigmatic ambiguity of the narrative itself, the purposeful confluence of these three heterogeneous and seemingly contradictory figures highlights Quaderna's enigmatic and polysemous nature, which is highlighted further through his movements in a crouched posture, distorting his body in a way that evokes a question mark (see figure 4.15). What is more, this type of posturing and the dissonant visual combination of the figure of the *cangaceiro* and clown are minor motifs that run through much of Carvalho's shorter-format productions, appearing in the director's work as early as *Uma Mulher*

FIGURE 4.16. Makeup from *Uma Mulher Vestida de Sol* (1994). Right to reproduce granted by TV Globo.

FIGURE 4.17. Makeup from *A Farsa da Boa Preguiça* (1995). Right to reproduce granted by TV Globo.

FIGURE 4.18. Makeup from *Hoje é Dia de Maria* (2005). Right to reproduce granted by TV Globo.

FIGURE 4.19. Makeup from *Capitu* (2008). Right to reproduce granted by TV Globo.

Vestida de Sol and repeated in *A Farsa da Boa Preguiça, Hoje é Dia de Maria,* and *Capitu* (figures 4.16, 4.17, 4.18, and 4.19).

Although the music and *mise-en-scène* each represent varied cultural and temporal artifacts, their true power to communicate with the spectator comes through their interaction and juxtaposition with one another. For example, when added to the already present grouping of aesthetic elements, the choreographed dance in *A Pedra do Reino* reinforces the idea of an indeterminate and fanciful space, while visually symbolizing the circular narration employed throughout the microseries. Itself a cultural amalgam, the dance is a blend of Irish, Israeli, and Russian circular dances, designed to represent a mandala, a spiritual tool used to designate a sacred space. While Quaderna dances about the space with the local children, he glances over at the square's main gate as if summoning the narrative's characters out of his memory to enter the mythical and sacred space. Once in the square, Quaderna both orchestrates and is the focal point of the dance. In doing so, he introduces—although neither didactically nor explicitly—the characters that populate his memory and make up his story. That this story will be nonlinear and somewhat disorienting is suggested by the way the camera playfully and sensorially moves around Quaderna and the characters as they consecrate the forthcoming epic tale.

Then, out of nowhere, in the same way Quaderna magically fell from the sky, a *mambembe* or itinerant stage appears in the middle of the village square. Suggesting a circular movement in time, like the dance before it, the stage rotates to reveal Quaderna telling his story. On the stage, the camera always captures Quaderna from either a low or a high angle; a framing that mimics Quaderna's cryptic, never quite forthright narration. Finally, after nearly four minutes, Quaderna recites Suassuna's novel's prologue and, as is characteristic of epic poetry, invokes the muses in preparation for the pending narrative. The hybridization in this sequence of cinematography (framing, camera movements, flashbacks, seamless editing), soft, emotive music (the use of the fife flute, fiddle, and accordion), the physical presence of the makeshift wooden stage, the recitation of literature, and Quaderna's exaggerated theatrical body movements result in an end product that is neither cinema, music, theater, nor literature, but something that singularly embodies all at once.

While *A Pedra do Reino's* opening scene gives continuity to the defamiliarized aesthetic hybridity in *Uma Mulher Vestida de Sol* and *Hoje é Dia de Maria*, it also represents an important change in narration that will continue in *Capitu* and *Afinal, o que Querem as Mulheres?* The special and the 2005 microseries have omniscient third-person narrators that share the stories of female protagonists navigating a harsh, patriarchal world. However, beginning with *A Pedra do Reino* in 2007 and continuing through *Afinal, o que Querem as Mulheres?* in 2010, Carvalho utilizes male protagonists, each of whom narrate their own stories in the first person. Additionally, for each of the three protagonists, a psychological or emotional crisis functions as the driving force of their backward-looking narration. As in all of Carvalho's work, the aesthetic that brings these male character's respective narrations to life is intended to be an audiovisual representation of their troubled states. This is the case, for example, with Quaderna; one minute he is dancing playfully in the tombstone city, dressed as an aristocratic *cangaceiro* clown, while the next he dramatically begins his dark, bloody saga. As such, the protagonist's conflicted state and the convoluted emotions his story sparks in him are communicated, not through expository dialogue, but through the combination of his movements, costume, the space itself, the symbolism and physical presence of theatrical stage, the tight, claustrophobic framing, and the sensorial camera that ensure that the spectator shares in Quaderna's inability to clearly grasp the chaotic narration.

DOM CASMURRO AND ANDRÉ NARRATE FROM RIO DE JANEIRO(S)

Although not as chaotic as Quaderna's recollection of his family's dark and bloody past, in *Capitu* Dom Casmurro also has a difficult time navigating the emotions that arise as he narrates the undoing of his marriage to his childhood sweetheart, Capitu. The slipperiness of Dom Casmurro's unreliable narration, a hallmark of Machado de Assis's masterpiece, is communicated from the very opening of the microseries through the introduction of chronologically disparate elements. Through this disjointed narration, which Dom Casmurro himself notes is an attempt to understand his present existence by connecting the two points of his life before and after Capitu, Dom Casmurro (Michel Melamed) constantly disconnects from the present in favor of a past that is never quite clear.

Unlike the lyrical opening of *Uma Mulher Vestida de Sol* and the explicitly antinaturalist openings of *Hoje é Dia de Maria* and *A Pedra do Reino*, *Capitu* complicates matters by first presenting the spectator with an inherently contradictory audiovisual construction. Following the opening credits, a rapid-fire collage of photographs of nineteenth-century Rio de Janeiro and old newspapers unfold to reveal an early map of the city. The images seemingly situate the action in the time period in which Machado's novel takes place. However, the rock n' roll guitar riffs from Jimi Hendrix's classic "Voodoo Child," which accompany the frenetic images, destabilizing the spectator's understanding of the setting. Indeed, this is the first of many temporal disconnects introduced in the opening scene and extended throughout the work. The confluence of period-specific images and historical artifacts—which are

FIGURE 4.20. Aerial shot of contemporary train, *Capitu* (2008). Right to reproduce granted by TV Globo.

themselves presented through collage, a technique that became famous in the early twentieth century with modernists such as Picasso—and of 1960s or later rock 'n' roll music, creates a level of uncertainty in the spectator as to what to expect next.

Meanwhile, on the old map of Rio de Janeiro, a red line traces the trajectory of an as yet nonvisible object. A cut transitions the movement of the red line from the map to a tracking aerial shot of contemporary Rio de Janeiro. Slowly, in the distance, the camera picks up and zooms in on a train covered in graffiti. Following a cut from the aerial shot to one that looks out the window from inside the front of the train, the spectator catches a ride as the train pushes forward, taking in images of the gritty urban landscape. The focus on these images, continuously accompanied by Hendrix's song, settles the spectator into the belief that this is going to be a contemporary adaptation of Machado's novel; perhaps something similar to Baz Luhrmann's *Romeo + Juliet*, a 1996 update of Shakespeare's most famous work.

Nonetheless, before the viewer can get too comfortable, the shot cuts to black and white footage of a nineteenth-century train in a rural landscape. From inside the modern-day train, the spectator sees this older train moving down the tracks (figures 4.20, 4.21, and 4.22).

A cut back to the contemporary train suggests the two spatiotemporally distinct vessels have just passed each other. Rather than continuing with the

FIGURE 4.21. Shot of surroundings from inside contemporary train, *Capitu* (2008). Right to reproduce granted by TV Globo.

FIGURE 4.22. Shot of nineteenth-century train, *Capitu* (2008). Right to reproduce granted by TV Globo.

FIGURE 4.23. Writing on screen, *Capitu* (2008). Right to reproduce granted by TV Globo.

perspective from inside the modern-day train, a subsequent shot to black and white footage appears to transport the spectator inside the older train. In this shot, the nineteenth-century, black and white train passes through a tunnel. However, we notice that, unlike before, here the train is not moving against the contemporary train, as was the case in the previous shot, but in the same direction. As such, despite initial appearances, the spectator has been transported to the older train; instead, the contemporary train has been transported back through the tunnel of time. The two distinct spatiotemporal moments of nineteenth- and twenty-first-century Rio de Janeiro have collided on the liminal space of the train tracks. Thus, it is not that the spectator is in one time period or the other; she is simultaneously in both.

Though this fusion of space and time is not yet entirely clear, the audio-visual construction of the shots leads the spectator toward the big reveal. At this point, everything has slowed down; the fast pace of the earlier images of the train, heightened by the presence of Hendrix's song, which has now faded out to give way to a softly played violin, have been replaced by black and white footage of a turn-of-the-century train station and its broader milieu. This new time-space, one that is neither exclusively Machado's nor Carvalho's but an osmotic combination of the two, is signaled further when Dom Casmurro begins to narrate the opening to Machado's novel: "One of these nights, coming from the city to Engenho Novo, on the Central Station train I met a young man from my neighborhood, whom I know by sight and the tipping of my hat"

FIGURE 4.24. Inside of contemporary train, *Capitu* (2008). Right to reproduce granted by TV Globo.

(*Capitu* DVD). Beginning with "I met" the words spoken by Dom Casmurro appear in characteristic nineteenth-century, black cursive handwriting over the archival footage (figure 4.23).

Although Carvalho had already adapted numerous canonical literary works, this represents the first time he cites the text by incorporating a visual representation of the written word. In a nod to Machado's ironic tone, the seriousness of the narration—reinforced by Michel Melamed's dramatic interpretation, the formality of the written word, which appears in cursive, and the presence of the violin—is undercut by the subsequent appearance of an arrow that extends from the end of the written sentence to a man in the archival footage who is wearing a hat. In addition to the ironic tone, the arrow serves as a transition, pointing the spectator to the next shot of an obscured window looking out from a moving train onto a modern-day train platform.

After continuously juxtaposing the distinct time periods only to have them eventually meld into a new whole, the spectator finally gets the first glimpse of this new world as represented in the interior of the train (figure 4.24).

Here, inside a twenty-first-century Rio de Janeiro train, Dom Casmurro and the young man from his neighborhood, both dressed in formal, nineteenth-century clothing, theatrically converse in the midst of present-day working-class *cariocas* (those born in the city of Rio de Janeiro). The interaction between the two characters is presented through slightly out-of-focus medium close-up shots captured from a below-eye-level angle. Like the inde-

FIGURE 4.25. Blurred wedding photo, *Capitu* (2008). Right to reproduce granted by TV Globo.

terminate, hybrid time-space of the train, the partially blurred images of Dom Casmurro's surroundings suggest his own clouded psychoemotional state. As stated previously, the protagonist's objective is to revisit his past in an attempt to understand what happened between him and Capitu. However, nothing is totally clear—that is, throughout the work, while always just on the verge of clarity, the blurred images of Dom Casmurro's immediate surroundings remind the spectator that everything about his narrative remains slightly askew.

This is made clearer still in the opening when, during a subsequent shot in this same sequence, Dom Casmurro dozes off as he listens to the young man recite one of his poems. As he does so, Dom Casmurro flashes back to his wedding with Capitu. While the initial image of the happy couple is in focus, the presence of a photographer in the foreground preparing to take their picture partially obscures her body. Thus, despite the clarity of the image, we do not see Capitu in her entirety because, in his recollection, Dom Casmurro himself does not see her in her entirety. Indeed, in the very next shot, the spectator sees the couple through the blurred frame of the photographer's camera lens, suggesting the complex and nebulous nature of their relationship (figure 4.25).

Before the image can come into focus, Dom Casmurro suddenly awakens to the words of the poet, who is offended by his listener's lack of attention. Through a hybrid aesthetic construction that fuses disparate artistic elements, *Capitu*'s opening scene informs the spectator that time, space, and memory are all dynamic and malleable. Though he continuously tries to reconstruct

FIGURE 4.26. Blue rose, *Uma Mulher Vestida de Sol* (1994). Right to reproduce granted by TV Globo.

FIGURE 4.27. Blue lighting, *Afinal, o que Querem as Mulheres?* (2010). Right to reproduce granted by TV Globo.

the space of the past by invoking his memories, Dom Casmurro is never fully able to grasp either the past or the present.

André, the protagonist of *Afinal, o que Querem as Mulheres?*, experiences a similar difficulty as he attempts to make sense of the dissolution of his own relationship with his girlfriend, Lívia. Unlike Quaderna and Dom Casmurro, both of whom actively narrate family histories directly related to their present existence, and as is the case later with Conceição in *Subúrbia*, André's first-person narration is reduced to the opening scene and functions, more than anything else, as a personal introduction. In the fragmented scene (discussed in detail in Chapter One), a visible camera captures André working feverishly at his desk. Nearly the same blue lighting used in *Uma Mulher Vestida de Sol* as a double signifier of the moon and serenity is accompanied by frenetic swing music; thus, here the tranquil emotional state implied by the color and its use in the special is inverted to convey agitation (figures 4.26 and 4.27).

André looks directly into the mirror placed above his desk to introduce himself to the unknown audience: "It is here that you guys see me for the first time. . . ." Before continuing his introduction, there is a cut to André, now facing the camera. With a clapperboard that reads "André" placed directly in front of his face, he continues: "I am writing my dissertation in psychology about the famous question proposed, though never answered, by Freud. . . ." Again, we are left with an ellipsis, visually represented through the insertion of a shot of André bathed in green lighting and reflected in a mirror. As the next shot returns to André, the protagonist now stands up and looks directly at the camera, enthusiastically declaring the title of both the microseries and his dissertation: "After all, what do women want!?"

Thus, in a manner that is simultaneously direct and highly fragmented, André has informed the spectator of the key narrative elements—that he is the protagonist, and that he is working on researching and answering a difficult question. The audiovisual construction that presents André and provides the context for his narrative, however, explicitly draws the spectator's attention to its artificiality. In terms of the narrative, this is a commentary on the artificiality of André's work and a foreshadowing of the search he undergoes to find a path back to his real self. Nonetheless, André's explicit, didactic narration is limited to the opening scene. For the rest of the microseries, Carvalho avoids providing the viewer with any semblance of facile, expository dialogue or narration. Instead, as the continuation of the opening scene exemplifies, much of the rest of the work moves freely, and often inexplicably, between different moments of André's past and present. Thus, like Quaderna in *A Pedra do Reino* and Dom Casmurro in *Capitu*, André's narration transcends strict spatiotemporal parameters.

In the scene described above, the spectator first encounters André in the present tense—that is, at the very moment he is working on his dissertation. This suggests that the narrative will move us toward some resolution regarding his work. The continuation of this scene, however, disorients the spectator when André suddenly appears in a number of different locations, all of which initially appear to be unrelated to one another. Moreover, the fast pace of the narrative and the expressive and highly formalized presentation of these locations make it difficult to identify any concrete time-space. For example, after André declares his dissertation's title, the camera cuts to a typewriter that emits the sound of keys being punched and of the carriage release lever giving way. This last sound is picked up in the next shot of a blonde woman in a salon looking at the camera and wiggling her bracelet. In a point-of-view panning from left to right and then right to left, meant to represent André's gaze as he walks slowly through the salon, the spectator sees a row of attractive women sitting in hair and makeup chairs. As André peruses the women, he is met in turn with seductive stares and erotic actions from the women who lick their lips or caress their bodies. In response, in what reads as more of what André wants, the protagonist's gaze fragments the women, reducing them to a mixture of legs, lips, faces, arms, and eyes.

The female fragmentation in question here is not merely physical. A linguistic fragmentation is also emphasized. As the spectator sees the women's fragmented bodies, in voice-over André asks, "After all, what do women want?" Their superficial responses include: "to be loved by your man, and desired by all men!"; "ask the fortune teller"; "to put my career above all else"; "to be young and beautiful twenty years from now." Such responses evoke the subjective and instantaneous nature of our technology-driven culture. That is, on sites like Facebook and Twitter, individuals might respond to a profound question, such as the one André proposes, with quick, artificial answers that, rather than seeking reflection, depth, and perhaps objectivity, appeal to the immediacy of the respondent's technologically supported domain. But how do the responses fit into this opening scene? Similar to *Capitu*'s opening, the fast back-and-forth between the spatiotemporalities and the general lack of spatiotemporal and narrative contextualization make it difficult for the spectator to grasp exactly what, when, and where something is happening.

As the scene moves deliriously forward, the female body continues to be objectified. Shots of Dr. Naomi, about whom we know nothing, interrupt the eroticism of the beauty parlor. Though Dr. Naomi is dressed in a low-cut red blouse, a form-fitting gray pencil skirt, and high heels, she is lecturing in a classroom setting about females as the dominant gender. Then André, appearing back at his apartment, far removed from both the hair salon and

Dr. Naomi's classroom, places a red high heel on his head, seemingly transporting him back to the hair salon, which is now a bathhouse. The same women from the salon appear naked and wet, moaning and moving sensually in a visual milieu that recalls a setting from Baz Luhrmann's *Moulin Rouge!* (2001). While the spectator does not actually hear the words "What do women want?" when one of the women happily declares that she was born to be a housewife, the repeated fragmented responses lead the spectator to assume safely that it was André's question that prompted this response.

The nature of the responses and the audiovisual representation of the objectification of the women's bodies signal that the spectator is now deep inside André's fantasy world. The women are presented in the manner that André desires them to be—that is, submissive and naked and longing, as one barely dressed woman says, "to take care of my man." André's own thoughts regarding how he would like women to respond to his question are contradicted in the following scene. In a highly stylized 1950s American soda fountain, which is perhaps meant to symbolize the outdatedness of Andre's chauvinistic thoughts, the same three women from the hair salon and the bathhouse respond to Andre's question in a way that undermines any notion of a docile, sexualized woman who solely seeks to serve her husband. The first woman says, "To be a widow. Of course I want to get married, but later, I want him to die!" This response causes André, again back at his apartment, to fall flat on the ground. The second woman explicitly states her financial interest in any future relationship with a man: "I want a man to take care of me!" The third woman, initially more hesitant than the other two, finally finds the courage to announce her desire for a biodegradable man.

One way of making sense of the chaotic confluence of different time-spaces in this long opening scene is to look at it as the audiovisual manifestation of André's incessant work on his dissertation. A highly accelerated form of editing takes the spectator back to André, who is either listening to some of the women's responses or typing at his desk. As a result, what at first appears to be a steady flow of narrative and visual fragmentation is actually a representation of the extensive time-lapse of André working deliriously on his research. This is not to say that the spectator can locate André's act of writing in any one specific spatiotemporal moment. On the contrary, the flow of his flashbacks signifies the period over which he conducts his research and writes his dissertation. Evidence of this is found in the presence of intermittent visual references to an ever-changing bedside alarm clock, suggesting a flow of time. Furthermore, the scene is held together by the nondiegetic upbeat jazz music that first begins during the title presentation and plays continuously until the 4:40 mark. Thus, in the midst of varying spatiotemporal settings,

André's imagined erotic fantasies, and mixed lighting, the unifying factor is the early-twentieth-century jazz/swing music, which appropriately mimics what Carvalho does visually.

OPENING(S) TOWARD CONTINUITY—THE COLOR RED AND THE STAGE

In addition to the centrality of the opening scene, *Uma Mulher Vestida de Sol* introduces the spectator to two motifs that are present and often intertwined in all of Carvalho's work since 2005. The first is the color red, which serves as a signifier of three of the most important themes that run throughout the director's work—passion, jealousy, and death. The second motif is the presence of an actual or evoked theatrical stage. In the many instances where a stage appears or is evoked, it exists as the space upon which a performance occurs or implies the presence of an underlying performance. As such, the stage also functions as a metaphor for Carvalho's broader aim to reimagine standardized television fiction by constructing an aesthetic that asserts an explicit level of artificiality whose very existence is in direct contrast to the field's norm of naturalism.

In *Uma Mulher Vestida de Sol*, red is a nonverbal sign of the underlying importance of passion and jealousy, which will lead to the destruction of Rosas's family. In *Hoje é Dia de Maria*, it represents both Maria's love for Amado and the jealousy of Quirino and Asmodeu, which represses the heroine and impedes her journey. Through the figures of Sinésio and *Moça Caetana*, in *A Pedra do Reino*, the color evokes bloodshed and death. In *Capitu*, red points to Dom Casmurro's passion for and jealousy of Capitu, eventually leading to the destruction of his family. And, finally, in *Afinal, o que Querem as Mulheres?* the color elicits the problematic nature of Andre's meaningless sexual conquests, which nearly overtake his life and lead to his death. Though each of these themes is also central to the melodramatic Brazilian telenovela—made explicit in that genre through the use of dialogue—in Carvalho's work, they are manifested first at the level of the preverbal. As I will show below, they thus exist "not as the physical reflection of the written text, the mere projection of physical doubles that is derived from the written work, but as the burning projection of all the objective consequences of a gesture, word, sound, music, and their combinations" (Artaud, *The Theater* 73).

In *Uma Mulher Vestida de Sol*, each of the on-screen spaces is lit either exclusively by or in combination with a deep-red, a sealike blue, or a brighter, white light. The dominant red lighting is diffused through a large and expressionistic red rose situated on the back of the center of the sound stage's wall. In narrative terms the red lighting represents the sun and therefore suggests daytime settings. However, instead of creating a bright, radiant milieu, depending

Figure 4.28. Projection of a room onto the floor, *Uma Mulher Vestida de Sol* (1994). Right to reproduce granted by TV Globo.

on the narrative moment, the back-lit rose evokes a suppressed infernal or passionate environment. The special's most important narrative prop, then, is also a double, whose presence transcends its role as portraying the sun to also emphasize Rosa's complicated familial and amorous situation. In addition to the rose and the lighting that accompanies it, Carvalho expands the use of the color red to other elements of the *mise-en-scène* and the cinematography as a way to nonverbally emphasize not only Rosa's emotional state, but also that of her father. In doing so, Carvalho visually portrays the interconnectedness of Rosa's passion for Francisco, Joaquim's jealousy of their relationship, and the bloodshed that results from his jealousy.

The interconnectedness of the characters' distinct emotions as embodied in the color red is best exemplified in one of the work's most important scenes—a flashback to Joaquim visiting Rosa's room, where he learns his daughter has run away to marry Francisco, the nephew he so despises. Gavião, Joaquim's farmhand, breaks the news by informing his boss that Rosa "is with him [Francisco] at home." Joaquim's facial expressions make it clear that this news renders him infuriated with his daughter. From Joaquim's face, the image cuts to an extreme close-up of the backlit red rose, which fills the entire screen. Depending on the character's perspective, at that crucial narrative moment, the insertion of the red stands for either passion or anger. That is, for Rosa, who is at home with Francisco, the red signifies the love and passion-

FIGURE 4.29. Furniture in miniature, *Uma Mulher Vestida de Sol* (1994). Right to reproduce granted by TV Globo.

filled consummation of her recent marriage. However, for Joaquim, the red represents his rage. Set on retrieving his daughter, Joaquim instructs Gavião to prepare everyone for an attack to get Rosa back. While in Suassuna's play this scene is simply a dialogue between the two characters, serving as a narrative bridge that explicates both the cause (Rosa's absence) and the reaction (Joaquim stealing her back), Carvalho pauses to reflect visually on Joaquim's state at the moment of learning this devastating news.

In the above scene, a bracketed, audiovisual insertion interrupts the already nontraditional dialogue between Gavião and Joaquim. Instead of a shot reverse-shot setup, a fundamental characteristic of the Brazilian telenovela, the spectator sees Joaquim in medium close-up with Gavião standing behind him, as if whispering in his boss's ear. Then, with no explanation, the image cuts from the place where the two are conversing to Rosa's empty room. There the camera captures the space and Joaquim from high above (figure 4.28).

Mimicking the camera's gaze from above, Joaquim looks down upon some very small objects grouped together on the floor. A cut to a ground-level shot of the objects reveals them to be Rosa's bed, dresser, and chair in miniature (figure 4.29). From a now nearly ground-level perspective, the spectator then sees Joaquim gently bending down to contemplate the furniture. As Joaquim reaches down, taking a piece of the furniture into his hands, another bracketed extreme close-up of the backlit red rose interrupts the shot, filling the screen.

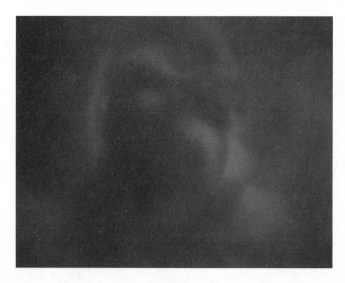

FIGURE 4.30. Red fills screen, *Uma Mulher Vestida de Sol* (1994). Right to reproduce granted by TV Globo.

The interplay between the high and low angle shots combined with Joaquim's physical presence relative to the miniature furniture emphasizes the patriarch's power and authority. However, for the first time, Rosa has challenged her father. That she has done so is for Joaquim both shocking and enraging. With the screen still filled by the image of the red rose, Joaquim declares, "This is due to the impure blood of her mother!" Whereas up until this point, the red rose has symbolized Rosa's passion for Francisco or Joaquim's jealous anger directed at Rosa and Francisco's family, the mention of Rosa's mother's impure blood alludes to her death and foreshadows pending tragedies. Moreover, the fact that it is likely that Joaquim himself killed Rosa's mother in a jealous rage situates him as the point on which all three of these emotions converge.

The bracketed visual insertion comes to an end after a cut from the red rose–filled screen back to a medium close-up of Joaquim trembling with anger. We are finally transported back to the spatiotemporal moment when Joaquim and Gavião converse. "Get everybody together!," Joaquim declares, almost uncontrollably. "Tell them to hide around my house because I am going to get my daughter back and that dog [Francisco] is going to die today!" (*Uma Mulher* DVD). Upon the completion of Joaquim's orders, the image cuts to yet another extreme close-up of the backlit red rose, which takes over the entire space of the screen (figure 4.30).

It is now clear that the interconnectedness of passion and jealousy will likely end in at least the death of Francisco. But what is passion or jealousy?

Figure 4.31. Maria's red cloak, *Hoje é Dia de Maria* (2005). Right to reproduce granted by TV Globo.

That is, it is one thing to discuss such abstract concepts, but because it so often done and in a quotidian manner, Carvalho would argue that they become overly familiar, therefore losing their essence. Instead, the director's objective, as exemplified in this scene, is to move beyond the spoken word and the figurative or pictorial. To this end, Carvalho seeks out the more open-ended communicative power of the preverbal, suggesting that passion, jealousy, and death are simply—beyond any definitions or descriptions one might provide—red.

Similar instances can also be found in Carvalho's later works.[4] In *Hoje é Dia de Maria*, for example, jealousy nearly results in the death of Maria's lover, Amado. As in *Uma Mulher Vestida de Sol*, Carvalho uses red in costumes, makeup, and other elements of the *mise-en-scène* of *Hoje é Dia de Maria* to signify and reinforce the psychological and emotional states driving the characters' actions. One element of the *mise-en-scène* that deserves special attention in this work is the theatrical stage. As already mentioned, along with the color red, the stage is one of the motifs that runs throughout Carvalho's work, and not surprisingly, the two motifs often share the same narrative space and serve the same narrative ends.

For example, shortly after Asmodeu—the diabolical figure who incessantly hounds the young heroine and whose body is entirely covered in red paint—

FIGURE 4.32. Red curtains, *Hoje é Dia de Maria* (2005). Right to reproduce granted by TV Globo.

marvelously transforms Maria into a woman, she finds herself working in a small traveling theater owned by the brother and sister Quirino and Rosa. Every night Maria leaves her new friends to encounter her faithful companion and protector the *Pássaro Incomum* (Uncommon Bird), who at sunset is magically transformed into the princely Amado, Maria's lover. Having fallen madly in love with Maria, Quirino follows her in hopes of learning where she goes each night in her red cloak and what she does there. To his dismay, he encounters her in the arms of Amado. After his discovery, the next time Quirino appears before Maria, his face has been theatrically painted to feature a light-blue tear falling from his eye and bright, full red lips forming a frown (see figure 4.18). Often playing the part of a clown, Quirino's painted face makes perfect sense within the narrative context. Until this point, however, his makeup has always been that of a cheerful clown. Unlike Maria, the spectator already knows of Quirino's feelings for her and of his disappointment with the situation. His change in appearance is a nonverbal signifier, communicating to Maria and reinforcing to the audience his sadness and dismay because she does not reciprocate his feelings (figures 4.31 and 4.32).

FIGURE 4.33. Stage, *A Pedra do Reino* (2007). Right to reproduce granted by TV Globo.

As is characteristic of Carvalho's work, nonverbal forms of communication are preferred to the spoken word whenever possible because, in addition to diminishing the power of the writer, these forms of communication augment the director's creative input and engagement with the spectator. Along these lines, singing and theatrically performed monologues and dialogues directly follow the nonverbal in Carvalho's communicative hierarchy. Considering the importance performance and artificiality maintain in Carvalho's work, it is not at all surprising that the director prefers any of these forms of communication to a shot/countershot composition centered on spoken dialogue between two or more characters. The overuse of this conventional form has become so familiar to the spectator that for Carvalho it has lost the power to incite the spectator beyond expected, even predetermined interpretations.

In the sequence in question, Carvalho utilizes each of these three forms of communication as a means of highlighting the narrative's key psychological and emotional moments. It does not take long for Quirino's heartache and disappointment to become uncontrollable jealousy, and he devises a plan to separate Maria and Amado forever. The next time the spectator sees Quirino his tear-stained cheek has been replaced with his usual cheerful countenance. In a red costume evoking that of a court jester, Quirino appears from behind the red curtains of the traveling stage to perform for the rural audience (figure 4.33).

FIGURE 4.34. Red curtains, *Capitu* (2008). Right to reproduce granted by TV Globo.

The red curtains might seem like an insignificant detail, since they are typical of so many theatrical stages. In the broader context of Carvalho's work, however, along with the stage itself, the curtains function as a metaphor for the revelation of those aspects of life that exist beyond our consciousness. That is, the stage and the red curtains constitute a liminal space wherein the characters and the spectator engage in an exploration of a state of being that exists somewhere slightly beyond that seemingly tangible reality that informs so much of our daily lives and what we do.

If we consider the scene in which Quirino steps out onto the stage from behind the red curtains within Carvalho's broader artistic trajectory, it becomes readily apparent that in each case, the stage, physically present or evoked, is the space from which the director examines those themes he finds most important: love, jealousy, and death. Thus, in *A Pedra do Reino,* the spectator encounters Quaderna, the Quirino-like figure standing atop his own traveling stage, theatrically calling attention to his family's bloody past. In *Capitu,* Dom Casmurro's operatic attempt to understand his past begins with enormous red curtains pulling back to reveal the protagonist posing on a stagelike space, illuminated by a spotlight (figure 4.34).

The evocation of the stage in *Hoje é Dia de Maria* invites the spectator to enter the indeterminate space of memory and performance, something that is reiterated a number of times throughout that microseries. In the same way,

FIGURE 4.35. Red curtains, *Afinal, o que Querem as Mulheres* (2010). Right to reproduce granted by TV Globo.

FIGURE 4.36. Operatic setting, *Afinal, o que Querem as Mulheres* (2010). Right to reproduce granted by TV Globo.

the red curtains are evoked in two very important moments in *Afinal, o que Querem as Mulheres?*, signaling to the spectator the ongoing, theatrical performance that characterizes Carvalho's work. First, in a flashback, the origin of André's relationship with Lívia is introduced through a red countdown of numbers, which function like the red theatrical curtains, pulled back to reveal the artificially constructed performance. In the space of memory, André's relationship takes on a performative aspect, nostalgically romanticizing the couple's first moments together. Similarly, André's near-death experience summons the presence of both the stage and the red curtains during a nine-minute operatic performance set in a closed red room (figures 4.35 and 4.36).

As I have shown in this chapter, along with the motifs of the color red and the theatrical stage, the hybrid accumulation of aesthetic elements and artistic fields come together in Carvalho's work as defining characteristics of the director's reimagining of contemporary Brazilian television fiction—one in which the figure of the director emphasizes an audiovisual construction both to express and arouse emotion. The theatricality and aesthetic accumulation that distinguishes Carvalho's work from everything else on Brazilian television is on full display beginning with his 2005 microseries *Hoje é Dia de Maria*. As I discuss in the next chapter, messages about nationalism and citizenship are embedded in Carvalho's aesthetic forms. What is more, the inclusion of these two issues in *Hoje é Dia de Maria* is in line with TV Globo's broader mission statement. However, Carvalho's aesthetic treatment of nationalism and citizenship positions the director in a long tradition of Brazilian intellectuals and artists attempting to reimagine the nation and what it means to be Brazilian.

Chapter Five

REDISCOVERING AND REAPPROPRIATING ANCESTRAL ROOTS

According to the Agência Nacional de Telecomunicações (ANATEL—The National Agency of Telecommunications), 18,908,827 homes, approximately 28.35 percent of all Brazilian homes, had pay television as of April 2016 ("TV paga registra"). As a point of comparison, during the same month in 2012, 13,959,159 homes had pay television ("TV por assinatura cresce"). In contrast, Brazil's dominant network, TV Globo, reaches approximately 99.5 percent of all homes. Thus, while the numbers indicate that pay television in Brazil is increasingly pushing the network era into a period of multichannel transition (discussed in further detail in Chapter Seven), those same numbers reveal the reality of pay television's limited reach and access compared to network television. Specifically, TV Globo continues to capture far and away the largest audiences.

Very much aware of its reach and enormous audiences, TV Globo has long positioned itself as the primary disseminator of Brazilian culture. This is clear in one of the network's oft-used slogans, *Globo, a gente se vê por aqui* (Globo, we see ourselves here). The slogan suggests that TV Globo is the source for and platform upon which *brasilidade* (Brazilian-ness) is represented and negotiated. To celebrate its fiftieth anniversary, in 2015 the network used *Somos Brasil, somos 50 anos, somos Globo* (We are Brazil, we are 50, we are Globo) as its slogan. Here, the point is made more explicitly: TV Globo is Brazil, and Brazil is TV Globo.

Such positioning by the network goes far beyond mere slogans, however. Parts of the company's mission statement speak of its social responsibility, which, according to the media empire, is a "result of being in contact with hundreds of millions of people, in almost every Brazilian home" ("Social Mission"). According to the Rio de Janeiro network's conception of itself, its task is more than just entertainment: "Globo's high-standard dramaturgy includes the dissemination of knowledge, the transmission of socio-educational messages and the incentive for debate and behavioral change" ("Social Mission"). In recognizing its nearly ubiquitous reach, TV Globo conflates its massive and extremely diverse audiences—especially in socioeconomic terms—with an obligation to disseminate didactic and ideological messages through fictional content—a practice known as social merchandising. To this end, a telenovela can at moments feel like a school classroom where a teacher gives a lesson on citizenship issues ranging from pollution to the perils of human trafficking. In such social merchandising and the positioning of itself as representing what it means to be Brazilian, TV Globo determines what these issues of citizenship and pressing socioeducational messages are. This raises a number of ethical concerns related to the fact that because of its reach and declared mission, the network does not passively reflect on or represent what it means to be Brazilian but, to a certain degree, actively creates or dictates what it means, or should mean.

Carvalho's thirty-plus years of professional tenure at the network necessarily places him within the company's overarching mission of entertaining, informing, and shaping citizens. Indeed, on more than one occasion Carvalho himself has made reference to what he understands to be his own social responsibility in light of TV Globo's huge audiences. For example, referring to his desire to create an ethical aesthetic, he says:

> Considering television's reach in Brazil, to treat it as merely a diversion seems very questionable. We need entertainment, but we also need to orient ourselves and understand the world. My aesthetic is just a small consequence of this. I seek a dialogue between those *who know* and those *who do not know*; a simple, sober, and fraternal dialogue through which what for the average man of culture has already been securely acquired will also become more common patrimony for the common, poor man, who, in regard to many issues still finds himself abandoned. (emphasis added, "Educação" 23)

Clearly, the language and logic Carvalho employs in the above statement is strikingly similar to TV Globo's definition of its self-determined social mission. Both are paternalistic in their implicit recognition of the socioeconomic and class disconnect between the country's very large impoverished and undereducated population, a significant portion of the television-viewing public, and the significantly smaller, wealthier, and more educated population that creates content.

Nonetheless, while it would be easy to do so, it would be overly simplistic to reduce Carvalho's position and work to a mere form of elite manipulation. A more productive path for comprehending Carvalho's self-positioning as a creative figure can be found in Anthony D. Smith's suggestion that scholars "seek to understand the underlying impulse to moral regeneration and authentication that inspires their researches and activities, and to sift the novel national categories and interpretations from pre-existing traditions of ethnic myth, memory, symbol and value" (*The Antiquity* 21). Indeed, a closer look reveals that, while Carvalho is furthering the mission of TV Globo, the messages he chooses to disseminate, which are intrinsically linked to the manner in which he presents and disseminates them, diverge from the norm to such a degree that he is in fact constructing an alternative voice—though not without its own problems at times, as I will discuss in Chapter Seven—from within the dominant structure.

Despite the similarities between their respective discourses and despite their professional relationship, Carvalho's work deviates strongly from other TV Globo–produced fiction, in terms of both its production and its aesthetic. As such, the increasingly glocalized, neoliberal Brazil created and represented by TV Globo's telenovelas, which the network sells to over 130 countries throughout the world, is drastically different from the oft-portrayed folkloric Brazil in Carvalho's artisanal, artificial, and aesthetically hybrid productions. Behind this central difference are two interconnected forces that drive Carvalho's unique work and distinguish it from everything else on Brazilian television. First, more than anything, Carvalho conceives of himself as an artist who happens to be a television director. Second, Carvalho can be placed within a long tradition of Brazilian left-leaning artists and intellectuals who view themselves as activating the masses through the creation of symbolic goods. In an aggressive and rebellious tone, some of the Brazilian modernists of the 1920s forever altered the path of their country's literature and its arts in general by engaging in the production of artistic creations representative of the nation's cultural specificities. Similarly, Carvalho takes aim at the influx and the local production and reproduction of imported culture with the intention of constructing an audiovisual language that is both "authentic and essentially Brazilian" ("Educação" 23).

In the face of the locally situated global popular culture that characterizes so much of contemporary Brazilian television fiction, nearly all of Carvalho's work in television looks to the past in an attempt to rediscover and appropriate a cultural heritage that is both Brazilian and universal—what the director refers to as *ancestralidade* (ancestrality). *Ancestralidade* is the creative source from which the director claims his aesthetic emerges. In his own words, it "represents that which is most modern and, at the same time, that which is most archaic" ("Educação" 24). In fact, according to the director, "Everything is reflected in *ancestralidade*, be it biological or spiritual" ("Educação" 24).[1] More specifically, one can think about ancestrality as it relates to Carvalho's work in television as a return to a distant past in search of "authentic" myths and memories that will encapsulate the "origins" and "essence" of the national identity (Smith, *The Antiquity* 26). Nonetheless, ancestrality is not merely located in ancient times. Instead, it "is revealed as an *amalgam* of the *modern*—that is, the recent and the novel—and the *ancient*—that is, the rooted, original and persistent elements" (emphasis added, Smith, *The Antiquity* 26).

In the already mentioned 2008 essay "Educação Pelos Sentidos,"[2] Carvalho offers some of his thoughts on television production, his role in the medium, and *ancestralidade* as the creative metaphor for his audiovisual production. Although not nearly as ironic or caustic, the essay recalls the nationalistic *manifestos* of some of Brazilian modernism's leading proponents. Like the iconoclastic modernist Oswald de Andrade in his *Manifesto Pau-Brasil* (1924) and later in his *Manifesto Antropófago* (1928), Carvalho advocates on behalf of the "obligatory" development of a televisual language that is unique to Brazil ("Educação" 23). In search of his country's "origins" and "essence," the director explicitly asks, "Who are we? What face do we have? Where, in this exact moment, does someone write a history for us?" ("Educação" 25). Carvalho then declares his mission: "I am in search of a narrative drama that represents us" ("Educação" 25). In an entirely different tone, Oswald de Andrade also clamored for what he believed was the necessary development of a truly Brazilian artistic expression. Against the importation and copying of the European literary tradition, he argued for: "A type of language without archaisms, without erudition. Natural and neologistic. The millionaire contribution of all the errors. *As we speak. As we are . . .* " (emphasis added, *Obras Completas* 6). Later, in 1928, Oswald more radically argued in favor of a metaphorical cannibalism as a means of creating a singular Brazilian literary production: "Only Anthropophagy unites us. Socially. Economically. Philosophically. . . . Tupi or not Tupi, that is the question" (*Obras Completas* 13). For Oswald, the issue was no longer—as it was only four years prior in his own *Manifesto Pau-Brasil* (1924)—a matter of importing or exporting cultural production. Instead, Brazilian letters would reach its maximum potential if it actively consumed all the best at its disposal, independent of origin, so as to then incorporate it into its own tradition, producing a uniquely Brazilian symbolic good. The answer, then, as proposed by Oswald, was a form of artistic and cultural anthropophagy wherein Brazilian artists consumed the "enemy" (foreign culture), so as to ultimately transform it into a "totem" (a novel and distinctive mark of Brazilian culture) (*Obras Completas* 15).

Over eighty years later, Carvalho's devouring of myriad forms of artistic expression from all parts of the world can be understood as a twenty-first century technological reappropriation of Oswald's radical proposal. Indeed, Carvalho's delineation of ancestrality in "Educação Pelos Sentidos" shares Oswald's anthropophagic understanding of artistic production as a way to create a unique national language. He also sees the source for such a language as deriving from any age and anywhere, yet concretely localized in individual Brazilians. He says: "Brazil's genetic patrimony, stories, races, languages, sounds. . . . *Ancestralidade* is something that allows us to create, rather than copy; to feel, rather than to describe or explain. It is a metaphor available to all of us and should be utilized. . . . It is a sensorial tool kit, a playful imagination that inhabits us because it lives on from our earliest memories" ("Educação" 24). In this multifaceted definition, Carvalho outlines the contours of *ancestralidade* by comparing it to Brazil's genetic patrimony. Neither visible nor tangible, like one's DNA, *ancestralidade* is in and all around us; it helps to shape our thoughts and actions; and it is ultimately the source from which Brazilian culture derives. Smith arrives at a similar conclusion regarding a more expansive, long-view understanding of the nation, arguing that "cultural and symbolic elements of myth, value, memory and symbol provide frameworks for understanding and aspiration, and these are often, although not exclusively, *embodied in a sense of common ethnic identity and of belonging to a cultural community of imputed common ancestry*" (emphasis added, *Ethno-Symbolism* 18). For Carvalho, *ancestralidade* carries within it a sensorial kit of dispositions. These dispositions, which *nos habitam* (inhabit us), which are "embodied," develop over time and are a result of circumstances relating to family upbringing, educational experiences, and, more broadly, one's cultural context. It follows then that *ancestralidade* is not something of which the individual agent, in this case the artist or spectator, is wholly conscious. Consequently, it is more akin to what Pierre Bourdieu refers to as *habitus*.

Bourdieu's development and use of the term *habitus* is an explicit attempt to move beyond the limiting dichotomous interpretive tools he believed characterized structuralism and other intellectual modes of analyzing society or cultural production (Johnson, "Pierre Bourdieu," 22; Maton 53). Bourdieu surmised that habitus comprises a "structured and structuring structure" (*In Other Words* 170). Habitus is "structured" insofar as it is shaped by both past and present circumstances, including, but not limited to, such aspects as family upbringing, geographical context, and educational background. The use of the adjective "structured" suggests the organization of something continuing over time, thus occurring in the past yet also existing in and helping to inform the present. Something that is "structured," then, is not static, but is instead dynamic, potentially changing according to an agent's circumstances and position within a particular field at a given moment. Nonetheless, that which was "structured" in the past does not simply disappear in new contexts. Instead it helps to shape or influence one's present and future actions, decisions, and worldview. Thus, habitus is also "structuring" as it pushes a "structured" accumulation of dispositions onward into the future. Finally, habitus is a "structure" in that it is the home to these dispositions, which foment certain perceptions, appreciations, and practices. Regarding dispositions, Bourdieu says that they express "first the result of an organizing action, with a meaning close to that of words such as structure; it [disposition] also designates a way of being, a habitual state (especially of the body) and, in particular, a predisposition, tendency, propensity or inclination" (*Outline* 214).

Although not an attempt to repurpose or expand on Bourdieu's concept of habitus, Carvalho's *ancestralidade*, as a metaphorical representation of a source for the creation and interpretation of an audiovisual language, is strikingly similar to the sociologist's analytical tool. Encompassing *all* of Brazilian cultural production, both past and present, *ancestralidade* represents an artistic and hermeneutic source present in each individual. It is thus accessible by artists and spectators alike in a communicative interaction potentially resulting in the creation and understanding of a unique audiovisual language. Karl Maton affirms that habitus "links the social and the individual because the experiences of one's life course may be unique in their particular *contents*, but are shared in terms of their *structure* with others of the same social class, gender, ethnicity, sexuality, occupation, nationality, region and so forth" (53). The capacity to recognize and reconcile the link between the individual and the particular within a shared structure, like habitus, may also be found in *ancestralidade*. As with habitus, *ancestralidade* denotes the passing on of both individual and communal characteristics between generations. Consequently, these characteristics may range from the local (specific family traditions, for example); the regional, such as shared dialects; the national (nation-building narratives, among others); or to the universal, as in fairy tales or tragedies.

Bourdieu elaborates on the theoretical link between the individual and the communal made possible by habitus, arguing: "The *habitus*, as the word implies, is that which one had acquired, but which has become durably incorporated in the body in the form of permanent dispositions. So the term constantly reminds us that it refers to something historical, linked to individual history, and that it belongs to a genetic mode of thought, as opposed to existentialist modes of thought" . . . (*Sociology in Question* 86). Again, the language used here by Bourdieu is very similar to that used later by Carvalho (e.g., "genetic patrimony," "histories," "inhabit us," etc.). Like habitus, *ancestralidade* is also a structured and structuring structure insofar as it perpetuates geographically distinct cultures through national pillar social institutions. In individual agents, *ancestralidade* is structured by way of such institutions, resulting in unique manifestations and helping to broadly inform an agent's way of being, her habitual state, and her predispositions, tendencies, propensities or inclinations. Finally, *ancestralidade* is a spatiotemporally transcendent structure—that is, a platform on which the traces of past generations potentially meet in the present and are subsequently carried forward into the future—from which both creators and spectators can draw on the hermeneutic and communicative process of the construction of an audiovisual language.[3]

FOLKLORIC AND AESTHETICALLY HYBRID *ANCESTRALIDADE*

Hoje é Dia de Maria is Carvalho's first attempt to create a work that uses an artistically hybrid audiovisual construction to engage what he understands as his *ethical* obligation to his television audience. While the *Primeira Jornada* (the first part of the microseries) draws primarily from Brazilian popular culture, and therefore a more explicitly Brazilian *ancestralidade*, elements from universal fables and fairy tales also influence the work. The *Segunda Jornada* (the microseries' second part), however, assumes the references to a global *ancestralidade* in a more direct manner, through the incorporation of an urban setting, non-Brazilian popular and classical music, and the *quixotesque* figure Dom Chico Chicote. Broadly speaking, both *jornadas* attempt to locate and explore some of the antiquated and diverse cultural symbols that, together, compose a wide-ranging idea of what it means to be Brazilian—namely as conceptualized through the *campo/cidade* (countryside/city) dichotomy.

As Randal Johnson notes, one of the historical characteristics of the Brazilian intellectual elite has been, "a self-attributed 'mission,' frequently assuming the shape of the national 'conscience,' 'guide,' 'mentor,' or 'voice'" ("The Dynamics" 8). Assuming "the right to intervene in the process of national organization, reorganization, or transformation," the Brazilian intellectual elite has, according to Johnson, been consistently engaged in the mission of establishing a national culture for their country since the beginning of Romanticism in 1836, shortly after Brazil's independence from Portugal in 1822:

> Romantic writers—most of them closely associated with the Imperial government—took upon themselves the herculean task of forging a national culture. Thus the concern, in the Indianism of such writers such as Gonçalves Dias and José de Alencar, with creating symbols of national identity. With the declaration of the Republic (1889), many intellectuals saw themselves as "guides" in the process of modernization and, armed with positivist theories and ideological liberalism, instrumental in the remodeling of the state. In the 1920s, the "scientistic" concerns of Republicans were replaced with cultural nationalism in a search for the roots of Brazilian-ness as a part of broader process of national discovery. ("The Dynamics" 8)

It is precisely within this last period that Carvalho located a model for the eclectic construction of a folkloric nationalism. In fact, though vastly different in content and tone, one could argue that the aesthetic and ideological roots of Carvalho's exploration in *Hoje é Dia de Maria*—especially as it pertains to the *Primeira Jornada*—can be found in Mário de Andrade's 1928 rhapsody *Macunaíma, o herói sem nenhum caráter*. Ironic, ludic, sarcastic, and aggressive, Andrade's literary masterpiece appropriates stories, legends, and myths from myriad sources to create the fantastical world of Macunaíma, the work's lazy, morally ambiguous antihero. The result is a highly innovative work that explores the complexities of Brazilian Portuguese's linguistic hybridity, while also establishing what David Haberly refers to as both an "etiological myth of national creation [and] a myth of national destruction" (159).

In the 1920s, roughly one hundred years after Dom Pedro II peacefully declared Brazil's independence from Portugal, Andrade and other Brazilian modernists were still searching, through the written word, to understand what exactly it meant to be Brazilian. Nearly one hundred years after the publication of Andrade's rhapsody, Carvalho takes up the task through television of understanding what it means to be Brazilian in the twenty-first century. Indeed, those questions regarding what it means to be Brazilian and how to express that through literature and other art forms, which were at the center of the first phase of Brazilian modernism (1922–1930), also inform the ethical aesthetic project Carvalho initiates in *Hoje é Dia de Maria*.

The connection between Andrade's and Carvalho's respective works is an example of the long-standing concern, highlighted by Johnson, among some Brazilian artists and intellectuals with understanding what defines Brazil as such. Both artists, via their distinct mediums, seek to create a unique artistic language that represents the nation's singularity. To this end, both look to the past, away from the technological advancements of their respective modernities, to those symbols, stories, songs, and myths that have persisted through time and inform what it means to be Brazilian. In his work on ethnosymbolism, Smith highlights the central role of an intellectual and artistic elite in exploring its nation's roots: "This is the goal of intellectuals (I would add artists as well) and professionals who seek out, select and reinterpret strands from the cultural heritage of local populations whom they designate as 'their nation,' usually an ethnic core. Rather than simply inventing national traditions (though that occurs too), the nationalist intellectuals, inspired by Romantic ideals, turn to folk cultures and ethnic memories and symbols in their search for authentic 'roots' for themselves and their community" (*The Antiquity* 21). Though distinct in their specificities, Andrade's and Carvalho's creations search out "authentic roots" by relying heavily on folk cultures and shared memories and symbols. It is well known that Andrade conducted extensive research into the impressive accumulation of myths, superstitions, sayings, proverbs, and idiomatic phrases that make up *Macunaíma, o herói sem nenhum caráter,* which, as the story goes, the author wrote in only six days while lying on his back in a hammock (Proença 5). The result was the construction of Macunaíma, Brazil's first literary (anti)hero. Interestingly, there is very little that is redeeming about Macunaíma. Indeed, as the work's title states, Macunaíma is the hero without any character. A reading of the work reveals that the title's ambiguous reference to Macunaíma's absence of character is purposeful insofar as he lacks any one defining characteristic, whether moral or physical. That is, Macunaíma is both good and bad; both physically mature and mentally immature. He is both lazy and industrious. Manoel Calvacanti Proença's characterization of Macunaíma highlights the antihero's connection to Sérgio Buarque de Holanda's description of the Portuguese adventurer who played a central role in colonizing Brazil: "taking advantage of situations; he lacks that worker's spirit that demands persistence. His is a mentality of adventure; of fabulous and easy wealth . . . " (14). Additionally, he is simultaneously the physical embodiment of the tripartite racial miscegenation of indigenous, African, and European cultures that in part comprises the Brazil's national identity. More importantly, Macunaíma is the hero of the Brazilian people ("herói da nossa gente") (*Macunaíma* 214). As such, he is, by extension, a metaphor for Brazil. In short, as Proença notes, "because he is a condensation of Brazilian characteristics, we [Brazilians] are all a little bit Macunaíma" (24).

Like Andrade's modernist rhapsody, *Hoje é Dia de Maria* tells a fantastical story of the protagonist's journey through Brazil's vast territory. Whereas Andrade's hero is complex and problematic yet likeable, Carvalho's new Brazilian hero, Maria (Carolina Oliveira), is neither lazy nor selfish. Moreover, if Macunaíma's moral compass is at best ambiguous, Maria's is clearly pointed in the direction of the common good. Though only a child, like her religious namesake, Maria symbolizes *the* maternal figure, representing an example of the country's value system in its most pure form. Maria simultaneously embodies, then, the maternal generator of Brazil, both as the mother figure and as the land, and, as a child, the country's future. In short, Maria is the personification of some of the major preoccupations Carvalho has taken up in select works: the figure of mother, the land, and the nation.

In part, the constructed symbolism of Maria along these lines has to do with Carvalho's distrust of globalized culture, which for him eliminates what is interesting about his country in favor of some rootless, universal cultural product. He says:

On the other side, a globalized world awaits us, with its arms full of formulas and successful models. I'm in a fight against these "monsters," that is, against the ignorance, the aberrations of their reasoning, their formulas, and their illusions. . . . In *Hoje é Dia de Maria*, as in a harvest, we work to return to Brazil the fruit Brazilians themselves planted in the midst of their preparation. The tales taken from Brazilian popular oral traditions were the seed. In the eyes of today's globalized world, I feel that is a work of extreme importance. Using a cliché, I would say, even resistance, as there is no country that easily gives up its memories. The series was born out of joy that I had when I was faced for the first time as an adult with the popular fables collected by Romero and Cascudo, among others. Soon after came the paintings by Candido Portinari and the *cirandas* recreated by Villa-Lobos. ("Educação" 23–24)

Of course, as Néstor Garcia Canclini argues in *Imagined Globalization,* one need not be forced to choose between the local and the global (13). Nonetheless, despite his search for the local in what he views as an increasingly globalized world, in *Hoje é Dia de Maria* Carvalho engages in a process of rediscovering and reinterpreting a selection of the country's traditions, while situating these in or alongside universal traditions. To have any success in doing this, as Smith notes, "he or she must dig down to the '*authentic past'* of the community, like some political archaeologist, so that the nation can be built in its *ancestral* homeland on its *true foundations*" (emphasis added, *The Antiquity* 23).

Highly eclectic in both narrative and aesthetic terms, in addition to those influences already mentioned and those and cited by Carvalho in the quote above, *Hoje é Dia de Maria* is loosely based on playwright Carlos Alberto Soffredini's investigations into the *fala caipira*.[4] Each of the influences highlights Carvalho's need to reassert a *brasilidade* (Brazilian-ness). In so far as nationalism is, as Benedict Anderson has shown, to at least some degree a social construct, what it exactly means to be Brazilian, or any nationality for that matter, is debatable. However, it is clear that Carvalho believes that—like many of the Romantics and Modernists before him—Brazilian-ness exists in the country's folktales and popular culture, which have dialogically moved through multiple generations. Thus, by directly or indirectly incorporating, referencing, citing, and dialoging with works by Luís da Câmara Cascudo, Sílvio Romero, Mário de Andrade, Candido Portinari, Heitor Villa-Lobos, and others, Carvalho constructs a televisual language that offers the spectator an opportunity to explore their shared Brazilian ancestrality.

MARIA EXPLORES BRAZIL'S COUNTRYSIDE

Sweet and innocent Maria lives in the Sol Levante (Rising Sun) with her widowed father, Pai (Osmar Prado[5]). Early on, her innocence is challenged when, in one of his inebriated states, Pai makes a sexual advance toward his daughter. Saddened by the tragic event, her father's increasing degradation, and yearning for her deceased mother, Maria plays matchmaker by introducing her father to Madrasta (Stepmother), a widowed neighbor (Fernanda Montenegro[6]). To Maria's dismay, however, Madrasta turns out to be a wicked stepmother who has little patience for her new stepdaughter. While her own daughter, Joaninha (Thaynná Pina and Rafaella de Oliveira), gluttonously devours corn and lazily plays with her dolls, Madrasta incessantly orders Maria to do domestic chores such as cooking, cleaning, and washing clothes.

It is during this initial part of the microseries that the spectator first encounters the familiar and problematic stepmother/stepdaughter relationship. As Vladimir Propp notes in his book *Morphology of the Folktale*, the figure of the stepmother is "either present from the very beginning, or the story of an old man's remarriage after the death of his first wife is recounted. Through the old man's second marriage the villain is introduced into the tale" (86). Thus, *Hoje é Dia de Maria* inserts itself into the world of the folktale while making clear reference to *Cinderella*, which is later reinforced in a sequence depicting a beautiful computer-generated, stop-motion regal ball, where, upon trying to escape before midnight, Maria loses her red slipper. However, even if the spectator has never heard of *Cinderella*, she will likely recognize the tenuous daughter/stepmother relationship from similar portrayals of it in a telenovela.

Importantly, then, in narrative terms, Carvalho's interest in *ancestralidade* begins with a common European folktale. The suggestion here is twofold: first, this is, at least in part, a story of oppression, which Maria will need to escape and subsequently overcome; second, when we think about something as being uniquely Brazilian, as Carvalho aims to do with this work, it is clear that we are not dealing with an overly nationalistic sentiment. That is, instead, Carvalho's creative path forward is closer to what Oswald proposes through his artistic anthropophagy—to copy and consume anything that comes from abroad is acceptable, but only insofar as it results in something new. With *ancestralidade* as his creative source, Carvalho casts his artistic net far and wide, allowing himself the freedom to cite, reference, appropriate, or reappropriate whatever he finds interesting. However, the director is careful to note that the point of departure is always the local. This is why, as we will see shortly, in addition to the Brazilian creative sources that serve as the microseries' base, Maria's journey is also always brought back to and grounded in the domestic context, defined in the microseries by the underdeveloped countryside or the modern city.

Disillusioned with her home life and her stepmother's constant attacks, Maria decides to embark on a journey in search of the distant, enigmatic, and mythical edge of the sea (*franjas do mar*). Like Macunaíma's magic talisman, the *muiraquitã* (amulet), which serves as the narrative engine for the hero's travels throughout Brazil and South America and, more specifically, to São Paulo, Maria puts the small key (*chavinha*) she inherited from her mother around her neck and sets off in search of the sea. Prior to leaving, however, Madrasta, in what Propp refers to as the "interdiction," warns her that in order to reach the ocean she will need to pass through the harsh País do Sol a Pino (Land of the High Sun) where the sun never sets (121). Undeterred, Maria departs on her journey, thereby constituting what Propp refers to as the "violation of the interdiction" (121).

Instead of faithful brothers who accompany and constantly aid the mischievous Macunaíma, throughout her search for the franjas do mar, it is the Pássaro Incomum (Uncommon Bird), a puppet in the form of a beautiful golden bird, who watcheds over Maria. Again, according to Propp, like Macunáima's brothers, the bird represents "The Helper (Magical Agent)" (124). Moreover, as the spectator later learns, the bird is actually the princely Amado (the Beloved), who has been maliciously transformed by the villain, Asmodeu. Widely considered to have derived from the book of Tobias in the Old Testament, Asmodeu, or Asmodeus in English, is known as the destroyer of marriages (*Asmodeu*). Although Maria never marries, Asmodeu incessantly attempts to destroy the heroine's relationship with Amado and works to keep her separated from her estranged father. While in Andrade's rhapsody it is Macunaíma who seeks out the villain Piamã in hopes of recovering his talisman, Asmodeu and his five incarnations—Asmodeu Bonito (Pretty Asmodeu) (João Sabiá), Asmodeu Sátiro (Satirical Asmodeu) (Ricardo Blat), Asmodeu Velho (Old Asmodeu) (Emiliano Queiroz), Asmodeu Mágico (Magical Asmodeu) (André Valli), and Asmodeu Poeta (Poetic Asmodeu) (Luiz Damasceno)—constantly impede Maria's progress by making veiled (and sometimes not so veiled) attempts to steal her shadow or her little key.[7] By inverting this process, Carvalho makes Maria a more likeable figure. Rather than being the cause of suffering, she is the object of persecution. Despite the difficulties she experiences—losing her mother, attempted violation by her father, being forced to live with a wicked stepmother, and being bothered at all turns by Asmodeu—Maria always does what is right, purposefully situating her as a powerful example for the spectators.

Indeed, it is due to his frustration with his inability to stop Maria and his disgust with her infallible wholesomeness that Asmodeu decides to steal Maria's childhood, magically transforming her into a young woman (played by Letícia Sabatella). During this period, Maria learns of the Pássaro Incomum's true identity—the princely Amado, who subsequently becomes her lover. Disappointed with his failed attempts to ruin Maria's life, Asmodeu separates her from Amado by returning her to her childhood. However, to his surprise, he realizes that he has sent the protagonist too far back in time. Upon returning to the Sol Levante from which she first departed, Maria recognizes that she is in the time-space prior to her mother's death, her brothers leaving the family farm, her father violating her and marrying Madrasta. Finally, overcome with happiness, Maria, along with her new friend, Ciganinho (Phillipe Louis), who is Amado as a child, before he was punished to eternally roam the skies, achieves her initial objective of reaching the *franjas do mar*. The "Return" as Propp calls it, represents Maria's journey having come full circle. Moreover, with the "lack" resolved—that is, Maria's family once again intact—Maria's happiness is restored (125). However, before Maria can get home, she must push through eternal, scalding days that characterize the País do Sol a Pino.

After some time in the País do Sol a Pino, Maria finally is granted a reprise by unlocking the cool, damp night from its unlikely imprisonment in a coconut possessed by the Xavante indigenous tribe. The hero's discovery of the night is a direct reference to the indigenous legend "*Como a noite apareceu*" ("How the Night Appeared"). The legend maintains that in the beginning night did not exist; there was only day. However, when a young man, who had recently married the daughter of the *Cobra Grande* (Large Snake), wanted to consummate his marriage, his bride informed him that she would only do so under the cover of nightfall. Perplexed, the young man tells her that night does not exist, to which his bride responds by telling him that her father has it. In response, the young man sends out his helpers to obtain the night from the *Cobra Grande*, and the helpers eventually return with the night trapped in a *caroço de tucumã* (palm tree seed) (Cascudo, *Antologia* 209–11). Indeed, in another connection to Brazilian modernism, in his epic poem *Martim Cererê* (1928), Cassiano Ricardo adapted the legend *Como a noite apareceu* for the development of a narrative about how nationhood in Brazil was formed.[8] What is more, *Macunaíma*'s narrator informs us that Macunaíma is "filho do medo da noite" ("the son of fear and the night").

This, when combined with the *Cinderella* reference discussed above, is a good example of the multiple intertextual layers—or the intermedial phenomenon Irinia Rajewsky refers to as medial transpositions, media combination, and media references—at play in Carvalho's work (51–54). In the first instance, the director draws upon a European folktale as a central element for the development of Maria's fantastical journey and as an opportunity to utilize computer-generated images for an elaborate formal dance scene. In the second, he references an indigenous myth, allowing Maria to enter into a new narrative space. Both of these cultural references, however, are not in and of themselves "Brazilian." Nonetheless, the two are, as is the case in Ricardo's poem or Andrade's rhapsody, appropriated and subsequently mediated by a contemporary artistic construction—in this case the microseries—in an effort that both looks back in time and across geographical borders to locate the cultural and ancestral roots that give rise to notions of *brasilidade*. Along these lines, in his poem "O Trovador," part of *Paulicéia Desvairada* (1922), a collection of poems that initiated Brazilian modernism, Mário de Andrade declares: "Sou um tupi tangendo um alaúde" ("I am a Tupi strumming a lute") (83). In "Inspiração," a poem from the same collection, the author writes: "Galicismo a berrar nos desertos da América" ("Gallicism screaming in the wilderness of America") (83). Similarly, in his *Manifesto Pau-Brasil* (1924), Oswald de Andrade sums up his position by grouping together the *floresta* (forest) and the *escola* (school). In each of these examples, the poets explicitly highlight the seemingly contradictory relationship between the European and indigenous cultures that in part comprise Brazil. The inclusion of the distinct narrative and aesthetic sources within the confines of Maria's fictional universe suggest that Brazil's roots, as portrayed in Mário and Oswald's poetic formulations, are far-reaching and culturally diverse.

The referential, intertextual flexibility that transcends spatiotemporal boundaries to inform Maria's journey is also present in the very spaces through which she passes. After discovering the night, and with her hope now renewed, Maria continues onward through the *Agreste* (Woodlands), *Vilarejo* (Village), *Despenhadeiro* (Crag), *Fazenda* (Plantation), and *Bosque* (Forest). The snowcapped European mountains that characterize the *Despenhadeiro* appear alongside the *Bosque*—which itself evokes both a space from *Alice in Wonderland* and the Amazon—and the very familiar space of the *Fazenda*, a nod to the country's history of slavery. Like the cultural references, the interplay of distinctly Brazilian spaces and seemingly far-off or even mythical spaces symbolizes the geographical diversity embodied in the country's territory and ethnic makeup. These references and their broader symbolism evoke, yet again, similar efforts made during the heroic phase (1922–1930) of Brazilian modernism.

As Maria moves through these different spaces, she encounters a number of archetypal characters. Her interactions with the different characters present her with ethical dilemmas that situate her progress toward the sea within the localized context of pressing contemporary Brazilian social issues. Unlike Macunaíma, however, who during his own journey almost always chooses his own well-being over any notion of the common good, Maria serves as an example of "appropriate" citizenship, consistently electing to sacrifice her own needs for the betterment of her newfound acquaintances. This is particularly apparent in the microseries' second and third episodes, during which Carvalho develops the notion of *ancestralidade* through an aesthetically hybrid audiovisual construction that places Maria in a number of ethical dilemmas. Of particular interest here are the scenes leading up to and immediately following Maria's encounter with the Dois Executivos (two businessmen) and Pai's interaction with the three Cangaceiros (bandits).

In the first example, Maria is moving through the País do Sol a Pino when she comes upon the Maltrapilho (Ragamuffin) sitting alone alongside a small creek. Rather than exchanging greetings, the two initially communicate with one another through song. More specifically, they sing the well-known Brazilian folk song "Sapo Jururu," also referred to at times as "Sapo Cururú." The inspiration for the inclusion of this particular version of the song comes from renowned Brazilian composer Heitor Villa-Lobos's adaptations of traditional rounds in the 1920s. Like Mário de Andrade and Oswald de Andrade in literature, Villa-Lobos's rounds were also aimed at producing music in line with Brazil's cultural heritage and therefore supposedly unique to the country. As David P. Appleby states: "The *Cirandas* represent the Brazilian nationalist movement in music at its best" (123–24). Though I will take this up in more detail at the end of the chapter, it is worth mentioning now that what is most interesting about the appearance of the Villa-Lobos rounds and the other intertextual references and citations in *Hoje é Dia de Maria* is the way in which they form part of a palimpsest of national construction. That is, in the 1920s, the modernists found themselves looking back, deep into the past, in search of authentic roots. In the early 2000s, Carvalho does something similar, but rather than going back to the roots themselves, in a technological recycling he reappropriates the modernists and that which they had already reappropriated.

As such, "Sapo Jururu" is not merely a folk song; it is the aestheticized version of a folk song as conceived by perhaps Brazil's greatest composer. Nonetheless, insofar as the song has transcended space and time, becoming, as Carvalho would put it, a part of Brazil's genetic patrimony, the spectator need not know of this version of the song's history in order for the song to engage her senses. Thus, that a young girl and a middle-aged male ragamuffin, having never met before, can communicate in such a manner suggests that two very distinct individuals actually partake in a shared *ancestralidade*. In other words, "Sapo Jururu" connects the two characters' respective individualities and their interaction with one another in that particular moment to a broader cultural past, which they share and through which they become in part who they are.

As is the case throughout *Hoje é Dia de Maria*, references to the characters' common *ancestralidade* precedes some type of ethical reflection. Once they

Figure 5.1. Retirantes, *Hoje é Dia de Maria* (2005). Right to reproduce granted by TV Globo.

finish singing, the Maltrapilho breaks the fourth wall by looking directly into the camera as if speaking to the spectator and letting her in on what Maria does not yet know. Importantly, the breaking of the fourth wall in this particular scene represents one of the earliest examples of a technique that will come to be a common occurrence in nearly all of Carvalho's subsequent work. Representative of the artificiality that characterizes Carvalho's microseries, as he ruptures the narrative universe, the Maltrapilho theatrically shares his wisdom in a brief monologue: "This is a world that oughta be made and, when it is all said an' done, a defect is an important step in the perfect ladder. Bent, poor, or shoddy, all living can walk straight because to be human is not bad. Not good, is to be an incomplete human"[9] (*Hoje é Dia* DVD). Looking directly into the camera, the Maltrapilho speaks to the Brazilian spectator, who, like Maria, probably recognizes the folk song, thereby sharing in the broader ancestral consciousness. The message, then, which alludes to one of the primary lessons of Maria's journey, explicitly extrapolates beyond the fictional universe to inform the viewer that no matter what, do the best you can and always continue your journey toward betterment.

Shortly after her encounter with the Maltrapilho, Maria comes across the wandering Retirantes. As with the inclusion of Villa-Lobos's version of "Sapo Jururu," this scene activates and evokes multiple artistic and cultural layers, so many that the spectator will almost assuredly identify at least one. First, the presence of the dislocated migrants elicits a well-known northeastern Brazilian reality in which harsh and extensive droughts force workers to leave

FIGURE 5.2. Candido Portinari, *Retirantes* (1944), 190 × 180 cm. Right to reproduce granted by João Candido Portinari / Fundação Portinari / Projecto Portinari.

their jobs and homes in search of water and employment. Within the broader context of the Brazilian social imaginary, this reality was made well known through its artistic representation in Graciliano Ramos's literary masterpiece *Vidas Secas* (1938) and Nelson Pereira dos Santos's 1963 homonymous filmic adaptation of Ramos's novel, a masterpiece in its own right. Not unlike the Brazilian artists mentioned thus far, Ramos, although he disassociated himself with *modernismo*, was a key figure during Brazilian modernism's second, socially engaged phase (1930–1945). For his part, Santos was, along with Glauber Rocha, the most important director behind the Cinema Novo movement in the 1960s and 1970s. Importantly, during that movement's first phase

(1960–1964), as was the case with Brazilian modernism, there was an explicit focus on the nation, as represented, for example, by a concerted effort on the part of the directors to construct an aesthetic that mirrored the country's impoverished reality. Carvalho recognizes the importance of the movement's early concern with the nation and its relationship to his own work: [The land as nation] "has a direct relationship with Cinema Novo, which has a direct relationship with the Motherland" (*Luiz Fernando Carvalho* 27) (figures 5.1 and 5.2).

Second, the depiction of the migrants is a direct citation of Candido Portinari's series *Retirantes* (1944). Arguably the country's greatest painter of the twentieth century, Portinari was also, like the other artists already mentioned, deeply concerned with rediscovering and representing his nation:

> In 1928 Portinari won the Travel Award to Europe, with *O Retrato de Olegário Mariano*. This fact is a milestone in the artistic and existential trajectory of the young painter. Throughout 1930, Portinari remains in Paris. From this distance, he can better see his land. He decides: "I'll paint those people [Brazilians] with those clothes and that color. . . ." Toward the end of 1931 Portinari returns to his homeland. There, he puts into practice his decision to portray in his paintings Brazil—its history, people, culture, flora, fauna. . . . His paintings, prints, murals reveal the *Brazilian soul*. Concerned, too, with those who suffer, through bold colors Portinari shows poverty, difficulties, and pain. ("Candido Portinari")

The outlining of a key moment in Portinari's artistic trajectory emphasizes the painter's desire to represent his country, something he discovers while in Europe, not unlike some Brazilian artists before him. Additionally, like in the work of the aforementioned Graciliano Ramos and Nelson Pereira dos Santos, Portinari was interested in an artistic creation that was socially engaged. This is clear in the painter's many macabre depictions of the migrants, which serve as a social critique of a nation that has forsaken at least some of its citizens.

In *Hoje é Dia de Maria*, Carvalho revisits this critique by visually citing Portinari's painting. But in doing so, he is also visually citing his own work, since in *Uma Mulher Vestida de Sol* Carvalho had already included a similar *Retirantes* scene (figure 5.3). In both the 1994 year-end special and the 2005 microseries, notwithstanding the eleven years that separate the two works, Carvalho uses the same actor (Nanego Lira) as the primary migrant figure. Similar to the *Uma Mulher Vestida de Sol* scene, in *Hoje é Dia de Maria* the migrants appear in white linen suits and dresses, singing in unison to the sound of a traditional Brazilian string instrument, the *rabeca*, and a deep bass drum, both of which are played by the renowned in-scene folk musicians, Mestre Salustiano and his son Pedro Salustiano. As is the case in *Uma Mul-*

FIGURE 5.3. Retirantes, *Uma Mulher Vestida de Sol* (1994). Right to reproduce granted by TV Globo.

her Vestida de Sol, Carvalho purposefully shoots the migrants out of focus as they move slowly toward the camera. The blurred image simultaneously echoes the macabre tone and impressionist technique used by Portinari while also suggesting Maria's fatigue and resulting difficulty in seeing them clearly. The dialogic interaction between the distinct works represents an intermedial recycling that, depending on the spectator's cultural disposition, offers a number of possibilities for interpreting the presence of the Retirantes.

The richness of intertextual and aesthetic layers in this scene, like the allusion to a shared *ancestralidade* in the Maltrapilho scene, comes before the ethical lesson, therefore giving it priority. In their brief conversation, the migrants encourage Maria to continue her travels by informing the weary young heroine that "we're all on same journey" (*Hoje é Dia* DVD). Later, the Mendiga (the homeless woman) echoes this sentiment when she says, "I've been here as long as the world has been the world. It's you who hasn't noticed" (*Hoje é Dia* DVD). Along with the Maltrapilho exchange, each of these encounters further reinforces the message that, despite a perceived disconnectedness brought on by the influx of globalization, we all partake in the journey together and we share an ancestrality that extends through time beyond the individual via myriad vehicles. Maria, who represents all that is good, seems to understand this message inherently; always doing what she thinks is best. Not surprisingly, and in clear departure from Macunaíma's attitudes, for Maria this means placing her newfound acquaintances' needs before her own. She thus treats the Maltrapilho's leg wound; she tells the migrants she will cross the desert and never forget them; and she gives the Mendiga her last drop of water. Finally, in the Dois Executivos's scene, she saves an indebted dead man from another spanking by two insufferably insistent and nonsensical businessmen.

Like the previous examples, the Dois Executivos's scene fleshes out the ethical message through its aesthetic construction, which is, in this instance, a hybridization of experimental cinematography, music, stop-motion animation or pixilation, and theatrical body movements. Exhausted after having left the Mendiga behind, Maria searches for some shade where she can momentarily rest and seek refuge from the blistering sun. Here, there is a nontraditional cut that works against classical audiovisual narration, potentially disorienting the spectator. Facing the camera, Maria moves toward a barren tree; once there, she turns 180 degrees to her left so her back is now to the camera. As soon as she does so, there is cut to a tracking shot of the flying Pássaro Incomum, captured closely from above. Below the bird, Maria is now facing the camera while she looks for a place to sit at the base of the tree. As a result, in this particular shot, Carvalho breaks the 180-degree rule of continuity editing by crossing the axis of action. Moreover, in line with his use of objects to fragment, obscure, or frame a particular shot, Carvalho places the puppet bird in a position where it is initially the subject, but later, as the image unfolds, becomes the obscuring object that eventually moves to reveal Maria at the base of the tree. These nontraditional forms of editing and framing are a precursor to the strange amalgam of aesthetic elements that follows with the appearance of the Dois Executivos.

Sitting beneath the tree, Maria talks to the Pássaro Incomum. As she utters the word "*noite*" ("night"), there is a cut to a profile of her sitting and resting her head against the tree. The cut, however, is masked by the sound and out-of-focus image of a hand striking a match. Hearing the sound, Maria turns quickly to see a man, the Homem do Olhar Triste (the Man with the Sad Face) (Rodolfo Paz). Even before he tells Maria that they [the Dois Executivos] are coming, one can hear the rumble of an engine in the distance. As the rumble grows louder, the sound of a vehicle backfiring masks a cut to the businessmen appearing on a vintage beat-up motorcycle and sidecar. In this sequence, the editing—which is in this case aural, but is also at other times visual and is a constant throughout Carvalho's work—exemplifies the detail with which Carvalho seeks a seamless narrative construction, but one that also potentially calls attention to itself.

Indeed, in this particular case, it is directly through sound that the Dois Executivos burst into Maria's fictional universe. Caricatures of businessmen, the Dois Executivos emerge driving a motorcycle and sidecar and wearing black suits and ties and black rubber wigs. Lying in the middle of the sun-

FIGURE 5.4. Os Dois Executivos, *Hoje é Dia de Maria* (2005). Right to reproduce granted by TV Globo.

drenched *sertão* is the Defunto, an abandoned dead body. After circling chaotically and nonsensically around Maria, the mannequin body, and the Homem do Olhar Triste, the executives get off their motorcycle and do a playful choreographed dance before beating the cadaver with wooden sticks. Carvalho mixes the cartoonish music with pixilation to animate the actors' overtly theatrical and absurd body movements and facial expressions, thus linking the two to the figures of Tweedle Dee and Tweedle Dum from Disney's animated *Alice and Wonderland* (figure 5.4).

Cuts back and forth between the men and Maria, who also exchanges gazes of disbelief with the Homem do Olhar Triste, reveal that she finds the situation to be utterly ridiculous. Maria learns that the executives have appeared to collect an unpaid debt from the dead man. She also learns that they do this daily and will continue to do so until they receive their money. Obviously, this situation is silly, and for Maria, who is still an innocent child unconcerned with such issues as money and debt, their malicious behavior is even more ludicrous. Thus, what the spectator sees—the actors' theatrical or comical corporal movements, their over-the-top manner of speaking, and their costumes and black rubber wigs, combined with the music and pixilation—is actually the manifestation of Maria's perspective, which accentuates their ridiculous behavior, motivated by greed and capitalism. Upset by the absurdity of the situation, Maria comes to the dead man's rescue by using trickery to pay off the men with their own money. Thus, while Maria has

FIGURE 5.5. Spotlight on Pai and Os Cangaceiros, *Hoje é Dia de Maria* (2005). Right to reproduce granted by TV Globo.

clearly deceived the two men, their portrayal as overly greedy results in the spectator siding with and even applauding Maria for giving them a taste of their own medicine while also standing up for the defenseless Defunto.

Whereas Maria's encounters tend to deal with belonging to and participating in a social process for the broader good, Pai's encounter with the three *cangaceiros* (bandits) focuses on the specific question of corruption. In the third episode, there is a scene that is in many ways a near replication of Maria's experience with the Dois Executivos. As he searches through the harsh *sertão* for his lost daughter, hoping to one day redeem his deplorable behavior, Pai seeks a momentary rest at the base of a barren tree. From beneath the tree, the approaching sound of horses galloping can be heard. Suddenly, a bright light fills the screen. In the lower half of the image, through the light, three cangaceiros appear on horses. Realistic noises seemingly emitted from the animals accompany a harsh screeching sound coming from a nondiegetic *rabeca*. Although the horses' heads and bodies are to scale and move in a realistic manner, which the onomatopoeic sounds also help to underscore, their glass and plastic construction and the wheels upon which they are mounted clearly reveal their artificial nature. If there is any doubt regarding their artificiality on the spectator's part, Carvalho dispels it through an establishing shot from behind Pai, who stands directly in front of the three cangaceiros on their horses. In this shot, which is symmetrically framed, Pai stands nearest the camera and is bathed in a dark shadow. The cangaceiros and horses,

FIGURE 5.6. Candido Portinari, *Bumba-meu-boi* (1959), 32.5 × 32.5 cm. Right to reproduce granted by João Candido Portinari / Fundação Portinari / Projecto Portinari.

however, are brightly lit by a spotlight, which shines directly down upon them (figure 5.5).

The horses' artificiality, juxtaposed with a realist interpretation on the part of the actors and real sounds emitting from the soundtrack, exemplify the creative dichotomy characterized by the juxtaposition of antinaturalism with naturalism, present in all of Carvalho's microseries.[10]

This scene is important for two reasons. First, it underscores the reappropriation of a motif that is one of *Hoje é Dia de Maria*'s driving forces. Second, it is another example of Carvalho's effort to construct an aesthetic that embodies an ethical reflection. The rendering of an artificial horse is an aesthetic marker first used by Carvalho in *Renascer*.[11] In the first episode of that work, Carvalho depicts a *bumba-meu-boi* festivity. Dating as far back as 1840 in the

FIGURE 5.7. Bumba-meu-boi, *Uma Mulher Vestida de Sol* (1994). Right to reproduce granted by TV Globo.

northeastern city of Recife, the folkloric tradition of the *bumba-meu-boi* combines theater, circus, dance, and traditional music. In line with *Hoje é Dia de
Maria's* ethical mission—that is, the linkage of all Brazilians, independent of
race, place, or socioeconomic status, through their shared ancestrality—"the
[*bumba-meu-boi*] drama represents the total solidarity of a local group, from
the highest to the lowest social class" (Queiroz 92). A rich cultural practice,
the tradition's most notable visual characteristic is that of a man who, dressed
in a colorful bull costume, dances about, threatening to attack onlookers at
any moment.

In his work, Carvalho develops the *bumba-meu-boi* into the motif of the
artificial horse or bull. The purpose of this is twofold: first, it represents Carvalho's broader concern with rediscovering in and through his work in television Brazil's authentic past; second, it functions as one of the main markers
of the director's artificial aesthetic. Once again, Portinari's work serves as an
important point-of-reference and influence for Carvalho's visual reimagination of the figure of the *bumba-meu-boi* (figures 5.6, 5.7, 5.8 and 5.9). As is
the case with the Retirantes and the Cangaceiros, with the *bumba-meu-boi,*
Carvalho draws upon and activates the Brazilian social imaginary while also
referencing an entire artistic tradition that surrounds and informs these ancestral symbols.

Figure 5.8. Artificial horse, *A Pedra do Reino* (2007). Right to reproduce granted by TV Globo.

FIGURE 5.9. Artificial horse, *Capitu* (2008). Right to reproduce granted by TV Globo.

Once Carvalho draws spectators into the ancestral realm he invites them to consider a very real and contemporary Brazilian social issue, namely corruption. At the narrative and audiovisual levels, Pai's journey for redemption could not be more disconnected from matters of contemporary corruption. However, it is precisely because of the aesthetic disconnect from a realist portrayal that the message carries more weight. In order to pass through the *sertão*, the armed cangaceiros demand that Pai pay them a *propina*, or an illicit fee. Like his daughter before him, Pai exhibits morally sound behavior, informing the cangaceiros that "I don't pay bribes to any man in this world. What I have to pay, I figure that out with God" (*Hoje é Dia* DVD). Pai's moral turn suggests he is on the road to redemption and therefore closer to finding his daughter. Additionally, his ethical positioning communicates to the audience that corruption is wrong and that it is necessary to take a stand, no matter who one is or what one has done in the past, against those that destroy society through their selfish behavior, even if death is a possibility.

In each of the encounters analyzed above, Carvalho provides spectators with an aesthetic depiction of contemporary social issues. In doing so, Carvalho puts into practice Shklovsky's idea of the transformational power of art. Put differently, the explicit defamiliarization of current social issues, achieved through their aesthetic portrayal, functions to extract pressing social matters from their ubiquitous place in the, news headlines, potentially infusing them with renewed meaning for the spectator.

THE CITY EXPLORES MARIA

In the *Segunda Jornada*, an urban musical replaces Maria's rural journey in the *Primeira Jornada*. Broadly speaking, the insertion of an urban space in the *Segunda Jornada* functions as a narrative and aesthetic counterpoint to the *Primeira Jornada*'s largely rural settings. In narrative terms, it completes the fantastical depiction of the country by juxtaposing the nonurban/urban territorial dichotomy that, in large, part makes up Brazil and has long structured intellectual discourse surrounding it. Maria's arrival in the city from rural origins evokes a journey made by millions of Brazilians over the past century. Though the distinct spaces (the rural and the urban) both have serious social problems, Carvalho's aesthetic construction of the city suggests that these problems emanate outward from the urban space. Thus, much as in the *Primeira Jornada*, in the *Segunda Jornada,* Carvalho frequently presents the spectator with a unique audiovisual construction that is followed by an ethical reflection. At the heart of the ethical aesthetic of the *Segunda Jornada* is Maria's narrative as told through an urban musical that draws upon a broader *ancestralidade.*

In the urban setting, the slow-paced narrative of the *Primeira Jornada* drastically accelerates. The freedom that accompanies Maria's seemingly limitless journey through rural spaces is replaced by a pervasive claustrophobia in the city, a closed and dark milieu populated by masses of people. In the city, loud, sometimes abrasive, global pop and rock music replaces the light-hearted traditional Brazilian music that characterizes Maria's Arcadian expedition in the *Primeira Jornada*. Nonetheless, despite some of the clear visual differences between the *Primeira* and *Segunda Jornada*'s *mise-en-scènes*, Carvalho's broader objective is still to construct an aesthetic that expresses an ethic. As such, Maria finds herself once again faced with socially relevant issues ranging from homelessness to the exploitation of child labor. As she does in the first part of the work, Maria consistently takes a stand against inequalities and injustices, further distinguishing herself as the exemplary national hero.

From the beginning, Carvalho makes it clear that the *Segunda Jornada* is the result of Maria's dream and that music is one of the primary vehicles of expression in this dream. In fact, music, primarily in the form of Maria's *cirandas* from the *Primeira Jornada,* whether used to comfort herself or as a form of identification and communication with strangers, is expanded upon in the *Segunda Jornada*, where roughly half of the dialogue is transmitted through song and dance. The story picks up where the *Primeira Jornada* ends—with

Maria's arrival at the *franjas do mar*. Meanwhile, the omniscient third-person narrator (Laura Cardoso) invites all listening and watching to participate in the mysterious and fantastical tale to follow: "Night! So I begin like this suddenly, speaking to anyone who believes that the world is full of mystery and that it is still an empire where everything is possible" (*Hoje é Dia* DVD). Already, for those who have seen the *Primeira Jornada*, there is a clear aesthetic departure from the beginning of that initial journey. Gone is the bright sunshine and lush green vegetation of her father's farm. Maria is now at the verge of a doubly mysterious time-space—night is quickly approaching and before her lies the endless sea, which both soothes the protagonist and threatens to swallow her up. As is the case throughout much of Carvalho's work, the narrator's invitation to the spectator to participate in this enigmatic, fantastical universe is reinforced by the clearly artificial construction of the space.

Despite the sound of the crashing waves, a number of shots of Maria and the surrounding space purposefully reveal the ocean to be a man-made construction, wherein real, native vegetation contrasts with the fake waves. In fact, these waves, which were later recycled for use in *Capitu* and represent one of the many visual references to Fellini's work employed by Carvalho, are made of twenty canvases attached to hand-turned rotating levers (*Segunda Jornada*). To further highlight the aquatic universe's artificiality a spotlight shines down on the heroine as she, along with the spectator who has accepted the narrator's invitation, prepares to give herself over to the unknown mystery of the moonlit sea. Softly, a chorus of female voices accompanies the sounds of the waves crashing, singing "Ah-mar, Ah-mar, Ah-mar! Maior mistério da vida é amar . . . " (*Hoje é Dia* DVD). This first part of the chorus, which is a play on the words to love (amar) and oh-sea! (ah-mar), is complemented by the second half which reads: "Life's greatest mystery is to love" (*Hoje é Dia* DVD). Though seemingly nondiegetic, a cut reveals the music to be taking place in scene as the narrator, along with the other main characters from the *Segunda Jornada*, sing directly below where Maria is standing. The characters are seated like puppets against a wooden wall, which sways back and forth as if floating above the waves. As they sing, encouraging Maria with the chorus, "Go, Maria, come . . . float in the waters, submerge your smile. Come, Maria, go . . . ," their voices, which mimic the fluctuation of the ocean, soothe Maria, putting her into a state of sleepiness and inviting her—and, by extension, the spectator—to lose herself in the depths of her imagination (*Hoje é Dia* DVD) (figure 5.10).

In this surreal, sleep-inducing scene, Carvalho pulls back the metaphorical curtain to reveal the artifice behind the moving waves. The director uses a long panning shot to show a small orchestra of men dressed in black suits and

Figure 5.10. Waves, *Hoje é Dia de Maria* (2005). Right to reproduce granted by TV Globo.

wearing black top hats, playing string instruments and a fife and a steel bicycle wheel being turned manually to make the waves move. As the camera continues to survey the space, there is shot of the artificial waves from the bottom up, showing Maria standing, bathed in sunlight, looking out over the waves. It is as if Maria teeters on the border between reality and the dream world. However, the dream world ultimately wins out when, suddenly, an animated version of the protagonist falls into an animated ocean, initiating her transportation through time and space to a far-off land, she eventually ends up in a city from the 1920s (figures 5.11 and 5.12).

Inspired by an eclectic accumulation of global artistic sources, including the paintings of Robert Rauschenberg and Paul Klee, Jean Tinguely's sculptures, and Fritz Lang's *Metropolis* (1927), Carvalho's city—like the rural space from the *Primeira Jornada*—is set inside the dome. The city encompasses a space measuring nearly 25,000 square feet. Within that space, there are four bustling city blocks largely composed of paper mâché and complete with traffic, stoplights, apartments, stores, a theater, a bus station, and a shoreline ("*Hoje é Dia*" *Memória Globo*). Additionally, all the city's inhabitants are dolls. Artist Raimundo Rodrigues, a key member of Carvalho's artistic team, and his crew created 120 heads, each with a different facial expression. Depending on the scene, the heads alternately appear atop fifteen different moveable bodies constructed of fiberglass ("*Hoje é Dia*" *Memória Globo*).

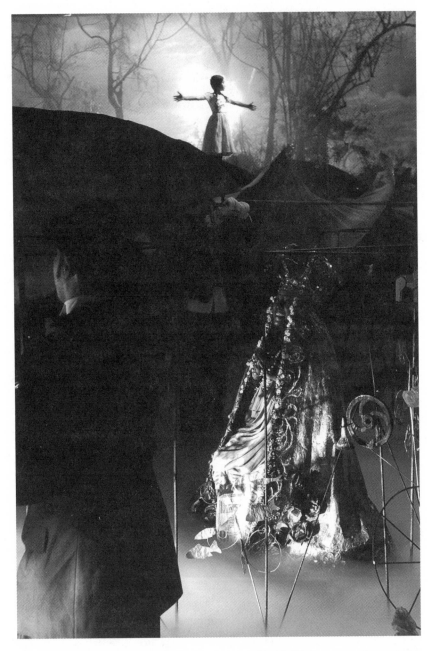

FIGURE 5.11. Waves choir, *Hoje é Dia de Maria* (2005). Right to reproduce granted by TV Globo.

FIGURE 5.12. Urban city, *Hoje é Dia de Maria* (2005). Right to reproduce granted by TV Globo.

Although it possesses a high degree of visual depth, especially when compared to the *Primeira Jornada*'s relative minimalism, this urban space functions much like a stage upon which the characters constantly perform, sing, and dance. Indeed, the singing from the opening scene just described is taken a step further in the urban space as it becomes the primary means by which characters communicate. For example, Maria's first encounter with an individual in the city occurs when a salesman (Daniel de Oliveira) asks her what her dream or wish is (*sonho*). In an instance of what Rajwesky calls an intermedial reference, he like all the city's nonanimated habitants, is made up "as if" he were a puppet or doll (54). When Maria replies that she wants to go home to be with her family, the salesman breaks out in song and dance, informing Maria of the wonderful homes available in the city. Moreover, in addition to the great number of scenes that are presented through song and dance, a choir composed of nearly the entire *Segunda Jornada* cast appears at different moments, moving throughout the city in a choreographed manner and singing songs about the dream world (figures 5.13 and 5.14).

Indeed, Maria herself, desperate to make her way back home, unwittingly takes a job in a vaudeville theater in hopes of earning enough money to leave the city. In a critical commentary on child labor—a subject also dealt with during the scenes from the *Primeira Jornada* depicting child slavery—Asmodeu Cartola (Asmodeu Boss) (Stênio Garcia) takes advantage of Maria

FIGURE 5.13. Doll-like salesman, *Hoje é Dia de Maria* (2005). Right to reproduce granted by TV Globo.

FIGURE 5.14. Choir, *Hoje é Dia de Maria* (2005). Right to reproduce granted by TV Globo.

by encouraging her, under the pretense that he wants what is best for her, to take the stage as one of his theater's female performers. Maria, as her stage persona Piano Baby—a reference to Marlena Dietrich's character Lola Lola in Josef von Sternberg's 1930 *The Blue Angel*—becomes a huge hit among the audience of older men. After Maria realizes that the shrewd businessman is exploiting her through sexual objectification, she finds a way to escape the theater (figure 5.15).

Although it is not the primary focus of the *Segunda Jornada*, Maria's tenuous relationship with the commercially driven entertainment business is a subtext of the work; one that serves as a precursor to Carvalho's metafictional critique of Brazilian television in *Afinal, o que Querem as Mulheres?* Not long after she arrives in the city, Maria finds herself on the verge of losing her characteristic innocence. This potential loss occurs as a result of her newfound relationship with the entertainment industry, and is perhaps the earliest fictional representation of Carvalho's complex relationship with his profession. Time and time again over the years, Carvalho has commented on how television's overly commercial structure seems to impede the creative endeavor and alienate the creative artist: "My generation was already characterized by the consumer model; it already tended to be a generation that valued copying, name-brand clothing, fashionable music, and all those other codes that constituted the *carioca* bourgeoisie. I never felt right in that situation; I forced the communication, but it never felt right, and the harder you try to make it work, the greater the sensation of exclusion" (*Luiz Fernando Carvalho* 25). In this way, Carvalho's work is like Maria's fantastical journey. With the exception of a few key helpers, he feels that he is a loner, fighting against the aberrations of a greedy, overly commercialized world that has forced out those individual and ancestral qualities that characterize people and places as unique.

With this in mind, it is not surprising that after her escape, Maria befriends the whimsical, idealistic, imaginative—and yet destitute—poet, Dom Chico Chicote (Rodrigo Santoro). Chicote's character is a literal reference to Miguel Cervante's *El ingenioso hidalgo don Quijote de la Mancha* (1605) and a visual reference to Portinari's series of colored pencil drawings, *D. Quixote* (1956–1961) (figures 5.16 and 5.17).

Dom Chico Chicote also represents the pure artist who dreams of constructing a world uninhibited by the strictures of a consumer-driven society. His name, when spoken, sounds similar to the Brazilian Portuguese *Dom Quixote*. However, it literally means Sir Chico Whip—"whip" as in lashes received as punishment. If there were any doubts regarding the broader structures at play, Carvalho introduces capitalist financiers who further complicate Maria's efforts at getting home. These individuals impede her return to inno-

166

FIGURE 5.15. Maria on stage, *Hoje é Dia de Maria* (2005). Right to reproduce granted by TV Globo.

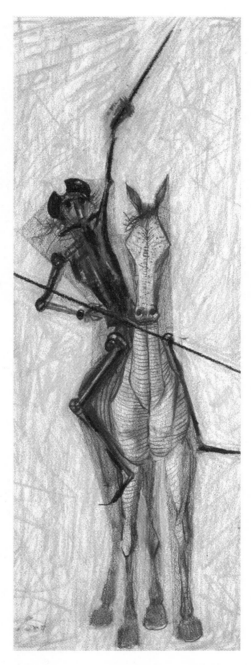

FIGURE 5.16. Candido Portinari, *Dom Quixote a cavalo com lança e espada* (1956), 42 × 16 cm. Right to reproduce granted by João Candido Portinari / Fundação Portinari / Projecto Portinari.

FIGURE 5.17. Dom Chico Chicote, *Hoje é Dia de Maria* (2005). Right to reproduce granted by TV Globo.

cence and freedom as they urge soldiers to incessantly engage in a battle that destroys the city and its inhabitants. The constant fighting in the city makes it increasingly difficult for Maria to escape.

Moreover, it is the capitalist financiers, represented by the Dois Executivos from the *Primeira Jornada,* who help put Dom Chico Chicote on trial for being an outlier who dreams of great, mythical objects and worlds. In a scene that evokes the Crucifixion, implicating the entertainment industry by revealing the artifice behind the production, Dom Chico Chicote is found guilty and, as his punishment, is to be thrown into the sea of forgetfulness. The suggestion here is that whoever dreams big or thinks outside the box, not unlike a "true" artist seemingly does, suffers at the hands of a commercial structure that, having no place for such individuals, goes so far as to make her existence forgotten entirely (figure 5.18).

As is the case with virtually all of Carvalho's aesthetic experimentation and hybridization, the creation of this urban musical is his attempt to distance his audiovisual language from that of everyday Brazilian television. In addition, Carvalho's inclusion of the urban space and non-Brazilian music into the *Segunda Jornada* demonstrates his recognition of a broader *ancestralidade*, one that, insofar as it borrows freely from both national and universal folklore,

FIGURE 5.18. Artifice in Dom Chico Chicote sentencing, *Hoje é Dia de Maria*
(2005). Right to reproduce granted by TV Globo.

transcends Brazil's expansive territory, and which also serves as a creative
source from which he can borrow. In this way, Carvalho adapts Oswald de
Andrade's theorization of an anthropophagic mode of production for the
creation of a uniquely Brazilian symbolic good.

From the beginning of *Hoje é Dia de Maria*'s preproduction process, one
of the guiding creative concepts was the reappropriation of discarded objects.
The general idea was to create most elements of Carvalho's fictional world by
repurposing "used objects that had been thrown aside and forgotten" ("Figurino" *Hoje é Dia*). *Hoje é Dia de Maria* exemplifies such repurposing on the
level of the macro (for example, the dome) and that of the micro (for example,
most of the costumes—some of which are made of or adorned with discarded
candy wrappers). Carvalho's conceptualization of reappropriation in *Hoje é
Dia de Maria,* however, extends beyond the realm of the discarded or forgotten physical objects to include ideas, stories (oral and written), and cultural
artifacts as intertextual references or instances of artistic influence. That is,
there is both a physical and a narrative recycling that is ongoing in *Hoje é Dia
Maria*'s first and second journeys (Nakagawa 90, 103–04).

Thus, the director's desire to reappropriate the discarded or undesirable
broadly falls within the context of Brazilian cultural production's long artistic tradition of aesthetic recycling. In "Hybridity and Aesthetics: The Case of

FIGURE 5.19. Rural space, *Hoje é Dia de Maria* (2005). Right to reproduce granted by TV Globo.

Brazilian Cinema," Robert Stam astutely argues that Brazilian cultural discourse, in addition to those of Latin America and the Caribbean, has been characterized by the conceptualization of "alternative aesthetics," aesthetics aimed at positively reassessing that which was formerly viewed as a negative through a process of artistic inversion ("Hybridity"). Using the example of the abjectly viewed ritual of cannibalism, made famous by Oswald's *Manifesto Antropófago*, mentioned earlier, Stam argues that the concept "becomes with the Brazilian *modernistas* an anti-colonialist trope and a term of value. At the same time, these aesthetics share the jujitsu trait of turning strategic weakness into tactical strength. By appropriating an existing discourse for their own ends, they deploy the force of the dominant against domination . . ." ("Hybridity").

Stam's argument points to the politicization of aesthetic hybridity as it enacts an artistic inversion of an existing power structure through the incorporation of distinct formal sources. On this basis, it would be easy to exclude Carvalho's work from Stam's argument: after all, Carvalho is still employed by the socially, politically, culturally, and economically dominant TV Globo. However, in *Hoje é Dia de Maria*, as in his other microseries, Carvalho practices his own jujitsu, both utilizing and inverting TV Globo's power by taking advantage of its immense resources—resources normally reserved for the factorylike production of telenovelas—to create a highly intimate and artisanal product rarely seen on Brazilian television. In doing so, Carvalho and his cast

FIGURE 5.20. Rural space, *A Pedra do Reino* (2007). Right to reproduce granted by TV Globo.

FIGURE 5.21. Urban space, *Hoje é Dia de Maria* (2005). Right to reproduce granted by TV Globo.

FIGURE 5.22. Formal dance, *Capitu* (2008). Right to reproduce granted by TV Globo.

and crew reappropriate both Brazilian television fiction and folk culture's formal styles and narrative constructions, ultimately combining the two into an organic whole that is *ancestralidade* as a *novidade* (ancestrality as novelty).

Additionally, the inclusion of a universal *ancestralidade*, especially when juxtaposed with the decidedly more local elements that characterize the *Primeira Jornada*, foreshadows Carvalho's subsequent development of the *Projeto Quadrante*. Throughout the two microseries that so far compose this project—the topic of Chapter Six—Carvalho includes, elaborates on, and sometimes even simplifies all of the aesthetic elements represented in the *Primeira* and *Segunda Jornadas*. *A Pedra do Reino*, for example, is a visual elaboration of many of the aspects pertaining to the *Primeira Jornada*, mainly those that have to do with the País do Sol a Pino. On the other hand, *Capitu* simplifies the visual excesses of the *Segunda Jornada*, while maintaining and elaborating upon the overt mixture of Brazilian and global *ancestralidades*, transforming *Hoje é Dia de Maria*'s urban musical into an introspective opera (figures 5.19, 5.20, 5.21, and 5.22).

Chapter Six

TAKING THE SHOW ON THE ROAD
ITINERANT TELEVISION

From its origins in 1950 to the present, Brazilian television has had a long tradition of adapting literary texts to the small screen. Drawing from Antonio Candido's *Literatura e Sociedade* and Renato Ortiz's *A Moderna Tradição Brasileira*, Randal Johnson argues:

> In Brazil the market for symbolic goods historically has been highly restricted and concentrated, especially given the lack of generalized access to public education and the nation's high levels of illiteracy (1890—84%, 1920—75%, 1940—57%. . . . Although the decrease in illiteracy would seem to indicate an increase in the potential reading public, which would occasion a diversification of both publics and producers, legitimate literature (i.e., that which disavows commercial interests as a primary motivation and is recognized as "serious" literature by the critical establishment) has continued to be a form of cultural expression directed at an educated elite, despite the considerable expansion of the publishing industry in the 1930s. ("The Dynamics" 11–12)

While Brazil's illiteracy rate has shrunk to around 10 percent, according to the country's most recent census (2010), Johnson's observation still holds true today ("The World Factbook"). Literature, along with theater and a significant portion of domestic film production, is still widely produced for and consumed by a small educated elite.[1]

In its drive for profit and the largest possible audience, television has long recognized and capitalized on the country's existing socioeconomic obstacles, serving as a bridge that connects its enormous audiences to canonical literary works adapted as highly popular telenovelas, miniseries, microseries, and specials. Hélio Guimarães highlights this practice in "Literatura em Televisão." Expounding upon Candido's seminal essay "Literatura e Subdesenvolvimento," Guimarães emphasizes the sociohistorical importance of Brazilian television in the dissemination of both international and national literature. According to Candido, large numbers of Brazilians experience a process in which more traditional cultural fields like literature are passed over due to social, political, and economic issues. As a result, Candido argues that a technologically urbanized folkloric tradition, like the telenovela, becomes the primary cultural source for these Brazilians ("Literatura e Subdesenvolvimento" 142). Considering, then, that a disproportionate amount of Brazilians' cultural competence is the result of contact with television, Candido's argument is especially relevant to Carvalho's *Projeto Quadrante* (*Quadrant Project*).

As discussed in the previous chapter, *Hoje é Dia de Maria* exemplifies Carvalho's interest in communicating with the television audience in a way that is ethical, at least as he understands the definition of that term. In that microseries, Carvalho's interest in ethics is in part revealed through explicit lessons on citizenship. Nonetheless, for Carvalho, there is more to an ethical form of communication than providing the spectator with educational messages regarding citizenship. Equally important is the effort to bring to the audience a complex aesthetic embedded with and informed by national and universal ancestral roots that simultaneously challenges and activates the spectator's senses. The aim is to eschew the facile, dialogue-driven of standardized television fiction in favor of an experimental process and an aesthetic where the primary objective is to defamiliarize the spectator's experience. In the *Projeto Quadrante*, Carvalho even challenges exactly what such an experience is within the Brazilian context, taking his show on the road in what can be described as the director's televisual version of *mambembe*, or low-budget, makeshift traveling theater. With the *Projeto Quadrante*, Carvalho not only extrapolates beyond the confines of TV Globo's studios; he also moves beyond the historically dominant production and cultural axis of Rio–São Paulo, providing the spectator with possibilities for engagement that transcend traditional television-viewing practices.

MAMBEMBE TELEVISION: COMMUNICATING WITH BRAZIL

As an adjective, the word *mambembe* connotes something ordinary or of poor quality (Houaiss and Salles Villar 474). However, as Ana Beatriz Wiltgen da Costa Guimarães points out, "As a noun, the *mambembe* can be a place, an actor or theater group, but, inevitably, on the margins, outside the center, out of the light, out of the spotlight" (7). Important in this latter definition is the physical dislocation to the periphery that it implies. The origins of *mambembe*'s marginalization lie in the development of the medieval Italian itinerant theater groups known as the *saltimbancos* (from the Italian *Saltare in Banco*) and then later from the *commedia dell'arte*. The *commedia dell'arte*, for example, managed over time to break the barrier between the theater of the court and the theater of the city (Guimarães, "Itinerância teatral" 6). It moved to the streets, selling inexpensive tickets to a largely illiterate population and allowing such individuals to consume what was, up until that point, predominately a luxury of royalty and court officials (Guimarães, "Itinerância teatral" 6).

Though numerous small circus groups have long performed throughout the interior of the country, *mambembe* troupes first appeared in Brazil around the end of the nineteenth century. Located primarily in Rio de Janeiro, the performers traveled to different areas in and around the city to present low-budget, circus-inspired plays to diverse audiences. The phenomenon gained widespread recognition only in 1959. However, as early as 1904 Artur Azevedo and José Piza's *O Mambembe*, a three-act play, portrayed a small national theater company as it traveled through and performed for audiences in the interior of Brazil, and in doing so, garnered the domestic practice of itinerant theater some notoriety (Guimarães, "Itinerância teatral" 3).

Importantly, by jumping ahead to 1977, one can establish a direct connection between *mambembe* theater and Carvalho's later work in television. During that year in São Paulo, playwright Carlos Alberto Soffredini created the Grupo Teatro Mambembe (The *Mambembe* Theater Group). The reader will recall that Soffredini's research into the *caipira* dialect was in large part what initially inspired Carvalho to begin working on *Hoje é Dia de Maria*. Moreover, Luís Alberto de Abreu, Carvalho's co-screen writer for both *Hoje é Dia de Maria* and *A Pedra do Reino* and a writing collaborator for *Capitu* and *Velho Chico*, wrote his first play, *Foi bom, meu bem?* in 1979 specifically for the Grupo Teatro Mambembe. At the core of Soffredini's company was an attempt to create a type of popular theater that integrated traditional Brazilian dramatic theatrical texts and styles with the language of the circus theater. After having updated the more archaic language of their source-texts, the group would then travel throughout the vast periphery of São Paulo, performing impromptu shows ("Grupo de Teatro Mambembe"). More importantly, like its medieval Italian itinerant theater precursors, by taking theatrical works from fixed locations and performing them in different regions, Soffredini's group introduced the theater to areas that would otherwise not have contact with this less accessible art form. Indeed, such physical dislocation from the center—that is, TV Globo's studios in Rio de Janeiro—would be one of the central concerns of Carvalho's *Projeto Quadrante*.

In early 2006, shortly after the completion of *Hoje é Dia de Maria*, Carvalho began working on the *Projeto Quadrante*. Conceived as a four-work special, the project's first two microseries were *A Pedra do Reino* (2007), an adaptation of Ariano Suassuna's epic novel *Romance d'A Pedra do Reino e o Príncipe do Sangue do Vai e Volta* (1971), and *Capitu* (2008), an adaptation of Machado de Assis's 1899 masterpiece *Dom Casmurro*.[2] The other two are to be Milton Hatoum's *Dois Irmãos* (2000) and Sérgio Faraco's collection of short stories as *Dançar Tango em Porto Alegre* (1998).³ The *Projeto Quadrante* has four primary objectives: (1) to adapt national literary works from different regions of the country's expansive territory; (2) to shoot and produce those works in the geographical region in which their narratives take place; (3) to identify and train new television professionals; and (4) to create an educational exchange ("*A Pedra*").

Broadly speaking, each of the four objectives is a response to the centralization of production—both industrial and cultural—in the country's southeastern urban centers, Rio de Janeiro and São Paulo. Moreover, to differing degrees, each objective conjures television's unique ability to function as an educational tool. Responding to the geographical centralization of production and evoking television as means for engaging audiences on a level that transcends pure entertainment, Carvalho's *Projeto Quadrante*, like *mambembe* theater, used a self-imposed relocation to the margins of Brazil's culture industry in order to interact with individuals who otherwise would not have access to such an experience. As such, the communicative interaction initiated by the project occurs at multiple levels: the traditional interaction that entails audiences consuming the cultural commodity as well as other supplemental content aired on television or on the radio; the Internet-mediated interaction that draws spectators to other forms of information related to the narrative, its participants, or its construction; the more intimate, nontechnological interactions between audiences and cast and crewmembers at special screenings of the different microseries throughout Brazil; and last, the interaction that occurs between crewmembers and television executives from the Rio–São Paulo cultural and economic axis, seminar and workshop leaders, local actors, local crewmembers, and those that live in the communities where the production occurs.

Encompassing these multiple levels, the *Projeto Quadrante* was the first TV Globo program to span Globo's diverse media platform ("*A Pedra*"). To use Henry Jenkins's term, the project's microseries embodies the network's first foray into "convergence culture." According to Jenkins, convergence culture, "where old and new media collide . . . represents a cultural shift as consumers are encouraged to seek out new information and make connections among dispersed media content" (2, 3). First published in 2006, Jenkins was concerned with addressing what were then relatively recent changes to the way that media content was produced, distributed, and consumed. At around the same time, in 2007, with the airing of *A Pedra do Reino*, TV Globo began to explore the early stages of this then incipient reality of convergence culture.

Produced in part to celebrate Ariano Suassuna's eightieth birthday, shortly before the premiere of *A Pedra do Reino*, Globo's GNT, a pay television channel focused on news and journalism, aired a documentary about Suassuna's life and work. Another of TV Globo's pay television channels, Multishow, aired a special edition of *Revista Bastidor*, documenting the making and filming of the microseries. Meanwhile, Globo's radio stations transmitted interviews with some of the work's actors as well as with artists who adhere to the *Movimento Armorial* (Heraldic or Armorial Movement), which Suassuna had developed in the early 1970s. These supplemental texts gave distinct cross sections of Brazilian society an opportunity for deeper contact with Carvalho's microseries and associated topics. Because subscription television was still expensive and therefore out of reach for many Brazilians, the two programs on Globosat (Globo's pay television subsidiary) channels were targeted to upper-middle-class spectators. Moreover, GNT and Multishow's respective specials were aimed at different audiences. That is, to place the channels in a familiar, comparative context, whereas GNT's demographic is akin to that of CNN, Multishow caters to an audience that would be similar to that of MTV. Meanwhile, the interviews on the radio—the most accessible mass communication vehicle in Brazil along with network television—were directed at all classes.

Following *A Pedra do Reino*'s completion and in line with the *Projeto Quadrante*'s aim of cultural and structural inclusivity extending beyond Rio de Janeiro and São Paulo, special screenings were held in August and September 2007 in movie theaters in Belo Horizonte, Brasília, Fortaleza, João Pessoa, and Porto Alegre, in addition to Rio de Janeiro and São Paulo. While these large cities are by no means representative of Brazil's huge territory, they do represent a concerted effort to engage diverse geographical regions. The screenings were divided into two parts: the first showed episodes one, two, and three; and the second, following an intermission, showed episodes four and five. These screenings marked the first time in Brazil's history that a program created specifically for television had been shown in movie theaters without alteration ("A Pedra"). Particularly for those who had closely followed the microseries, the screenings represented an opportunity to experience the work in an entirely different context. Considering the microseries' cinematic nature—it was shot using 16mm film, which allowed for it to later be amplified and projected in 35mm—the opportunity to screen it on the big screen provides the spectator with a richer audiovisual experience than on the much smaller television screen. Adding to this sensorial experience, Carvalho and members of his cast and creative team were present at some of the screenings in different cities, where they participated in question-and-answer sessions with audiences ("A Pedra").

Editora Globo, the media conglomerate's publishing company, also released two separate volumes dealing with the production of the microseries.

The first volume is a beautiful six-piece box set of the facsimile of the annotated shooting script and a cast and crew diary. The shooting script, divided into five separate books corresponding to the work's five chapters, includes Carvalho's personal notes, commentaries, and drawings. The *Diários de Elenco* (*Diaries of the Cast*) is a collection of comments and musings from a selection of the cast and crew. The second volume is a photo book that captures different moments during the preproduction and filming processes. Also, during the month the microseries was airing, the Centro Cultural da Ação da Cidadania (Cultural Center for Citizen Action) put on an exhibit of some of the work's set and costume designs and a selection of the visual art pieces created specifically for the microseries.

A similar but more extensive form of convergence culture was also an intricate part of the production, airing, and postproduction of *Capitu*. Two instances are of particular interest. First, for the release of the DVD, Carvalho and TV Globo promoted a widespread technological interaction with unknown spectators. Two thousand *Capitu* DVDs were left in undisclosed public places in São Paulo, Rio de Janeiro, Belo Horizonte, Recife, and Brasília, in what Carvalho and TV Globo called a "DVD-crossing." In addition to the thrill of finding one of the special DVDs, the fans were enticed by the fact that these DVDs contained a previously unreleased scene. Those who found the DVDs received instructions to watch them and then publish their reactions at the site *Passe Adiante Capitu* (*Pass Capitu Forward*), which was especially created for the event.[4] After completing these steps, as the Portuguese name of the site suggests, the participants were asked to pass the DVDs on to someone else so as to create a cultural chain of interaction ("*Capitu*").

Second, Carvalho and TV Globo put on the largest-ever collective reading of a Machado de Assis work. Once again, TV Globo created a special site called *Mil Casmurros* (*One Thousand Casmurros*), where they divided *Dom Casmurro* into a thousand distinct passages.[5] Internet users from all over the county were invited to read and film specific passages, in addition to some of TV Globo's most famous actors who also appeared reading select passages. Once this step was finished, the collected readings were edited together on the website as a complete audiovisual reading of the novel ("*Capitu*" *Memória Globo*).

Though certainly not as developed as the convergence culture surrounding the *Matrix* films, one of the preferred examples from Jenkins's book, both of these instances represent Globo's early interest in mixing its older, structural forms of media—the radio, television, and print—with newly emerging forms such as the DVD and the Internet. Whatever the medium, it is clear that these different communication levels are intended to attract an increasingly disperse audience and engage it in a more meaningful interaction, one that represents some of society's important ongoing technological changes. However, the efforts made at extrapolating the communicative interchange beyond the confines of unidirectional television spectatorship are not limited to the clashing of old and new media. Through its decentralized, on-site production and shooting, the *Projeto Quadrante* also sought to engage those providing manual labor and other necessary production tasks in a practical educational exchange.

A Pedra do Reino executive producer Maria Clara Fernandez notes, "Any project that occurs beyond the confines of the Rio–São Paulo production axis is really difficult because it has to deal with production realities that lack the necessary infrastructure and manual labor" (*Diários* 14). In response to this reality, Fernandez notes that for *A Pedra do Reino* "we set up a strategy, which was in line with Luiz Fernando Carvalho's desire to elaborate an inclusive creative endeavor. To this end, we developed a preproduction scheme aimed at identifying local professionals" (*Diários* 14). These "local professionals" were not television professionals but individuals who, for example, had experience working with construction or similar forms of manual labor. Thus, the lack of individuals with the necessary skill set—more easily obtainable in the production centers of Rio de Janeiro and São Paulo—forced Carvalho and the producers to seek out participants willing to be trained in the specifics of audiovisual production. In practice, this meant that inhabitants of Taperoá, the small northeastern Brazilian town in the state of Paraíba where filming would take place, were recruited to fill various production needs. Thus, by shooting in the village, away from the entertainment centers in the southeast, and by training and incorporating locals into the production process, the *Projeto Quadrante* initiated an intercultural and interregional exchange. In this exchange, local patrimonies and cultural heritages came into contact with one another, serving as one of the primary bases for the artistic construction of the work. The professional interchange between workers from disparate fields and territories of the country is embedded in and therefore a manifestation of the individuals' respective *ancestralidades*. As with the *mambembe* theater, one of the most important points of this interaction is that it takes place on the margins. As Carvalho has said with regard to production for *A Pedra do Reino*: "Being in the *sertão* is critical for preparing everything. The territory is the seed. It is as if we were entering the space of *ancestralidade*; not only that of the author, Ariano Suassuna, but my own—part of my family is from the northeast—and that of the actors, who are all from the northeast" ("Sertão é 'semente'").

Carvalho's comments suggest that the artistic expression he seeks to create in the *Projeto Quadrante* already exists in its purest form, at least to some degree, in the land itself, which in turn helps to inform its inhabitants' dispositions. Thus, because one of the central tenets of the project is to move production to the geographical region where the source-text narrative takes place and, once there, to identify local workers and artists who can make up a significant portion of the work's cast and crew, in theory Carvalho seeks to draw upon the different participants' habituses as they exist far from the production center in the southeast. Consequently, a communicative and cultural interaction occurs, in different stages, at both the macro- and microlevels. That is, at the macrolevel the interaction occurs in the aforementioned paratexts related to the work and in the final product between the microseries itself and the audience. This level of interaction takes place in a time-space that is far removed from the production locale, though heavily informed by it. At the microlevel, the interaction occurs between the locals and Carvalho and the few members of his creative team who have traveled to the northeastern village; it occurs between the actors and the source-text, which the author himself, Ariano Suassuna, lectured on; finally, it occurs between the local cast and crew and Carvalho's crew during the intimate preproduction and production process that is characteristic of the director's work.

Although it is not uncommon for a Brazilian television program to use actors born in various regions of the country, the *Projeto Quadrante* is unique in that it makes a concerted effort to cast actors from the region where the particular work is being shot and many of whom come from theater or film and have not previously worked in television or have not gained any significant fame for having done so. Thus, with regard to *A Pedra do Reino*, a majority of the actors are originally from the northeastern region of the country. For example, Irandhir Santos, who plays Quaderna, is from Barreiros, Pernambuco; Mayana Neiva, who plays Heliana Swendson, is from Campina Grande, Paraíba; Jackson Costa, who plays Clemente, is from Itabuna, Bahia; and Luiz Carlos Vasconcelos, who plays Arésio, is from Umbuzeiro, Paraíba. Additionally, four of the cast members were actually from Taperoá itself and were selected during local casting calls ("A Pedra Reino"). Irandhir Santos, currently one of the most famous and critically acclaimed Brazilian actors, was largely unknown prior to *A Pedra do Reino*. He worked primarily in theater and film, having gained some notoriety for a supporting role in Marcelo Gomes's well-received 2005 film *Cinema, Aspirina e Urubus*. For her part, Mayana Neiva became quite famous following her participation in *A Pedra do Reino*, though the microseries was her first role in either film or television. To a certain extent—and this could be said about nearly all of Carvalho's shorter-format works—the casting of nonfamous actors or actors who have primarily worked outside the audiovisual center that is TV Globo serves the network's objective of using Carvalho's productions as an experimental space for discovering new talent as well as new narrative and aesthetic possibilities.

Broadly speaking, Carvalho is generally not interested in working with talent that has been coopted by a standardized mode of production, nor with individuals who are already famous. In comments about the casting process for *Lavoura Arcaica*, for example, the director reveals his position regarding the relationship between fame and art as it pertains to the actors he works with:

> Raduan [Nassar, author of *Lavoura Arcaica* (1975)] always pushed Selton for the role of André. And I would say, "I don't even want to listen to you. I'm over here, going through the interior of Brazil, interviewing people who come to see me with their feet dirtied by the red mud of the land . . . I am not going to stop rehearsals because so and so has to go to Rio de Janeiro to do a soap commercial. . . . Losing your vanity . . . you want to go to the bathroom; you, the TV Globo heartthrob, you want to go the bathroom and there is already someone in there. You are going have to wait with your little towel because this is not a five-star hotel; there is not a bathroom for each person. (*Luiz Fernando Carvalho* 82, 94–95)

Here, in reference to Selton Melo, the star of *Lavoura Arcaica* and long one of the most famous actors in Brazil, Carvalho is clear about the type of dedication he expects from those who work with him and the importance of the individual shedding fame-derived privilege. Rather than casting an already successful and famous actor, it is more advantageous for Carvalho to identify and train new talent. Of course, there are exceptions to this, which have to do both with Carvalho's past relationships or the network's desire or need to feature a particular actor. Regarding the first, for example, Antônio Fagundes is extremely famous in Brazil and has worked with Carvalho a number of times. However, precisely because the director and actor have a relationship that dates back to the early 1990s, Carvalho is open to working with someone that well known.

The point here is that Carvalho's preferred type of casting characterized by identifying local, nonfamous actors functions to eliminate celebrity baggage while also providing the director with a significant say over the type of work he wants to extract from the actor. What is more, although Carvalho is not formally concerned with realism per se, he does believe that it is important that the actors he chooses authentically embody—rather than simply represent or portray—their roles (*Luiz Fernando Carvalho* 82). That is, though he wants his actors to act, he also prefers that they have a direct connection to the roles they are interpreting. In theory, an actor's authentic connection to a role she is performing, results in—despite Carvalho's works' clear antinaturalist tendencies—a portrayal that is more real than any illustrative performance could ever be. Regarding the acting for the *Projeto Quadrante* microseries, Carvalho says, "It would be impossible (I would say) for an actor who does not have experience in the region; with its ethical and aesthetic coordinates (moral, geographical, climate, music, dance, song . . .)" ("Caderno de Anotações"). The ethical and aesthetic coordinates referred to by Carvalho exist in the source-culture and are carried through time in how people move, the words they speak, how they speak them, and the territory from which they hail. The *Projeto Quadrante* aims to materialize such coordinates insofar as it infuses Carvalho's characteristic formal hybridity with the inherited and embodied regional cultures of the cast and crew. He says:

> The *Projeto Quadrante* is a kind of passage that leads to a knowledge of a country that, in my way of feeling, is often wasted due to a centralized view coming from Rio and São Paulo. . . . The actors and all the local talent we work with, for example, in *A Pedra do Reino*, carry with them their individual surfaces, territories, and ancestries. In addition to the construction of the plot, all of them, even without a full awareness of this, naturally promote a fundamental reflection of our contemporary reality, which is the search for a more ethical representation of the country. ("Educação" 25–26)

In his search for a more just representation of the nation, Carvalho has frequently cited as a model Luchino Visconti's *La Terra Trema* (1948), shot on-site in the southern Italian fishing village of Aci Trezza (*Luiz Fernando Carvalho* 81, 82). One of the precursors to Cinema Novo, Visconti's neorealist film used nonprofessional actors and on-site shooting in order to most realistically depict them, their culture, and their physical environment. This is of the utmost importance for Carvalho, and is a driving factor in his realizing his artistic vision: "Creating a process through the participation of local talent is my joy. It is what in time becomes increasingly necessary and indispensable to me. It would seem sadly imitative if I were to talk about a country as complex as Brazil in an official, critically distant manner" (*Diários* 14). Thus, despite creating fantastic alternative universes characterized by formal hybridity, Carvalho achieves what is for him a more authentic depiction of the diversity of Brazilian culture via the *Projeto Quadrante*'s ideological tenet of on-site shooting and the use of local actors.

Despite the references to the northeast and its ancestrality and Carvalho's desire to create a televisual language unique to Brazil, he is careful not to promote an idea of Brazilian-ness as existing in any particular place or geographical culture. Instead, in all of Carvalho's work, but particularly in the *Projeto Quadrante* he seeks to create a fictional, mythical universe through which the spectator, at all of the different communicative levels, can explore what Brazilian culture is and what it means for her to be Brazilian ("*Lavoura Arcaica* estréia sábado"). Through the *Projeto Quadrante,* the search for what it means to be Brazilian, whatever that might be, and the ensuing multilevel communication begins with the country's most revered art form, literature. In line with a tradition that dates back to the very origins of Brazilian television, the first of the *Projeto Quadrante's* four objectives, and the one that puts the project in motion, is to adapt national literary works from different regions of the country's expansive territory.

ADAPTATIONS: CLOSE READING *APROXIMAÇÕES*

While every adaptation is a "reading" or interpretation of an existing work, it is also a response to both the time of the author and its own time. As Ismail Xavier argues, "the source-text and film are separated in time: the author and director do not have the same sensibilities and perspective, it is therefore expected that the adaptation dialogue not only with the source-text, but with its own context, including updating the agenda of the source-text, even when the aim is to identify with the values expressed in it" ("Do texto" 62). In addition to the specific sociohistorical contexts mentioned by Xavier, there is also a structural element to each medium that automatically results in differences played out across the cross-media adaptations. For example, a play generally takes place on a stage, itself normally limited to the confines of a closed theater space, in front of a live audience. Consequently, it falls to each individual spectator to follow the narrative as he or she sees fit. That is, while the production uses the *mise-en-scène* to call attention to the action, a spectator could potentially choose to focus exclusively on a specific character, independent of whether that character is central to the narrative at a given moment. A filmed television program, on the other hand, does not allow such arbitrary viewing freedom; the camera and editing direct the spectator's attention to what the director wants the spectator to see. Additionally, whereas a play may or may not have an intermission, the narrative flow of an hour-long program on Brazilian television will be disrupted by five commercials, totaling roughly fifteen minutes of advertising.

The inherent differences resulting from a cross-media adaptation are why Robert Stam, like Xavier, argues against fidelity discourse—the idea that a filmic or televisual adaptation of a particular work must remain faithful to its source or hypotext ("Introduction" 3–8).[6] For Stam, such a notion is problematic in that it points to a number of preconceived prejudices and hostilities, including the anteriority of the source-text, dichotomous thinking, iconophobia, logophilia (the valorization of the verbal), the myth of facility of the image, class prejudice, and parasitism ("Introduction" 3–8). These prejudices and hostilities, argues Stam, function to place the adapted work in an inferior position relative to the source-text (8). Like Xavier, Stam's overarching argument regarding adaptations is that "source-novel hypotexts are transformed by a complex series of operations" such as "selection, amplification, concretization, actualization, critique, extrapolation, popularization, reaccentuation, transculturation." In this sense, the resulting televisual or filmic adaptation, or what Stam calls the hypertext, is best analyzed not in the subjective terms of how well it extracts the source-text's assumed essence, but how it is itself a new, unique, and "automatically" different work ("Introduction" 45–47). Notably, both Xavier's and Stam's arguments regarding audiovisual adaptations point to the importance of the director's creative, hermeneutic reading of the source-text, as an entirely new work is created.

Carvalho is aware of the changes necessitated by the move from one medium to the next and conceives of his works as a creative reading of the plays, short stories, or novels in question. Nevertheless, Carvalho explicitly refuses to use the term adaptation (*Luiz Fernando Carvalho* 34). While "adaptation" implies a modification of something from a specific context or structure in order to make it fit a different context or structure, Carvalho prefers the term *aproximação* (approximation). Instead of adaptation's implied transposition of the text from one medium to the next, *aproximação* is the synergistic, dialogic interaction between the director and the text. Perhaps a simpler way to understand *aproximação* would be as a close rereading, or an exploration of a text as reader in search of extracting a creative response ("Entrevistas: Luiz Fernando"). In the *Projeto Quadrante*'s first two microseries, Carvalho's rereadings of *A Pedra do Reino* and *Dom Casmurro* are creative responses that manage to be both literally reverent and figuratively irreverent of the source-texts. The end result is two experimental audiovisual essays, both of which reflect how Carvalho interprets, augments, and interacts with the two novels, what in them interests him most, and how selected portions serve as creative sources for developing the theatrical and cannibalistic aesthetic hybridity that characterizes for his work.

REREADING *A PEDRA DO REINO*

Carvalho first began his artistic collaboration with Ariano Suassuna during the televisual staging of the author and playwright's *Uma Mulher Vestida de Sol* in the mid-1990s. Both Carvalho and Suassuna share a deep interest in theater, literature, and Brazilian popular culture. What is more, their respective interests similarly transcend individual artistic fields, as both the director and the author have worked to develop an art form that hybridizes distinct fields into a unique whole.

Suassuna accomplished this through the creation in 1970 of the *Movimento Armorial,* a nationalistic artistic movement open to artists from all fields that sought to fuse erudite and popular cultures, promoting "new artistic forms that translate the expansion of the imaginary, beyond the artificially established frontiers maintained by the cultured elite" (Santos, 20).[7] As Idelette Muzart Fonseca dos Santos notes, the movement "proposes an ambitious pioneering research program whose recognized goal is to participate in the development of Brazilian culture, where the national and regional character would become universalized thanks to the genius of its creators" (20). Here, as with *ancestralidade,* the creative individual has at his disposal an entire history of regional, national, and universal art forms, resulting in an endless range of artistic possibilities. This is, in part, why Suassuna's *Romance d'A Pedra do Reino,* published shortly after the advent of the Movement, simultaneously includes elements—as Bráulio Tavares notes—"from the *novela* [a fictional literary narrative shorter than a novel], the short story, the poem, the *feuilleton, cordel* literature, the dramatic monologue, philosophical dialogue, the period chronicle, and from the memoir" (qtd. in Suassuna, *Romance d'A Pedra* 1). Carvalho's *aproximação* of Suassuna's novel similarly includes diverse aesthetic elements, whose combination has been described as an attempt to incorporate, devour, and "totalize all forms of artistic manifestation" (Feldman 4). Indeed, while Suassuna's *A Pedra do Reino* draws from all of the sources Tavares mentions above, Carvalho's rereading of the novel maintains these elements while adding components from theater, dance, film, music, singing, literature, and even animation and computer-generated images. These are then melded together to construct Quaderna's temporally dialogic, fantastic narrative.

The microseries' complex nonlinear plot revolves around the whimsical, *quixotesque* protagonist and first-person narrator, D. Pedro Dinis Ferreira Quaderna (Irandhir Santos). After arriving with his *mambembe* theater in the small northeastern Brazilian town of Taperoá, in the state of Paraíba, Quaderna begins to tell the local audience the enigmatic tale of crime and bloodshed surrounding the 1930 assassination of his godfather Dom Pedro Sebastião Garcia-Barreto (Pedro Henrique) and the 1935 reappearance of Dom Pedro's youngest son Sinésio (Paulo César Ferreira), *O Rapaz do Cavalo Branco* (The Man on the White Horse). Quaderna's story centers on a long-ranging, transnational familial history, which includes the Sebastian myth of the Fifth Empire, Quaderna's ancestral connection to the mythical Dom Sebastião, Quaderna's family's violent past, the unexpected reappearance of the mysteriously disappeared Sinésio, the magistrate judge's probe into the assassination of Quaderna's godfather, the Brazilian sociopolitical unrest of the 1920s and 1930s surrounding these events, and Quaderna's subsequent imprisonment.

Nine distinct time periods shape the narrative's highly fragmented and nonchronological structure. Though not portrayed visually, the first period dates back to the sixteenth century. Quanderna's stories about this time period establish a familial connection to King Sebastião of Portugal, who, at twenty-one years of age, disappeared in 1578 while fighting in North Africa.[8] According to Samuel Wand'ernes (Frank Menezes), Quaderna's ultraconservative mentor and a faithful follower of Plínio Salgado,[9] Dom Sebastião fled to Brazil, where he left descendants tied to Quaderna's family. According to the story, one of these descendants was Quaderna's great-grandfather, João Ferreira Quaderna (Nil Padua), infamously referred to as *o Execrável* (the Execrable). During the 1800s, at the base of two long, steep rocks, known as the Pedra do Reino, o Execrável declared himself to be the legitimate king of Brazil. In doing so, he also caused the death of many of his followers as he called them to sacrifice themselves in the name of Dom Sebastião's return.

The subsequent time periods, 1897, 1912, and 1918, deal briefly with Quaderna's birth and early formation. Quaderna was born in 1897, coinciding with the final year of the Canudos War.[10] The year 1912 covers Quaderna's initial contact and early fascination with *cavalgadas* (cavalcades) and *cangaceiros* (bandits) and the development of his relationship with the politically left-leaning Clemente (Jackson Costa). Along with Samuel, Clemente serves as Quaderna's professor and mentor with regard to all social, political, and intellectual matters. Quaderna leaves Taperoá in 1918 to study for the priesthood: he is expelled shortly thereafter, however, due to his radical religious ideas. In 1930, within the broader sociopolitical context of the *Coluna Prestes* (Prestes Column) (1925–1927) and the 1930 Revolution,[11] Quaderna's godfather and uncle, Dom Pedro Sebastião, is inexplicably assassinated. On the very day of the assassination, Sinésio also disappears mysteriously and is later declared dead, only to miraculously reappear a few years later. Set between the 1935 attempted communist revolt and Getúlio Vargas's 1937 establishment of the *Estado Novo* (New State, 1937–1945), Sinésio's return sets off an ongoing battle between his supporters and those of Arésio (Luiz Carlos Vasconcelos), Quaderna's older cousin and Sinésio's brother.

Moved by an anonymous letter, the magistrate judge comes from the capital to Taperoá in 1938 to question Quaderna about his godfather's assassination and Sinésio's disappearance and subsequent return. Early on in the questioning, Quaderna reveals that his objective is to take advantage of the probe and the presence of the stenographer, Dona Margarida (Milene Ramalho), so that his epic, enigmatic story will be recorded. He notes that he would otherwise not be able to complete his novel, since, due to a bone spur on his coccyx, he is not capable of sitting for long periods of time. At the end of the investigation, despite being let free, Quaderna admits that it was he who wrote the anonymous letter that spurred the probe in the first place. Intent on creating for himself a "heroic biography" he asks to be sent to jail where, in a seeming state of madness, he frantically completes his epic novel. Finally, this is all told in 1970 by a visibly much older Quaderna, who theatrically shares his story as he travels the land with his *mambembe* theater.

As is always the case when adapting a novel to the big or small screen, the adaptor must select some and leave out other plot-related elements. In Carvalho's microseries, however, the aforementioned time periods adhere closely to those in Suassuna's novel. Despite the broad affinities between the two works, Carvalho's version unfolds through three distinct spatiotemporal structures, which together encompass all of the time periods of Suassuna's novel: the present, the past, and the convergence of the two, or the dialogic. The spatiotemporal structure of the present is the Taperoá square in 1970. Representative of a theatrical form of narration, this is the period in which the spectator sees an elderly Quaderna, his face painted like that of a clown, telling his story during a sun-drenched northeastern afternoon. Thus, while in Suassuna's novel, Quaderna writes from prison in 1938, Carvalho's version relocates him to 1970, the year Suassuna founded his *Movimento Armorial*. This subtle transition is symbolically very important because it transforms Quaderna's narrative vehicle from the written word, as it is in Suassuna's novel, into a *mambembe* theatrical presentation. Consequently, what the spectator sees is an audio-visual manifestation of Quaderna's imagination of the narrative developing as he relates it to the locals in the village square.

Unlike the singular setting of the square, the spatiotemporal structure of the past encompasses a number of different time periods and settings. Although most of the periods unfold within the relatively restricted space of the village square, the *mise-en-scène* necessarily fluctuates depending on which past moment Quaderna narrates. Subtle adjustments in lighting often indicate changes to the spatiotemporal setting. For example, while high-key lighting characterizes Quaderna's childhood, adolescent years, and early adulthood, darker, low-key lighting sets apart other moments in the past, particularly those marked by violence and death. Independent of a particular scene's degree of brightness, what is important is how the lighting is an expression of Quaderna's emotions and of his psychological clarity, or lack thereof, regarding the past events he narrates. Quaderna's adolescent years, then, are clear for him and evoke positive memories. His family's violent past, however, is both dark and delirious, simultaneously conjuring up feelings of guilt and a deranged pleasure (figures 6.1 and 6.2).

Figure 6.1. Lighting, *A Pedra do Reino* (2007). Right to reproduce granted by TV Globo.

Figure 6.2. Lighting, *A Pedra do Reino* (2007). Right to reproduce granted by TV Globo.

FIGURE 6.3. Converging pasts, *A Pedra do Reino* (2007). Right to reproduce granted by TV Globo.

FIGURE 6.4. Tombstone city, *A Pedra do Reino* (2007). Right to reproduce granted by TV Globo.

Finally, the dialogic spatiotemporal structure represents the moments in which the distinct pasts that Quaderna narrates audiovisually converge onto the present space of the village square, the locus of his narration. Unlike a flashback, for example, which is essentially what I am referring to as the spatiotemporal structure of the past, the juxtaposition of the present with the past in these scenes results in a mythical, hallucinatory representation of Quaderna's idealistically embellished tale.

By bringing together the present and past in the same scene, Carvalho uses the dialogic spatiotemporal structure to create a circular and oneiric form of storytelling, fusing together distinct narrative styles into a nonlinear, surreal whole (figure 6.3).

The village square itself symbolizes and therefore further emphasizes the circularity and dreamlike nature of Quaderna's mythical story. The space, especially when used to signify what I refer to as the dialogical spatiotemporal structure, is intended to evoke a medieval spectacle that mixes street theater with a sacramental act ("Sertão é 'semente'"). To this end, Carvalho and his team refashioned the small Taperoá village to look like a baroque tombstone city or, as he calls it "uma cidade lápide" (figure 6.4).

By constructing a universe that is supposed to evoke a tombstone city, which is home to an amalgam of popular entertainment and sacred religious ritual, Carvalho creates a narrative space that transcends the mere depiction of a place. The infusion of the space with distinct aesthetic elements that reference spatiotemporally diverse ancestralities transforms the space itself into one of the work's primary characters. As such, the enclosed tombstone city represents a mythical place where death and life converge, where memory as symbolized by the tombstone markings engage the living as they actively remember the past. In other words, the space represents the wholeness of time—not as a linear development, but as an all-encompassing circle. That this is the case is hinted at via the circular dance in the microseries' opening scene, discussed in greater detail in Chapter Four.

Both inside and outside this space, throughout the microseries Carvalho eclectically takes multiple art forms such as literature, theater, film, music, singing, dance, oral storytelling, and animation and combines them as if he were mixing colors before painting a picture. In keeping with the analogy, the director's canvas in this case is television—more specifically, a traveling television that has gone to northeastern Brazil in search of creating a site-specific microseries designed to be shared through television sets in every corner of Brazil. As a result, like the village square where Quaderna theatrically performs and dialogues with the past and present, with the dead and the living, Carvalho's traveling television becomes a space in which ancestralities converge, resulting in a work that is itself a rereading and interpretation of Suassuna's novel, is read and interpreted by the television audience, all while creating a space for the recognition of a shared cultural past.

REREADING *DOM CASMURRO*

Starting on December 9, 2008, *Capitu* aired on TV Globo at 11 PM over five consecutive nights. As was the case previously with *Hoje é Dia de Maria* and *A Pedra do Reino,* the former celebrating the network's fortieth anniversary and the latter Suassuna's eightieth birthday, *Capitu* was marketed as a special television event, marking the centennial of Machado de Assis's death. Like the two microseries that preceded it, *Capitu* is reflective of the director's overarching desire to ponder Brazilian culture and to defamiliarize Brazilian television. However, in *Capitu,* Carvalho moves away from theatrical, fantastic depictions of a mythical or folkloric regionalism toward a theatrical, or operatic pop depiction of a localized global urbanism. In doing so, Carvalho situates *Capitu,* and by extension his rereading of *Dom Casmurro,* within the broader context of contemporary Brazil's globalized pop culture.

Despite the microseries' title, which is a symbolic, perhaps even simplistic inversion of the main characters' roles, *Capitu* can be characterized as a literal adaptation of *Dom Casmurro.* This is because the microseries includes portions of the novel's written text verbatim and closely adheres to its plot. That is not to say that the microseries incorporates *all* of *Dom Casmurro*'s written text. Instead, it consists of a selection made by Carvalho. Nonetheless, the text the microseries does include—that is, *all* of the spoken or written text that appears on screen in *Capitu*—was taken directly from *Dom Casmurro*. In addition to leaving Machado's words as he wrote them, *Capitu* maintains *Dom Casmurro*'s ironic, ambiguous, and psychologically reflective tone. Despite the microseries' literal connection to the source-text, Carvalho uses it as a point of departure for exploring and dialoguing with the contemporary world. Thus, whereas *Dom Casmurro* is a superficially realist narrative set in the sociohistorical context of late-nineteenth-century Rio de Janeiro, Carvalho's postmodern reading of Machado's masterpiece maintains no definitive ties to a realistically represented time or place.

One important reason behind the postmodern treatment of *Dom Casmurro* is Carvalho and the network's broader objective of attracting and appealing to younger viewers, who might consider Machado's classic work overly difficult and disconnected from contemporary Brazilian culture ("Papéis Avulsos"). Nonetheless, rather than massacre a richly nuanced novel, Carvalho's popularization of *Dom Casmurro* does not sacrifice the playfulness and irony that characterize Machado's best fiction. In fact, like Bento Santiago's ambiguous narrative, the microseries is itself structurally ironic; it embodies the novel's superficially realist narrative while at the same time calling attention to certain aspects of that narrative through its audiovisual construction.

In his polemical study regarding the classification of Machado's later works as being realist novels, Gustavo Bernardo astutely highlights how *Capitu* calls the spectators' attention to the fact that what they are watching is not a depiction of reality but a work of art. Bernardo argues that Carvalho's frequent revealing of the microseries' construction is similar to the way in which Machado ensures *Dom Casmurro*'s readers that they are engaged in the act of reading an artificially constructed work of fiction (*O problema*).

For his part, Carvalho achieves this largely through a dissonant modernization of Machado's novel that is characterized by mixing the visual characteristics reminiscent of nineteenth-century Rio de Janeiro with blatantly anachronistic elements. In the microseries' opening scene, for example, Dom Casmurro rides on a modern-day train through contemporary Rio. Later, both he and his wife, Capitu, listen to an MP3 player while dancing at an elegant nineteenth-century ball. At other moments, in addition to a short clip from Orson Welles's film *Othello,* Dom Casmurro can be seen talking on a cell phone, while Capitu and her son, Ezequiel, stroll through modern-day downtown Rio de Janeiro. Additionally, an incongruous, jarring compilation of a wide range of music from artists including The Sex Pistols, Verdi, Pink Floyd,

FIGURE 6.5. Earbuds, *Capitu* (2008). Right to reproduce granted by TV Globo.

FIGURE 6.6. Orson Welles's *Othello*, *Capitu* (2008). Right to reproduce granted by TV Globo.

FIGURE 6.7. Capitu and Ezequiel, *Capitu* (2008). Right to reproduce granted by
TV Globo.

FIGURE 6.8. Converging pasts, *Capitu* (2008). Right to reproduce granted by TV Globo.

Brahms, Jimi Hendrix, Caetano Veloso, Black Sabbath, and Beirut, contrast with and undermine the theatrical caricature of Dom Casmurro as he narrates within an operatic setting (figures 6.5, 6.6, and 6.7).

As in *A Pedra do Reino*, in *Capitu*, Dom Casmurro's narration unfolds through the perspective of three different time frames or structures—(1) the present; (2) the past; and (3) the convergence of the two, or the dialogic spatiotemporal frame. Similar to the novel, the microseries presents Dom Casmurro's narration in the present tense as he attempts to "atar as duas pontas da vida, e restaurar na velhice a adolescência" ("to tie the two ends of life together, and bring back youth in old age") (*Dom Casmurro* 19 and *Dom Casmurro: A Novel* 5). Flashbacks to Bentinho's youth and his adult years of marriage to Capitu, compose the temporal structure of the past. As is the case in the novel, broadly speaking, this makes up the great majority of the narrative. However, as an audiovisual response to Machado's first-person narrator, Carvalho, creates a third time frame—the dialogic spatiotemporal structure—placing the present Dom Casmurro in direct physical contact with the memories he narrates (figures 6.8 and 6.9).

At different moments throughout the narrative, Dom Casmurro physically ruptures his memories in an attempt to reconnect to a period of innocence. Consequently, the spectator watches, for example, as he reaches out to, but is unable to touch, Bentinho or as he watches Capitu from a distance, in awe as she dances throughout the space. The narrator's inability to bridge the spatiotemporal rupture through physical contact is a subtle indicator of the

FIGURE 6.9. Converging pasts, *Capitu* (2008). Right to reproduce granted by TV Globo.

slipperiness of his memories and his ambiguous desire to share them with the viewer.

The spatiotemporal frame and the constant presence of anachronistic audiovisual juxtapositions eliminate any realistic expectations the spectator might have. Almost the entire microseries takes place within the confines of the Automobile Club in downtown Rio de Janeiro. Primarily filmed inside the beautiful nineteenth-century building, Carvalho uses Rio de Janeiro as the work's narrative setting and cultural springboard; at the same time, he neglects stereotypical, edenic, and realistic visual constructions of the city. Probably in favor of this decision, Machado, who expressed displeasure with the way in which Brazilians' creative and intellectual capacity was often overlooked in favor of the country's edenic nature, is quoted as saying: "My nativist sentiment . . . has always been hurt by this adoration of nature . . . I neither made nor asked anyone to make the sky, the mountains, the woods and the rivers. They were already there when I found them" (qtd. in Carvalho, "The Edenic" 111). Similarly, Carvalho's representation of Rio de Janeiro, as well as his many representations of the Brazilian *sertão,* could also be seen as a critique of telenovelas' frequent portrayals of Brazil as a paradise. In addition to not emphasizing Brazil's edenic nature, *Capitu*'s reappropriation of the Automobile Club further reinforces the defamiliarization already in play through the use of anachronistic music, props, and images. Together, these elements help to establish what becomes a mythical space of memory, much like the tombstone city in *A Pedra do Reino.* However, whereas in that microseries Carvalho mixes street theater with sacred religious rituals, the Automobile Club serves as an antinaturalist platform upon which Carvalho is able to experiment with theater and opera as a creative point of departure for his adaptation.

In a number of interviews leading up to the premiere of *Capitu,* perhaps as a justification for some of his own aesthetic choices, Carvalho frequently argued that Machado rejected realism in favor of defining life as "uma ópera bufa com alguns entremeios de música séria" ("a comic opera with some intervals of serious music") ("Oficinas"). Although this phrase actually belongs to Luís Batista, a character from *Ressurreição* (1872), it is an explicit representation of both Carvalho's reading of Machado's work and the heightened importance the director gives to opera as a resource for the creation of his antirealist microseries.[12] Indeed, by the end of the fourth minute of the first episode, Dom Casmurro echoes Carvalho's position when he breaks the fourth wall to inform the spectator that "a vida tanto podia ser uma ópera como uma viagem de mar ou uma batalha" ("life might just as well be a sea voyage or a battle as an opera") (*Dom Casmurro: A Novel* 18). Upon completing this phrase, which is taken from Chapter 9, "A Ópera," ("The Opera") in *Dom Casmurro,* there is a cut to one of the many title pages that signal a move to a new chapter taken from the source-text. Announced by a deep, masculine voice as it is shown on the screen, the title page reinforces the idea of opera through both the spoken and the written word. The image subsequently cuts from the title page to the interior of the Automobile Club, where, emphasizing the grandeur of the space, the camera rotates from an extremely low angle to reveal the red curtains typical of an operatic stage. As the curtains open to the sound of classical music, the stage lights turn on and a spotlight captures a distant Dom Casmurro standing on the improvised stage (see figure 4.34). At this point Dom Casmurro reinitiates the voice-over narration from the opening scene—"a vida tanto podia ser uma ópera como uma viagem de mar ou uma batalha"—finishing his explanation of how the novel received its name.

Therefore, in referencing what comes only eight chapters later in Machado's novel, the director inserts the opera scene, not to explicate the narrative, but to establish its centrality to *his* version of Dom Casmurro, the arc of the protagonist's life, and how Dom Casmurro understands the past he writes and narrates. If in *A Pedra do Reino* Carvalho transforms Quaderna's mode of narration from the written word to the theatrical presentation atop the *mambembe* stage so as to emphasize the theatricality that characterizes both the *Projeto Quadrante* and the microseries' aesthetic, in *Capitu,* Carvalho manipulates Machado's text so as to make Dom Casmurro narrate as if he were the protagonist of his own opera.

The theatrical space and the specific references to opera, along with the occasional anachronistic audiovisual insertions, are instances of the conspicuous artificiality that permeate Carvalho's reading of Machado's novel. All of the elements mentioned thus far fluidly interact with one another in an exemplary scene in which Dom Casmurro recounts an afternoon shortly after his marriage to Capitu. The result is an anachronistic dialogue between the novel, its nineteenth-century setting, and twentieth- and twenty-first-century popular culture, ranging from silent film to alternative rock music. The vehicle through which this dialogue plays out is Carvalho's artistically engaged version of twenty-first-century Brazilian television.

In this particular scene Dom Casmurro narrates verbatim from the chapter "De Casada" ("The Married Woman"), breaking the fourth wall to inform the spectator that he and Capitu, shortly after their marriage, wanted to get out of the house. During this brief scene, images of Dom Casmurro looking back in time are juxtaposed with images of the newlywed couple as they go out for a walk. Here, Carvalho eclectically joins the *mise-en-scène*, music, cinematography, and literature as a means to extrapolate beyond the space's physical and temporal limitations, ultimately deconstructing the spectator's expectations. Moreover, when together, the diverse array of aesthetic elements functions to supplant their own individuality. The result is an osmotic transformation that combines them into a singular audiovisual product that challenges both the physical limits of the narrative's spatial setting and the metaphysical limits of its temporal setting.

Narratively speaking, the first shot of the "De Casada" scene is of Dom Casmurro and Capitu, both of whom are supposed to be walking outside (figure 6.10). However, insofar as they are obviously within the enclosed space of the Automobile Club, this is not readily clear to the spectator. Although the interplay between lighting, decoration, camera movements, and framing multiplies the physical space into a seemingly much larger fictional universe, this fictional universe is only as large as the spectator's imagination will allow it to be. In what might seem contradictory, the narrative milieu includes less to spark the spectator's imagination. The point of this type of setting is to activate the spectator's imagination and therefore participation. In this particular scene, Carvalho further activates the spectator's participation through editing: he juxtaposes the images of the couple walking with the following shot of Dom Casmurro, both speaking and typing his story. Here, Machado's written word is inversely transposed onto the screen as if Dom Casmurro were reading what he is writing (figure 6.11).

The contrast between the dark, tight, distorted framing of Dom Casmurro typing and the relatively bright and more open framing of the previous shot

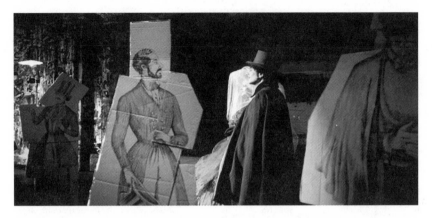

FIGURE 6.10. "De Casada," *Capitu* (2008). Right to reproduce granted by TV Globo.

of the couple suggests two distinct spaces: the space in which Dom Casmurro writes and the space of the memories he is writing. Here, as in other moments, Carvalho includes the written word among all the other disparate artistic elements so as to remind the spectator that he or she is engaged in a communicative process whose point of departure is an artificial work of art. In other words, Carvalho combines literature and cinematography, with different *mise-en-scènes,* to manipulate the physical space of the Automobile Club and to suggest narrative spaces that are distinct both visually and temporally. Rather than explicitly communicating to the spectator what these narrative spaces signify, the director pushes the spectator to arrive at her own conclusions.

In the subsequent shots, Carvalho heightens the defamiliarized narrative spaces by adding even more explicitly theatrical elements, archival footage, and music to the piece. After Dom Casmurro theatrically punctuates the first part of his monologue, the camera zooms out to reveal him standing on a kind of stage directly behind the footlights (figure 6.12).

As constituted, the space evokes the operatic stage from the opening scene, also suggesting a level of performance in Dom Casmurro's narration. The performative aspect, however, is distorted through the out-of-focus image of Dom Casmurro. In fact, the lens that exclusively captures Dom Casmurro or sometimes his point of view is distorted by placing a small filter filled with water directly in front of it. The 'Dom Casmurro Lens,' as Carvalho refers to it, was designed to depict specific scenes where the protagonist's fragile psychological state and nebulous memories were central to the narrative ("*Capitu*"). In this particular scene of Dom Casmurro performing before an imaginary audience, Carvalho employs the presence of the stage and the theatrical narration, cap-

FIGURE 6.11. Writing on screen, *Capitu* (2008). Right to reproduce granted by TV Globo.

FIGURE 6.12. Footlights, *Capitu* (2008). Right to reproduce granted by TV Globo.

tured by the distorted filter, to create an ambience of doubt. The artificiality intrinsic to such a performance encourages the spectator to question the reliability of the performer. Moreover, it is the director's way of hinting to the spectator, as Machado so often does in his novel, that he or she should be cautious of Dom Casmurro's broader account as it pertains to his wife's fidelity.

Immediately following the image of Dom Casmurro on the stage, there is a visual insertion of black and white archival footage of a bustling, turn-of-the century urban center. An explicit reference to the cinematic, the archival footage represents a rupture of the physical narrative space of the Automobile Club. Moreover, the footage's nineteenth-century milieu transports the spectator to a period of time more like that in which Machado sets his narrative. Finally, the documentary nature of the footage juxtaposed with the previous images of the theatrical space reinforces the artificiality of the narrative space in which Dom Casmurro writes and remembers. At the level of the narrative, then, the real/artificial dichotomy set up by such an audiovisual construction undermines Dom Casmurro's questioning of his wife's infidelity. That is, it further establishes an ambience of doubt because it situates the narrative and therefore the viewer in an in-between space; one that is neither wholly "real" nor "artificial." With regard to Dom Casmurro's slippery, ambiguous narration, one could extend this line of thought to argue that the audiovisual construction makes it such that the narration is neither wholly "true" nor "false," but somewhere in between. It is precisely in this in-between space that Dom Casmurro recognizes himself to be, and therefore desires to understand the end points of his life ("atar as duas pontas da vida")—from the age of sixteen when he meets Capitu to his time as a lonely middle-aged man. These temporal points symbolically function as anchors that allow Dom Casmurro to extrapolate beyond the ephemeral space of memory to a more grounded reality.

But, as is the case in Machado's novel, this can never actually happen. The point is that the artistic investigation cannot arrive at a definitive answer; it is precisely that such answers, when having to do with the human condition and our complex psychoemotional states, are always multiple—not unlike Carvalho's hybrid aesthetic. So, whereas the archival footage insertions visually extend the narrative beyond the enclosed theatrical space, while still corresponding to the nineteenth-century setting in which the novel takes place, the subsequent inclusion of Janis Joplin's "Mercedes-Benz" aurally extends the narrative beyond the immediate and concrete, in a blatantly anachronistic manner.[13] The addition of Joplin's 1970 hit to the dissonant use of the other televisual elements emphasizes Carvalho's disorienting audiovisual treatment of the novel's narrative, highlighting the always-indeterminate space of memory. As such, Carvalho's *Capitu* literally incorporates the original text

FIGURE 6.13. Capitu looking at Bentinho, *Capitu* (2008). Right to reproduce granted by TV Globo.

FIGURE 6.14. Archival footage, *Capitu* (2008). Right to reproduce granted by TV Globo.

FIGURE 6.15. Bentinho looking back at Capitu, *Capitu* (2008). Right to reproduce granted by TV Globo.

both through the spoken and written word, while at the same time radicalizing the figurative audiovisual treatment through an unlikely combination of aesthetic elements that transcend spatiotemporal and narrative expectations.

Another example of how *Capitu* is simultaneously representative of a literal and figurative treatment of Machado's novel is present in the scene that introduces Escobar, Bentinho's friend from seminary. The scene in question is taken from *Dom Casmurro*, Chapter 56, "Um Seminarista" ("A Seminarist"). Picking it up from just before the point when Dom Casmurro first mentions Escobar's name, the passage in Machado's novel reads as such:

> It was delightful to wander through it [the *Panegyric*—a poem Dom Casmurro began writing as a young man, but never completed]; at times, unconsciously, I turned the page over as if I were reading; I think it was when my eyes went to the bottom of the page, and the hand, so used to helping out, did its usual job. . . . *Here is another seminarist. His name was Ezequiel de Sousa Escobar. He was a slim youth, with pale eyes, a little elusive, like his hands, like his feet, like his speech, like everything about him.* (emphasis added, *Dom Casmurro: A Novel* 106)[14]

Although Escobar is the primary focus of this particular chapter, Dom Casmurro's first mention of him occurs almost in passing, as if his childhood friend suddenly popped into his memory, while he was remembering another seminary student—"Here is another seminarist." Of course, as is characteristic of Machado's unreliable first-person narrators, the reader would do well to be cautious of any seemingly random or unconscious insertion. As he continues his introduction of Escobar, Dom Casmurro comments on his friend's physical characteristics, hinting at a slipperiness that might perhaps characterize Escobar's personality, or, for the cautious reader, Dom Casmurro's very own narration. In the last part of the chapter Dom Casmurro describes how Escobar was able to gain his friendship and trust. Moreover, using a house as an analogy to describe his soul, Dom Casmurro alludes to how when he first met Escobar as a boy his identity was still in flux. He says,

> At first I was shy, but he found his way into my confidence. Those elusive ways ceased when he wanted them to, and time and the new environment made them settle down, too. Escobar opened up his whole soul, from the front door to the bottom of the garden. Our souls, as you know, are laid out like houses, often with windows on every side, lots of light and fresh air. There are also houses that are closed and dark, with no windows at all, or with a few barred windows, like convents or prisons. In the same way, there are chapels and bazaars, simple lean-tos and sumptuous palaces.
>
> *I don't know what mine was. I was not yet Casmurro, nor Dom Casmurro. Shyness prevented me from being open, but since the doors had neither keys nor locks, all that was needed was to push them, and Escobar pushed and entered. I found him inside, and here he stayed, until . . .* (emphasis added, *Dom Casmurro: A Novel,* 107)[15]

According to Dom Casmurro, Escobar did not just enter his "house," instead he pushed open the doors. Exactly what Dom Casmurro means by this is not entirely clear. That is, Machado's use of ambiguous prose in this passage opens itself up to an interpretation that locates subtle homosexual undertones between Bentinho and Escobar; whether anything materialized between the two is open to debate.

Carvalho's reading of the passage, as manifested in the audiovisual construction of the scene, places such an interpretation at the forefront, while maintaining the novel's characteristic ambiguity. Immediately prior to the chapter in question we see a montage of images of Bentinho leaving for the seminary while Capitu watches sadly from her window. Archival shots of papal processions fragment the cross-cut images of the young couple melancholically looking at one another (figures 6.13, 6.14, and 6.15).

Taken from Chapter 51, "Entre Luz e Fusco" ("In the Half-Light"), Dom Casmurro solemnly declares in voice-over, "Oh, sweet companion of my childhood, I was pure, and pure I remained, and entered the portals of São José pure, in appearance to seek priestly investiture, and before that, a vocation. But you were my vocation, you were my true investiture" (*Dom Casmurro: a Novel* 96).[16] It is at this point that Carvalho inverts what seems to be made

FIGURE 6.16. Capitu crying, *Capitu* (2008). Right to reproduce granted by TV Globo.

FIGURE 6.17. "Um Seminarista" title page, *Capitu* (2008). Right to reproduce granted by TV Globo.

FIGURE 6.18. Red curtains at the seminary, *Capitu* (2008). Right to reproduce granted by TV Globo.

clear in Dom Casmurro's narration—that is, that the narrator is in this passage referring to his relationship with Capitu. As visual reinforcement of Capitu as being the subject, the end of the narration is marked by another Dom Casmurro point-of-view shot of Capitu crying in the window (figure 6.16). However, the very next shot is that of the chapter title page, reading "A Seminarist," which is also announced in voice-over (figure 6.17).

The images of Capitu and the title page, as well as the distinct narrations placed in close proximity to each other, result in an audiovisual linkage between the written and spoken word. As such, by following a shot of Capitu with the pronounced title page, Carvalho creates a level of ambiguity where there seemingly is none. The effect is that together the voice-over narrations end up sounding like, "a investidura eras tu . . ." "um seminarista" ("you were my true investiture . . . a seminarist"). By placing the passage from Chapter 51, "In the Half-Light" wherein Dom Casmurro informs the reader of his last encounter with Capitu and their shared kiss before he left for the seminary, directly before the "A Seminarist" scene, Carvalho cuts out, at least as far as Dom Casmurro's narration is concerned, much of Chapters 52 through 55, making it no longer fully clear that Dom Casmurro is in fact referring to Capitu. The verbal references to Bentinho's purity, when juxtaposed with the visual depiction of Escobar in the following scene, reinforce the ambiguity created by Carvalho.

While in Machado's novel Dom Casmurro apparently remembers Escobar in passing, in Carvalho's microseries he bursts forth from the narrator's

FigURE 6.19. Escobar praying, *Capitu* (2008). Right to reproduce granted by TV Globo.

memory as a seemingly uncontrollable force. Whereas the focus of the narration in the novel falls entirely on Dom Casmurro, in this scene in the microseries Carvalho delays the voice-over narration, thus placing Escobar at center stage. In fact, the scene begins with red stage curtains opening to reveal a group of boys praying around a large table (figure 6.18). After a cut to a terrified Dom Casmurro, who seems to recall something he must repress, there is a shot of Escobar kneeling as if praying (figure 6.19).

Then, to the sound of Black Sabbath's "Iron Man" (1970), Escobar seductively dances into the space where the other students congregate. Escobar's initial physical distance from the group combined with the antireligious, heavy rock music and his erotic movements and gestures "dishonor" the space. Escobar is soon dancing diabolically on the dinner table, highlighting his position as an outsider and perhaps even a sinner (figures 6.20 and 6.21).

By prioritizing the audiovisual, that is, by delaying the literal narration of Machado's text, Carvalho accentuates the possibility of a homoerotic tension between Bentinho and Escobar. Through the hybridization of Machado's written word, cinematic editing, anachronistic music, dark lighting, Escobar's facial expressions and body movements, and Bentinho's seemingly overwhelmed reaction to them, Carvalho radicalizes the literal text, resulting in a figurative treatment that embodies the author's characteristic ambiguity while dialogically creating a new narrative possibility.

FIGURE 6.20. Escobar dancing, *Capitu* (2008). Right to reproduce granted by TV Globo.

FIGURE 6.21. Escobar seducing Bentinho, *Capitu* (2008). Right to reproduce granted by TV Globo.

The *Projeto Quadrante* represents Carvalho's attempt to create a type of television that is aesthetically innovative, going well beyond the standardized, more traditional, and easily consumable televisual symbolic good. In this way, the *Projeto Quadrante* is more than a group of microseries: it is a cultural event; a manifestation of the director's understanding of his responsibility as an artist to communicate with his audience socially, culturally, and artistically; and Carvalho's attempt to expand the possibilities for television production as well as its resulting aesthetic. Like *mambembe* theater, with national literature as its hypotext, the project moves to the periphery, experimenting with audiovisual possibilities and searching to meaningfully connect with the Brazilians that are so often excluded from participating in the centralized production of cultural goods. In his *Poema Acreano,* Mário de Andrade, the upper-middle-class author from São Paulo, suddenly realizes that far off in the northern state of Acre there is a rubber worker who is Brazilian just like him.[17] Like Andrade, Carvalho not only realizes this, but he also leaves TV Globo's Projac Studios, with his *mambembe* television in tow, in search of this symbolic other. However, as I will argue next chapter, this does not occur without some problems.

Chapter Seven

CHANGING WITH A CHANGING LANDSCAPE

As I have alluded to in the introduction and at different moments throughout this book, the field of Brazilian television production is experiencing significant changes to its modes of production, including who produces, what is produced, and how and where audiences consume the increasingly varied forms of television fiction. Modifications to the field have directly impacted TV Globo and, consequently, Carvalho's most recent television productions. A particularly good example of such modifications and of Carvalho himself changing with and within Brazil's changing landscape of television fiction is the director's 2012 microseries *Subúrbia* (*Periphery*).

Valério Cruz Brittos and Denis Gerson Simões situate the earliest moments of the changing landscape of Brazilian television, or what they refer to as the "multichannel transition," in the mid-1990s:

> Resulting from movements of capitalist globalization, the 1990s constituted itself as the moment of the weakening of the perception of national borders. The period was a foreshadowing of a media unfettered, independent of State wills, consolidated by the principle of free competition, and characterized by an increase in the number of television stations and the intensification of a market logic. Positioning themselves reactively, but seeking innovation, when faced with this new reality broadcast networks in Brazil set off for other sectors, such as pay television and business investments in other countries. This was a period that was especially marked by the characteristics of global capitalism, it was a time of transition to a business model that was different from those used previously. (220)

Nonetheless, despite the transnational sociohistorical, political, and economic developments highlighted by Brittos and Simões, the two scholars note that by the end of the first decade of the twenty-first century, pay television had failed to alter significantly the strongly entrenched and long-standing oligopoly that held sway over Brazilian television.

Along these lines, in a 2012 report on its own financial participation in the Brazilian audiovisual sector, the Banco Nacional de Desenvolvimento Econômico e Social (BNDES, National Bank of Economic and Social Development) described the Brazilian television industry in the mid-2000s as an anomaly within the broader global context. For report authors Gustavo Mello et al., the uniqueness of that industry was due to the fact that Brazilian broadcast television networks were characterized first and foremost by a commercially driven, vertically integrated business model: "Unlike the widely used model in other countries in which networks commission or purchase content from independent production companies, the model used by Brazilian networks absorbed almost all required programming through in-house production. Pay television on the other hand, still in its initial phase, showed little interest in locally produced programming, privileging content generated abroad, which, because its costs had already been covered in other markets, could be purchased for a rate lower than that of local production" (296). Like Brittos and Simões, the BNDES's description of Brazilian television in the mid-2000s reveals a medium still strongly linked to a business model characterized by the hegemony of a select few broadcast networks. As the report points out, the independent production sector's participation was minimal because broadcast networks controlled the field of production by producing largely in-house. Moreover, pay television's presence in market terms was primarily reduced to well-to-do audiences, who had both the money to pay the high subscription fees and interest in consuming international content, at that point the staple of the pay television programming grid. Looking forward to the beginning of the 2010s, Brittos and Simões were nonetheless hopeful that widespread digitalization would permit the deconcentration of media powers, thereby expanding the medium's potential beyond those select few networks that had traditionally controlled it (235–36). What neither Brittos and Simões nor the BNDES report foresaw was the way in which the sudden growth of the pay television sector would alter the landscape of Brazilian television.

THE PAY TELEVISION LAW

Over its approximately fifty-year history, TV Globo and its standardized production of extremely popular telenovelas have largely come to characterize Brazilian television as a whole. For decades, TV Globo's telenovelas have attracted enormous audiences that faithfully—and for the most part predictably—tuned in Monday through Saturday during the lucrative prime-time hours. More recently, however, this has changed. By early 2015, many in Brazil had come to believe that the network era was approaching the end of its six decades of dominance. Responding to a consistent downturn in ratings of TV Globo's telenovelas, for example, television critic Tony Goes declared that network Brazilian television was dead ("Novela da Globo"). At around the same time, an article in the *Folha de São Paulo* reported an expected growth of 11 to 12 percent for the Brazilian pay television sector in 2015 (Jimenez, "TV paga quer manter"). Interestingly, a similar article from *The Hollywood Reporter* proclaimed that the U.S. pay television sector experienced its first full-year drop in subscriptions in 2013 (Szalai, "Study: U.S. Posted"). Whereas such growth in Brazil would push the number of households subscribing to pay television to approximately 21 million, or 30 percent of all households, the decrease in the U.S. sector due to "cord-cutters" dropped the number of American household subscribers to roughly 100 million.[1]

Based on these numbers, Brazilian and U.S. television seem to be moving in opposite directions. However, if we consider Amanda Lotz's outlining of U.S. English-language television's trajectory from the network to the post-network era, we might understand Brazilian television to be on a similar path, albeit at a much earlier stage. Lotz argues that U.S. television transitioned to an as yet not wholly defined postnetwork era in the mid-2000s. Among other factors, an influx of distribution sources and the necessary generated content to fill the programming space of those sources are central to the burgeoning postnetwork era of U.S. English-language television. At least in theory, the proliferation and fragmentation of these distribution sources, as they pertain to the Internet, challenge the more traditional models of network and pay television, resulting in a decrease in the total number of households subscribing to pay television in the U.S. Nonetheless, rather than applying Lotz's model to Brazil, as if the latter was a carbon copy of the former, or oversimplifying the ongoing changes to Brazilian television and declaring, like Goes, that network television is dead, we can attempt to understand what has happened since the mid-2000s to bring about the media transition alluded to by Brittos and Simões and by the BNDES report.

At the center of this transition is the Lei 12.485/11 (Law 12.485/11), more commonly referred to as the Pay Television Law (Lei da TV Paga). Following a contentious nearly five-year dispute that began with the intention of updating the 1995 Lei do Cabo (Cable Television Law), President Dilma Rousseff signed Lei 12.485/11 into law on September 12, 2011. Designed to increase domestic production and competition in the audiovisual market, the law establishes quotas that require international pay television channels to broadcast a weekly minimum of three and a half hours of prime-time content created by Brazilian production companies (one and a half hours of the total must come from independent Brazilian production companies).[2] The quotas aim to prevent international pay television channels from dumping syndicated airings of inexpensive foreign content into the domestic programming grid, providing these channels with a legal incentive to use existing financing mechanisms for coproduction of Brazilian content to fill out their schedules.[3] In addition to the content requirement, the law also stipulates that for every three non-Brazilian pay television channels there must be one Brazilian channel.[4] Thus, during an era of increased globalization and of marketplaces heavily influenced by a neoliberal logic, the Brazilian government has elected to support the growth of the pay television sector by regulating it in such a manner that it promotes both local production and the creation of "Brazilian" content.

Each of Lei 12.485/11's primary objectives was designed to work in concert with the others to achieve the ultimate goal of maximizing the potential of the once-dormant pay television market. First, prime-time slots on pay television are set aside for Brazilian content, allowing such content to enter a previously untapped programming space. In turn, this creates a demand for independent production companies to supply said content while working outside the vertical monopoly controlled by networks like TV Globo. Moreover, as a larger number of pay television networks and, perhaps even more important, telecommunication companies get involved in distributing content and competition increases, customers acquire more access to Brazilian content at less expensive rates.[5] In short, the law is designed to function as a cycle that feeds on itself, ultimately increasing competition, production, distribution, and consumption of the Brazilian pay television sector.

In just over three years, Lei 12.485/11 has strongly impacted the already ongoing destabilization of network television's staggering dominance over the traditionally more elitist pay television sector. Manoel Rangel, for example, current president of ANCINE, the governmental entity charged with overseeing and administering the law, has gone so far as to declare that the law "transformed the Brazilian audiovisual field" ("*Ver TV*—Entrevista"). Rangel attributes the exponential jump in pay television subscribers, from roughly three million in 2004 to approximately 19 million in 2016, to the law eliminating competitive barriers and expanding pay television services. According to Marco Altberg, president of Associação Brasileira de Produtoras Independentes de Televisão (the Brazilian Independent Television Producers Association), by the end of 2015 a total of 600 member companies had registered, up from 215 in 2012 (125). Along these lines, Rangel also highlights a significant increase in production, pointing out that the number of projects registered with ANCINE—a prerequisite for any production company seeking to use government financing mechanisms and to be registered as content "qualified" to meet the quotas—went from 760 in 2011 to 1,059 in 2012; before jumping to 3,205 in 2013 ("*Ver TV*—Entrevista"). Rangel also comments on the law's goal of promoting national culture. Indeed, for the ANCINE president, the increase in Brazilian media production and the increase in designated spaces for its distribution has provided pay television with a "touch of Brazilian-ness," drawing audiences to a space previously dominated by international content (*"Ver TV*—Entrevista").

As Heverton Sousa Lima shows, one of Lei 12.485/11's most visible effects has indeed had to do with the exponential increase in the production of Brazilian series. According to Lima, between 2012 and 2014, 385 Brazilian television series received their necessary licenses from ANCINE (122). This number, up from 119 during the period between 2009 and 2011, represents a 224 percent increase (Lima 122). Producer and co-owner of O2 Filmes, another of Brazil's largest and most successful independent production companies, Andrea Barata Ribeiro illustrates how the numbers mentioned above have significantly altered her company's production and approach in recent years: "Lei 12.485/11 represents an important mark for independent production in Brazil. Prior to it passing, I think that independent production was basically non-existent. O2 Filmes has been around for 23 years. In our first 21 years we produced five series. In the last year-and-a-half, however, we produced eight and have another five series in development. . . . What is more, we are now producing for a number of different channels . . . before we only used to produce for Globo and HBO, but now, in addition to these, we are producing for Fox, Discovery, and GNT" (qtd. in Lima 105). Nonetheless, the law was not designed merely to support the production sector. Rather, the increased involvement of foreign telecommunication companies in distribution and deregulation allowing the necessary infrastructure to arrive to previously lacking areas provides customers greater access to Brazilian content at less expensive rates. Along these lines, the expansion of pay television in Brazil and its accompanying "triple-play" packages (pay television, Internet, and phone) have also played a central role in growing the Internet's reach to nearly 50 percent of all Brazilian households ("Celulares").[6]

Though Rangel, Altberg, and Ribeiro each have vested professional interests in declaring the Lei 12.485/11's success, their enthusiastic declarations along with the statistics representing significant growth both in terms of production and subscription reveal much about Brazilian television's current state. Again, if we apply Lotz's outlining of American television's evolution to Brazilian television, it is clear that the South American giant will first need to move through what Lotz refers to as the multichannel transition phase, before embarking fully on anything representative of even the earliest stage of a postnetwork era. Based on the recent increase in both pay-channel production and subscription, one could conclude that the days of the Brazilian broadcast networks are numbered. The reality, however, is more complicated. For example, as Siva Vaidhyanathan astutely argues with regard to U.S. television, the

views that "cord-cutting" is ubiquitous, or that the death of network television
is definitive, are problematic. Instead, Vaidhyanathan recognizes that while
this is true for certain U.S. demographics, namely those that are more socio-
economically privileged, the broader reality is complex:

> So we assume everybody is streaming video from tablets and settling in on Sunday
> evenings to watch *Game of Thrones* on HBO. After all, everyone we know is doing
> that. The assumption that Americans are significantly "cutting the cord" and
> opting to only stream Internet video instead of relying on cable and satellite pay
> television is also highly exaggerated. In 2013 cable and satellite subscriptions fell
> for the first time in history. But they only fell by about 250,000 people. Cord-cut-
> ting is a slow and so-far marginal phenomenon and services like HBO and ESPN
> are preparing for a more significant shift if it happens. The mantra that "broadcast
> television is dead" has been echoing for 20 years. Yet broadcast television lives on
> and plays important roles in the daily lives of millions of Americans. More than
> 50 million Americans rely on over-the-air free television. As you might assume,
> these viewers are disproportionately poor and/or live in rural areas. If cord-
> cutting grows, especially as purchasing power among lower-income working peo-
> ple falls, the percentage of viewers relying on free over-the-air television will rise,
> not fall. ("Big Bird")

To conclude that the growth of the pay television sector has or will soon re-
place broadcast network television in Brazil is, in the spirit of Vaidhyanathan's
argument, a position that fails to take into account both the reach of and re-
liance on broadcast network television in Brazil among rural, working-class
populations. Thus, even if we accept Lotz's trajectory for the postnetwork era
in the U.S. as a plausible model for Brazil, it is clear that despite the pay television sector's recent growth, Brazil is still in the early to middle stages of
this process of transition. Indeed, even the figure mentioned above, highlighting that nearly 30 percent of all Brazilian households have pay television, is
somewhat misleading, particularly when one considers the geographical distribution of subscribers. For example, nearly 12 million, or approximately 42
percent of all pay television subscribers in Brazil, are located in the southeast.
More specifically, Rio de Janeiro and São Paulo account for nearly 10 million
of that region's 12 million subscribers, or 83 percent of the total number ("TV
paga registra"). In contrast, the northeastern portion of the country is home to
approximately 13 percent of all pay television subscribers. The state of Bahia,
for example, is the country's fifth largest by area and the fourth most popu-
lous; however, it only has slightly less than 620,000 subscribers ("TV paga registra"). In contrast, TV Globo covers over 98 percent of the country's territory and reaches over 99 percent of Brazilian homes.

Nevertheless, even with Brazilian television in the early to middle stages of the multichannel transition phase, the changing state of the field is significant enough to have caught TV Globo's attention. Though the network remains the clear leader in terms of advertising revenue, production, and audience share, TV Globo has in recent years been preparing itself for a new, increasingly competitive reality. In this emerging reality, where pay television is becoming a viable market and where the Internet continues to expand, though access to new distribution channels and content remains largely unequal, audiences have more options than ever in the history of Brazilian audiovisual production. As such, TV Globo now finds itself having to compete as never before for audience share that over the past forty-plus years had become nearly automatic.

No demographic has been more important in this new field of competition than the C-Class. According to the Fundação de Getúlio Vargas's Centro de Políticas Sociais (Getúlio Vargas Foundation's Center for Social Politics), members of the C-Class are those households that earn an income between R$2,005 and R$8,640 per month (approximately $615 to $2,650) ("Qual a faixa"). Demographic research in the past few years from the Instituto Brasileiro de Geografia e Estatística (The Brazilian Institute of Geography and Statistics), among others, estimates that the C-Class makes up 54 percent of Brazil's population, approximately 105 million people ("Classe C já"). The meteoric rise of this particular demographic out of the impoverished D and E classes has resulted in a new consumer mass that is interested in purchasing products, services, and technologies that bring comfort and leisure to their lives. During Brazil's recent economic growth (2003–2014) it has been no secret that, like other economic sectors, Brazilian television has been particularly interested in creating content that appeals to this highly sought-after emerging socioeconomic group.

Brazilian media scholar Esther Hamburger foresaw the potential impact of the rise of the C-Class as early as 2005, noting that if telenovelas, and programming in general, were actually representative of the country's population, "The 'C-Class' would be the most important social class for broadcast networks" (55). More recently, in hopes of attracting this large consumer group, network television—TV Globo in particular—has adjusted its programming to suit C-Class tastes. The headline for a May 2012 article in *O Globo* announced that "A TV se rende à nova classe média" ("TV surrenders to the new middle class"). Also in May 2012, the public television program *Ver TV* did a special episode titled, "O *Ver TV* analisa os programas voltados para a chamada 'nova classe C'" ("*Ver TV* analyzes programs directed at the so-called new C-Class"). The program's press release and summary emphasized the importance the C-Class has had in recent TV Globo programming:

> The Brazilian Institute of Geography and Statistics (IBGE) concluded that the
> C-Class is the fastest growing in the country. It is for this gigantic audience that
> network television has been focusing its programming. Audience leader TV Globo
> has popularized the plots of its telenovelas, as seen in *Cheias de Charme* (*Sparkling
> Girls*, 2012) and *Avenida Brasil* (*Brazil Avenue*, 2012). Also, in addition to high-
> dollar investments in Faustão and Luciano Huck's weekend variety shows, the net-
> work has bet on comedies, such as *Zorra Total,* which are characterized by a sim-
> ple, straightforward language. The formula for attracting the C-Class is to show
> members of that class on screen, to recreate on TV that particular viewer's reality.
> A good example is the series, *Tapas e Beijos* (*Slaps and Kisses,* 2011–2015), which
> shows the lives of two store clerks, a common profession among the members of
> this new middle class. ("O *Ver TV* analisa")

While much consideration has been given to how this emerging population
has impacted TV Globo's content and overall programming grid, it turns out
that the C-Class has also been a major driver behind the recent growth of pay
television subscriptions.

At the NeoTV[7] Congress in April 2013, Renato Meirelles, the president of
the Instituto Data Popular (Popular Data Institute), presented a recent study
on the habits of the C-Class pay television subscriber. According to Meirelles,
at the time, 95 out of every 100 new pay television subscribers belonged to
the C and D classes ("95% de novos"). What is more, Meirelles states that the
report found that the C and D classes together made up 66 percent of the then
pay television subscription population, and that this number was only increasing ("95% de novos"). Indeed, reports have emerged that conclude that despite Brazil's recent (2015–) economic recession and dim long-term financial
outlook, the C-Class is showing tendencies of not giving up certain leisure
products and services gained during the country's economic boom. Pay television subscriptions are among these services. In fact, one article discussing the
recession as it pertains to the C-Class specifically states that this group "might
cut out going to a restaurant as a leisure activity, but they are not going to sur-
render having pay television and internet in their homes" ("Classe C elimina").

Thus, in 2015, when a *Folha de São Paulo* article announced in its headline that "Novela da Globo dar menos audiência é o 'novo normal'" ("Smaller
audiences for TV Globo *telenovelas* is the 'new normal'"), it was understood
that this was in large part due to a new middle-class portion of the population having subscriptions to pay television and increased access to the Internet. Newfound, and unprecedented, access to both new and more content
has drawn at least some C-Class audiences away from TV Globo's prime-time
telenovelas. As TV critic Tony Goes has noted: "In actuality, what we are wit-

nessing is the end of the 50-plus years the telenovela format has absolutely dominated television. . . . The world has changed. We are no longer in the late 1990s—a splendid period for TV Globo—when competition among networks was nearly nonexistent, pay television did not yet have an expressive presence, and the Internet was only getting started. Today, this reality has been inverted, and it has generated a dangerous situation for TV Globo. The network's audiences are not being reproduced" ("Novela da Globo"). Though Goes's declaration is perhaps a bit hyperbolic, it is clear that the landscape of Brazilian media is experiencing significant changes and that these changes have weakened TV Globo's power over its still relatively enormous audiences, and, as a result, threatened the company's stream of revenue from advertising. At the same time, through the proliferation of pay television and the quotas for nationally produced content, audiences have benefited from increased access to more programming options.

These changes have had an important impact on Carvalho's work. As a TV Globo employee—albeit one with relatively large degree of autonomy—Carvalho is ultimately subject to the network's overarching blueprint for maintaining its audiences. This is clearly the case in the director's most recent microseries *Subúrbia* (2012). As I will show in the rest of this chapter, though it employs Carvalho's characteristic production model and maintains traces of his singular aesthetic, *Subúrbia* is a problematic example of one of TV Globo's broader aims for television fiction in the field's changing landscape—to appeal to the C-Class.

THE C-CLASS AND THE *PERIPHERY*

Carvalho has been ambiguous about whether *Subúrbia*[8] was aimed at the C-Class. During an interview, Geraldo Bessa of the *Folha de São Paulo* asked the director if TV Globo pressured him to create something for the C-Class, along the lines of the hugely successful telenovela *Avenida Brasil* (2012).[9] Carvalho responded that there was no pressure at all from the network. Instead, the director said that it was he who approached TV Globo executives with the idea of making *Subúrbia* ("Diretor de *Subúrbia*"). Moreover, he was careful to say that *Subúrbia* was one of his most artistic and personal projects to date ("Diretor de *Subúrbia*").

Although TV Globo might not have pressured Carvalho to make a microseries for the C-Class, an *O Globo* article that came out right before *Subúrbia's* premiere indicates that the the work was in fact directed at the C-Class: "In the face of all of Brazilian television's efforts to portray the C-Class, many of which often resort to stereotypes, Luiz Fernando Carvalho's microseries, *Subúrbia*, promises to go against the grain in representing the periphery of Rio

FIGURE 7.1. Conceição and her family in the *sertão, Subúrbia* (2012). Right to reproduce granted by TV Globo.

de Janeiro" (Fonseca). In this same article, Carvalho reveals his awareness of the C-Class audience and his desire to represent that audience: "There is a reality invented by market conditions, called the C-Class. The market directed at reaching the C-Class has been manufacturing an excessively limited representation of the periphery, without realizing how much those representations lack the lyricism associated with the area. I wanted to talk about this world . . . about its real drama without prosaicism, about those mothers who stay at their doors, waiting for the arrival of their children, about those who take trains and buses to return home after work" (Fonseca). Thus, at the very least, it is clear from the above statements that both Carvalho and the network were aware of the C-Class in market terms (real or imagined, as Carvalho posits).

Perhaps more importantly, Carvalho's statements reveal the director's awareness of the C-Class in artistic terms. First, his narrative of how *Subúrbia* came into existence (he brought the concept to TV Globo, not the other way around) emphasizes a carefully constructed discourse regarding the artistic control Carvalho exerts over the work he does for TV Globo. Second, for Carvalho, recent representations of the C-Class are all too often both limited and stereotypical. Carvalho, then, positions himself and his work against other producers and their works that have also recently portrayed with the C-Class. As Bourdieu notes, "There is no position within the field of cultural production that does not call for a determinate type of position taking and which does not exclude, simultaneously, an entire gamut of theoretically possible

FIGURE 7.2. Conceição in the city, *Subúrbia* (2012). Right to reproduce granted by TV Globo.

position-takings" (132). Thus, as a director who has a significant amount of symbolic capital and artistic control over both the selection and production of the works he creates, Carvalho implies that *Subúrbia* is a "position-taking," the merit of which exists precisely in its formal divergence from the abundant run-of-the-mill representations of the C-Class.

Subúrbia tells the story of Conceição (Érika Januza), an illiterate eighteen-year-old Afro-Brazilian trying to find her way in the big city. Evoking the grainy, gritty, and saturated realist aesthetic that characterizes Fernando Merielles's *Cidade de Deus* (2002), *Subúrbia*'s narrative begins in the *sertão* of Minas Gerais, where a twelve-year-old Conceição (Débora L. Fidelix Nascimento) lives with her hardworking yet extremely impoverished and uneducated family (figure 7.1).

After her adolescent brother dies from a tragic coalbunker explosion—a theme also portrayed by Carvalho in *Hoje é Dia de Maria*—Conceição's heavyhearted mother encourages her to leave the family in hopes of finding a better life in Rio de Janeiro. The big city, however, proves to be a harsh place. That this is case is suggested both narratively and formally. There is a clear aesthetic transition from the opening scene's slow-paced, poetic images, which fluctuate between beautiful establishing shots of the land and close-up shots of the character's faces and bodies, to the rest of the work's fast-paced, vibrant colorful images captured by a highly mobile handheld camera that surfs through the urban and suburban spaces (figures 7.2 and 7.3).

FIGURE 7.3. Conceição and her family in the periphery, *Subúrbia* (2012). Right to reproduce granted by TV Globo.

Almost immediately upon arriving in the urban space, Conceição is wrongly mistaken by the police for ª street kid connected to a group of adolescent criminals. This mistake, which the narrative implies is tied up in police corruption and an institutionalized disregard for certain racial and socioeconomic groups of Brazilian citizens, results in Conceição being sent to a juvenile detention center. There, the young Conceição experiences the first of three attempted acts of sexual violence committed against her.

After having escaped, Conceição is once again thrust into the streets of the unforgiving city. Fearing the police will find her, she tries to hide, but is nearly hit by a car. The driver, Sylvia (Bruna Miglioranza), is a white, middle-class divorced mother of two who is completing her PhD in sociology. When she realizes that Conceição has nowhere to go, she takes in the girl. However, echoing Brazil's history of slavery and Brazilian television's long tradition of representing Afro-Brazilian in subaltern roles, rather than sending Conceição to school and providing her with a stable structure that would help her to progress as an individual citizen, this highly educated white woman decides to provide Conceição food and shelter in exchange for her work as a nanny and housekeeper (Araújo; Grijó and Sousa; Silva; Sovik). Instead of critiquing this form of quasi-forced labor, the microseries portrays Conceição as happily living and working in Sylvia's home, where she lovingly cares for Sylvia's two children for nearly six years. Nonetheless, Conceição's life is once again turned upside down when, in another evocation of Brazilian slavery, Cássio (Alex Teix), Sylvia's live-in boyfriend, attempts to sexually violate the now beautiful eighteen-year-old. Inherently aware of her subaltern state, Conceição is doubtful Sylvia would believe her if she were to tell of what Cássio had done. Left with few options, Conceição decides that her only choice is to leave. She accepts her only friend, Vera's (Dani Ornellas) invitation to go and live with her and her large family in Madureira, a neighborhood on the outskirts of Rio de Janeiro. There, Conceição encounters the three loves of her life—Vera's kind and generous Afro-Brazilian, working-class family, which accepts her as their own; samba and funk dancing, which is revealed to be her unique talent and becomes her passion; and Cleiton (Fabrício Boliveira), an Afro-Brazilian working-class young man from the neighborhood.

Though they differ in important ways—*Afinal, o que Querem as Mulheres?* has a male protagonist and only one Afro-Brazilian actor among its cast, whereas *Suburbia* has a female protagonist and an almost all Afro-Brazilian cast—within the broader context of Carvalho's artistic trajectory, *Suburbia* seems to have most in common with Carvalho's 2010 microseries. Importantly, as with *Afinal, o que Querem as Mulheres?*, Carvalho was the cowriter (along with Paulo Lins) of the original screenplay for *Suburbia*. Indeed, while Carvalho has had final say over the scripts for all his work since *Hoje é Dia de Maria*, and is listed as a cowriter of *adapted* screenplays, these two recent microseries represent the only times in the director's career in television when he has cowritten *original* screenplays. Moreover, like *Afinal, o que Que Querem as Mulheres?*, *Suburbia* is set in a more contemporary version of Rio de Janeiro. Again, since Carvalho has focused his creative efforts in the shorter microseries format, these two works are the only ones in which he explores anything remotely close to a realistic, contemporary urban space. Additionally, the visual treatment of the urban space in these two microseries is quite similar. For example, the vibrant colors, such as the artificial greens, reds, blues, and pinks that characterize *Afinal, o que Querem as Mulheres's?* 1960s pop-culture aesthetic, are also very present in *Suburbia's mise-en-scène*, which evokes its own Afro-influenced 1960s, 1970s aesthetic, not unlike that which characterizes the Blaxploitation films of the 1970s. In both works, the pop-culture aesthetic is reinforced and complemented by the inclusion of international (*Afinal*) and national pop music (*Suburbia*) from the twentieth and twenty-first centuries.

Nonetheless, despite Carvalho's participation as a coscreenwriter of *Suburbia* and the spatiotemporal and aesthetic similarities the microseries shares with the *Afinal, o que Que Querem as Mulheres?*, a closer look reveals *Suburbia* to actually be a rereading—or, to use Carvalho's preferred term, *uma aproximação*—of *Hoje é Dia de Maria*. Like Maria, Conceição is born into a simple, rural space, far from the chaos of the city. Both of these adolescent female protagonists set out on their respective journeys after realizing their lives are in danger. In Maria's case, her father attempts to molest her. Conceição, on the other hand, is nearly killed along with her brother following the coalbunker explosion. Upon leaving home, both the girls take with them amulets given to them by their mothers. Maria takes with her the *chavinha* (little key); Conceição holds dear a small wood carving of *Nossa Senhora da Conceição Aparecida* (Our Lady of the Immaculate Conception), the black patron saint of Brazil.[10] Once in the city, the girls experience different forms of repression and exploitation. The sly businessman Asmodeu Cartola imprisons Maria, putting the child to work as a dancer in a men's club. Like Maria, the innocent Conceição also finds herself alone and hungry. Though Sylvia does not imprison Conceição as Asmodeu does Maria, she exploits the child's innocence and vulnerability by putting her to work and keeping her out of school.

After a long journey, which I describe in greater detail in Chapter Five, Maria finally finds her way back to an even more utopian version of the rural countryside from where she first began. Confident that all will be okay, Maria finally gives into the sleepiness that has been summoning her since the opening scene of the *Segunda Jornada*, only to awake alongside her father and grandmother in an apartment in the Rio de Janeiro periphery, where she realizes it was all a dream. While Conceição never returns to her family's home in rural Minas Gerais, she does, like Maria, escape the harsh city for a romanticized periphery. Although she still faces a number of difficulties, in the end, as with the young protagonist from the 2005 microseries, Conceição finds herself safe and secure on the periphery, where she lives happily ever after with her new family and now husband, Cleiton.

As in *Hoje é Dia de Maria*, and to a lesser extent in some of Carvalho's other microseries, *Suburbia*'s narrative also touches on "appropriate" forms of behavior and citizenship. In Chapter Five, I analyzed some examples from *Hoje é Dia de Maria* in which Maria, and by extension the audience, are confronted with ethical questions about how one best interacts with and treats her neighbor. I contextualized such questions within Carvalho's own attempt to create an ethical aesthetic for television, as well as with TV Globo's broader objective of defining and representing what it means to be both Brazilian and a "good citizen" for its audience ("Social Mission"). While such definitions and representations might be understood as problematic and paternalistic in *Hoje é Dia de Maria*, they are certainly so in *Suburbia*. In large part, this is because the 2005 microseries makes no attempt at a realistic portrayal of Brazil. Instead, heavily grounded in folklore, *Hoje é Dia de Maria* takes advantage of its poetic license to share and express the values and morals extracted from the oral traditions it is adapting, while largely avoiding issues pertaining to race and identity politics. *Suburbia*, however, stands alone among Carvalho's works insofar as it lacks the playful, theatrical, operatic, and more explicit artificiality that characterizes each of the director's other microseries. Instead of the anthropophagic hybridization of artistic elements and overt artificiality that call attention to the characteristic theatricality that runs throughout Carvalho's work, *Subúrbia* tends toward a realistic, albeit poetic, representation of Conceição and the time and space she occupies. Moreover, Carvalho uses on-location shooting, nonprofessional actors, and a handheld camera—central production aspects of the Cinema Novo movement—with an eye toward authenticating the audiovisual discourse surrounding the work's marginalized object (the periphery) and subjects (working-class Afro-Brazilians).[11]

In choosing to shoot on location, Carvalho once again moved production of his microseries away from TV Globo's Projac Studios, shooting on-site in the Rio de Janeiro periphery. While *Hoje é Dia de Maria, A Pedra do Reino, Capitu,* and most of *Afinal, o que Querem as Mulheres?* were all shot outside the confines of Projac in spaces whose aesthetic composition served as physical extensions of the protagonists' psychological and emotional states, *Subúrbia* differs in that it does not reproduce the self-reflexive artificial spaces that characterize these microseries' fictional universes. Instead, Carvalho filmed *Subúrbia* in existing neighborhoods, which underwent little to no modifications. He says: "You cannot portray the periphery in the studio. It is ugly and 'fake.' It is much more labor-intensive and expensive to record only on-location. I have to adhere, for example, to a series of issues involving climate and even public safety. Nonetheless, it was the right option. We were in neighborhoods such as Madureira, Quintino, Ramos, Piedade, on the island of Paquetá and in some regions of Jacarepaguá. In the end, the periphery of Rio de Janeiro not only served as the setting for a love story, it was also a primary character" ("Diretor de *Subúrbia*"). By shooting on-location and by not altering the natural space, Carvalho juxtaposes *Subúrbia*'s realistic space—the periphery, which gives the work its title—with the overtly manufactured, artificial spaces from his earlier microseries and reveals the extent to which realism was a guiding force behind the construction and representation of Conceição's narrative.

The second reason *Subúrbia* differs from Carvalho's other works is, like the first, directly connected to the director's desire to achieve a realistic representation of the setting and its inhabitants. In addition to being shot on-location, *Subúrbia* features a number of nonprofessional, Afro-Brazilian actors.[12] For example, both Érika Januza, the actress portraying Conceição, and Ana Pérola, playing the villain Jéssica, made their television debuts in *Subúrbia*. Other actors were selected from the well-known *favela* or community-based theatrical troupe *Nós do Morro,* and from the Rio de Janeiro based

Afro-Brazilian theatrical troupe, *Companhia dos Comuns*. As discussed in previous chapters, this is not the first time Carvalho has shown an interest in nonprofessional actors or actors widely unknown to television audiences. In fact, since as early as casting for *Lavoura Arcaica* in 1998, Carvalho has sought out either nonprofessional actors or actors who had previously worked exclusively in theater. The clear difference in *Suburbia* from Carvalho's other works, and really from the majority of fictional programming on Brazilian television, is the overwhelming presence of Afro-Brazilian actors. This is precisely what makes the microseries an important achievement in the field of Brazilian television production. However, moving beyond the importance of featuring such actors, it is their portrayals and Carvalho's use of techniques to imply realism and authenticity that make the microseries Carvalho's most problematic work to date.

FROM THE *CITY (OF MEN)* TO THE *PERIPHERY*

Though casting Afro-Brazilian actors in mainstream network programming is not common, *Suburbia* was not the first long-form TV Globo production in the twenty-first century to feature primarily Afro-Brazilian actors from a marginalized space. Indeed, from 2002 to 2005, before the C-Class explicitly became the network's main target audience and in an early and rare instance of a TV Globo coproduction, the Fernando Meirelles–owned O2 Filmes coproduced *Cidade dos Homens* (*City of Men*), a series about the lives of Laranjinha and Acerola, two adolescent Afro-Brazilian boys from a South Zone favela in Rio de Janeiro. Like *Suburbia*, *Cidade dos Homens* featured a number of nonprofessional actors hailing from favelas in and around Rio de Janeiro. Additionally, it was Paulo Lins's 1997 novel, *Cidade de Deus*, that helped set off a string of cultural productions, eventually leading to the *Cidade dos Homens* series, for which the author also worked as a screenwriter. TV Globo's recent interest in attracting the C-Class and the presence of Lins as a coscreenwriter for Carvalho's microseries necessitates an analysis that places *Suburbia* within the context of those works that began with Lins's novel. What this analysis ultimately reveals is that, as is the case with the majority of his work, while Carvalho's microseries might offer formal advancements relative to the rest of the field of Brazilian television fiction, compared with *Cidade dos Homens*, *Suburbia* offers no ideological progression from the earlier work and in many ways functions as a regression in terms of representation of a racially and spatially marginalized group.

Lins's debut novel was unique for offering the reader an insider's view into the complex, marginalized space of the favela.[13] In a span of five years, film and television adaptations of Lins's perspective found their way to millions of spectators both in Brazil and around the world. In 2002, for example, Cidade de Deus, the community where Lins grew up and the focus of his novel, gained international fame (or infamy, depending on one's perspective) with the release of Fernando Meirelles's 2002 film *Cidade de Deus*. During the process of preparing for that film, long-time TV Globo director Guel Arraes approached Meirelles to gauge his interest in producing a year-end special for an Arraes-led, TV Globo special programming project called *Brava Gente*.[14] Meirelles accepted Arraes's invitation with the understanding that he was in the early production stages of *Cidade de Deus,* and that he would want the freedom to create something related to that project. Importantly, Meirelles was keen on using the special as an opportunity to test the actors who were participating in the *Nós do Morro* workshop in preparation for their roles in the upcoming film. Moreover, Meirelles saw the special as an opportunity to experiment with location, lighting, cameras, and other cinematographic and production elements in anticipation of shooting *Cidade de Deus* (Caetano 173).

With little publicity, at 11 p.m. on December 28, 2000, TV Globo aired the Meirelles-directed one-hour special *Palace II*. Taken from a portion of a chapter from Lins's novel, *Palace II* tells the story of two poor Afro-Brazilian boys (Laranjinha and Acerola) who concoct a plan to steal money so they can attend a musical concert. Much to the surprise of O2 Filmes and TV Globo, the episode captured relatively high ratings, prompting the network to request another eight episodes. However, because Meirelles wanted to finish *Cidade de Deus* first, those episodes were postponed until 2002, when O2 Filmes and TV Globo began production for the series *Cidade dos Homens* (Caetano 177).

Although *Cidade de Deus* was a commercial and critical success, garnering four Oscar nominations, a number of critics, scholars, and favela community members throughout Brazil criticized the film for its naturalist treatment of the favela as both disconnected from a broader social context and as the home to violent young men with little to no regard for human life.[15] In part as a response to this criticism, *Cidade dos Homens* made a concerted effort to portray everyday life in the favela not simply as a hotbed for violence, but as a home to a working-class population that was integral to Rio de Janeiro. Broadly speaking, one of the series' primary objectives was to deconstruct the numerous real and imagined barriers separating favelas and their inhabitants from the rest of Rio de Janeiro. Nowhere in the series' nineteen episodes is this clearer than in "Uólace e João Victor" ("Uólace and João Victor"), the fourth episode from the first season.

Like *Subúrbia*, "Uólace e João Victor" aired in the post–prime-time slot of 11 p.m. on October 18, 2002. Intent on arguing that the two protagonists share many similarities, the "Uólace e João Victor" episode juxtaposes a day in the life of Uólace (Darlan Cunha)—a poor Afro-Brazilian boy from a South Zone favela in Rio de Janeiro—with João Victor (Thiago Martins)—a white, middle-class adolescent who lives in the exclusive neighborhood of Leblon. As the spectator takes in the famous landmarks through the aerial shots, João Victor and Uólace take turns narrating in voice-over to the sound of a hip-hop beat. "This city that has sewage," João Victor begins, "is called Rio de Janeiro." In turn, Uólace echoes, "This city that doesn't have sewage is called Rio de Janeiro." João Victor follows with, "This city of asphalt is called Rio de Janeiro," before Uólace concludes with, "This city of dirt is called Rio de Janeiro" (Meirelles, "Uólace e" DVD). While the boys' narration recognizes the city's distinct realities, it emphasizes that it is ultimately one—that is, it is simply Rio de Janeiro.

A message attempting to deconstruct the real and imagined barriers dividing Rio de Janeiro and its citizens is, of course, not a negative one. Janice Perlman, author of the *Myth of Marginality* (1976), makes a similar argument in her 2010 book *Favela: Four Decades of Living on the Edge in Rio de Janeiro*. Ironically, Perlman's book's title functions to undermine her central position, which is that "the division of the urban space into formal and informal is no longer applicable, if it ever was" (30). On the very same page, however, two paragraphs below where she makes this argument, she states: "Even after the extensive 10-year Favela-Bairro upgrading program, which was carried out in 144 favelas and 24 loteamentos, with the aim of integrating them into surrounding neighborhoods . . . there is little doubt as to where the *asfalto* (pavement) ends and the *morro* begins" (30). Thus, though Perlman makes an attempt, successful at times, to problematize the dichotomous characterization of the Rio de Janeiro cityscape, she ultimately employs it herself.

The "Uólace e João Victor" episode engages in an audiovisual construction that does something similar to Perlman's rhetorical turns. Despite the voice-over narration's seeming recognition of the inequalities that structure and perpetuate the city's existing inequalities, the episode itself seems bent on erasing these divisions. Indeed, the episode concludes with the idea that, despite their city's socioeconomic and racial disparities, Uólace and João Victor are the same because they are just two innocent Brazilian boys with similar hopes and fears. Both, for example, live with their single mothers and have absent fathers; both like hamburgers; both have best friends; both want the same hot new tennis shoes; both worry about the future. While highlighting the boys' similarities encourages the spectator to focus on their shared humanity, it masks the stark contrast of their daily lives. For example, by the last scene, while this has served as reinforcement for the similarities highlighted above, an astute viewer will notice that while João Victor is upset with his father for being absent, Uólace does not even know who his father is. Both of the boys' mothers are hardworking women. However, whereas João Victor's mom is ever-present and overly concerned with her son, Uólace's mother is never home, due to her job as a live-in maid. In the morning, Uólace wakes up alone and hungry, so he decides to panhandle in the streets in hopes of raising enough money to purchase a hamburger. João Victor also wants a hamburger for breakfast, but his mother makes him eat buttered toast instead.

One might argue that the subtext of these events undercuts the broader emphasis on the boys' similarities, thereby revealing the episode to embody a complex dialectic, but I argue that the episode actually reinforces the unifying message initiated in the opening scene, problematically erasing the real inequalities that exist within Rio de Janeiro. In the last scene, for example, João Victor sits in his bedroom window looking down on Uólace, who walks alone, aimlessly, down the middle of the street. Instead of emphasizing the vast distance between the boys' positions, symbolically represented in the construction of the shot, the series melds them together, having them conclude in synchronous voice-over: "He looks so lost; just like me" (Meirelles,"Uólace e" DVD). The idea that João Victor is "lost" in the comfort of his loving mother's South Zone middle-class apartment is trivial at best when compared with Uólace's precarious situation. Nonetheless, the episode makes no effort to address the deeper underlying systemic issues that function to marginalize certain groups of people, such as Uólace, within certain spaces like the favela. Rather, by establishing tenuous similarities between the two boys and pointing to their shared existence within the broader space of Rio de Janeiro, the "Uólace e João Victor" episode promotes a discourse of racial democracy on the basis that they are all, independent of their skin color, human beings.

HARD WORK, RELIGION, AND FAMILY IN THE *SUBÚRBIA*

In his landmark study on representations of blackness in the telenovela from 1963 to 1997, Joel Zito Araújo argues that the emphasis on Brazil as a racial democracy is one of the central ideologies behind the structuring of Brazilian television's characteristic whiteness and underrepresentation of individuals of color (40). Interestingly, *Suburbia* does not adhere to the racial democracy discourse found in the "João Victor e Uólace" episode from *Cidade dos Homens*. However, whereas the 2002 episode makes a concerted, albeit problematic attempt to situate the favela within the broader social fabric of Rio de Janeiro, *Suburbia* isolates the periphery as a space cut off from an outside world. As already mentioned, this was precisely one of the major critiques of the representation of the Cidade de Deus community in Meirelles's film. By focusing intently on the isolated space of the periphery and its inhabitants, *Subúrbia* places a microscope over its object, examining their overtly melodramatic behavior from a top-down perspective that is evocative of a long Brazilian tradition of cultural production influenced by naturalism.

David Haberly argues convincingly, for example, that from the 1870s well into the twentieth century, a romantic regionalism infused with an "intensely pessimistic ideology" of naturalism characterized Brazilian literature ("The Brazilian Novel" 146–47). According to Haberly, the three central tenets of this ideology were: "the consequences of change, at the level of society or the individual, are certain to be negative; sexual desire is the single most powerful and controlling human emotion; and genetic heredity and environmental conditioning entirely determine character and behavior" ("The Brazilian Novel" 148). While the latter two tenets are at the center of Carvalho's microseries, *Subúrbia* inverts the first, promoting change and suggesting a path to productive citizenship for the C-Class viewer.

As mentioned previously, *Subúrbia* stands out for featuring not only a predominately Afro-Brazilian cast, but also an Afro-Brazilian female protagonist. Unfortunately, however, rather than a strong, independent woman, the work presents Conceição as a suffering, illiterate, hypersexualized object, an audiovisual construct recognized as being common practice in a number of studies focused on the Brazilian telenovela (Araújo 2000, Grijó and Sousa 2012, Mitchell 2013, and Silva 1999 are a few examples). But Conceição is also a loving and determined woman. We learn, for example, that she possessed these two positive traits from the very beginning, while still living with her hardworking family in the *sertão* of Minas Gerais. Conceição's adopted working-class family on the outskirts of Rio de Janeiro further reinforces these traits. In the broader context of the periphery, however, compared to the many villainous characters lurking about, Conceição and her new family are an anomaly. In fact, throughout the microseries—as is the case with Jerônimo in Aluísio Azevedo's famous 1890 naturalist novel *O Cortiço*—Conceição and her family run the risk of being overcome by the ills of the local environment.

Cleiton, Conceição's future husband, is the best example of this, as he is the embodiment of the second and third tenets of naturalism referred to by Haberly. The first time we encounter Cleiton, he is a quiet, gentle young man who quickly becomes smitten with Conceição—especially after he learns she is a virgin (figure 7.4). Stereotypically jealous, he helps his new girlfriend get a job at the gas station where he works, so that he can keep an eye on her. Within the broader context of the narrative, Cleiton's jealousy and impotence in the face of the overwhelming male attention directed at Conceição are supposed to explain his inexplicable behavior when one night, while inebriated, he at-

FIGURE 7.4. Cleiton the worker, *Subúrbia* (2012). Right to reproduce granted by TV Globo.

FIGURE 7.5. Cleiton the violent drug trafficker, *Subúrbia* (2012). Right to reproduce granted by TV Globo.

FIGURE 7.6. Cleiton the saintly pastor, *Subúrbia* (2012). Right to reproduce granted by TV Globo.

tempts to rape her. Almost immediately following the tragic event, Cleiton gets involved with local drug traffickers who help him avenge the death of his brother. After coldly killing a number of rivals, Cleiton becomes the head of the local favela's drug trade. During this transformative period, like his alcoholic mother, he begins to drink and do drugs excessively. Thus, rather inexplicably, the narrative positions Cleiton as a product of his race, environment, and historical moment. That is, Cleiton is presented as destined to succumb to the powers of his uncontrollable sexual desire, his family's past of alcoholism, and the favela's culture of violence (figure 7.5).

While the microseries' naturalist approach is problematic at best, Cleiton's subsequent transformation into an evangelical pastor is even worse. Cleiton's development is such that it takes him from the position of a normal working-class man to that of a murderous drug-trafficker—the negative extreme of the moral spectrum. After a near-death experience, however, he bypasses his previous position as a regular working-class man to settle at the "positive" end of the moral spectrum as an evangelical pastor (figure 7.6).

To use another literary reference, Cleiton's trajectory is similar to that of Leonardo Pataca's, the protagonist from Manuel Antônio de Almeida's 1852–1853 novel *Memórias de um sargento de milícias*. The juxtaposition of two ethical extremities and the elimination of a more neutral option positions the microseries didactically, implicitly educating the viewer in the most appropriate path for an impoverished individual to follow—something, as discussed previously, TV Globo openly declares as its social mission.

One way, then, to understand *Suburbia* is that it offers a model for how certain marginalized individuals might overcome their genetic heredity and subaltern position. Indeed, for Paulo Lins, who according to anthropologist Luiz Eduardo Soares gives Carvalho's microseries the same testimonial feel the author has given to all the works since *Cidade de Deus*, *Suburbia* is about characters "searching for a better life through hard work, culture, religion, and the network of solidarity that exists among the poor" ("*Suburbia*: A intensidade"). In other words, a better life comes through application of a neoliberal logic—the racial and social inequalities that limit upward mobility can be eliminated, if individuals work hard, follow the rules, and stick together. In line with this neoliberal discourse, *Suburbia* suggests that a "good" and law-abiding black male Brazilian citizen is heterosexual and dedicated to forming a family. Moreover, religion is the form of environmental conditioning that allows him to overcome his sexual, violent, and criminal tendencies. As for the black female Brazilian citizen, she is to be innocent, both physically and mentally, and devoted to her man at all costs, even if he has killed others and attempted to rape her.

Such positioning is in direct contrast with that of Glauber Rocha's 1962 film *Barravento*. The beginnings of what Rocha referred to as the new genre of the "black film," *Barravento* represents an important precursor to *Suburbia*—and any Brazilian audiovisual work representing a marginalized Afro-Brazilian population (qtd. in Xavier, "*Barravento*: Glauber" 54). In *Barravento*, Rocha presents the spectator with a formal rupture whose objective it is to criticize religion and its central role in subjecting impoverished Afro-Brazilian fishermen to a perpetual subaltern position in northeastern Brazilian society. Along these lines, Luiz Carlos Maciel has argued that: "*Barravento* reveals Glauber's central preoccupation with the religious alienation of the Brazilian people. In the film, the religious beliefs of fishermen from a Bahian beach represent the primary obstacle in the struggle for liberation from the economic yoke to which they are subjected. It is their beliefs that prevent the revolution" (qtd. in Xavier, "*Barravento*: Glauber" 54).[16] In *Suburbia*, however, religion is not the subjugating problem, but the answer. What is more, religion plays a central role in inverting the first tenet of naturalism referred to by Haberly—"the consequences of change are certain to be negative." Conceição finally finds true happiness after marrying Cleiton—a known murderer and a man who, earlier in their relationship, attempted to rape her. This is possible because, for his part, Cleiton becomes a man of God and a productive citizen. Like the "Uólace e João Victor" episode, *Suburbia* arrives at this overly simplistic conclusion by remaining silent with regard to the more deeply embedded systemic violence that characterizes the marginalized characters' daily lives.

In *The Contradictions of Media Power*, Des Freedman argues that silence is "a socially constructed phenomenon that reflects the unequal distribution of power in society" (73). Freedman contends that an examination of "policy silence" or "non-decision making" is a "valuable way of reflecting on an environment in which policies are developed on the basis of a limited palette of ideological values and preferences that further pre-empt the emergence of contrasting policy approaches" (64). Though Freedman's focus is on policy making, his understanding of the ways in which those in power remain silent when advantageous to their objectives could be applied to any number of situations—including the production of audiovisual works.

Cacilda Rêgo, for example, argues that in TV Globo's many telenovelas representing favela life since 2004, the locale "is portrayed not as the dwelling for blacks and the locus of violence and crime, but rather as the gentrified space inhabited by the country's emerging new middle class, also known as C-Class" (93). What Rêgo implicitly touches on is that, in its attempt to capture the enormous C-Class audience—both to "educate" it and to sell it to advertisers—the fiction produced by TV Globo has often remained silent with regard to the socioeconomic and racial inequalities that characterize the marginalized spaces it is increasingly representing ("Social Mission"). That is, television programs frequently portray impoverished spaces and individuals in an overly simplistic manner, one that provides a top-down ideal of how these spaces and its inhabitants should look and behave (Rial; Simpson; Silva; Araújo; Sovik; Dennison). In doing so, many of these programs, *Subúrbia* included, tend to reduce the inequality and suffering felt by impoverished groups and certain racial minorities living on the margins of society.

Octávio Florisbal, TV Globo's Chief Executive Officer from 2002 to 2012, hammers this point home by trying to excuse it with the paternalistic argument that "Brazilian people face enough difficulties in their everyday lives" and therefore, "don't want to see more suffering" (qtd. in Wheatley, "Brazil's Winning"). In *Subúrbia*, it is not that Carvalho precludes his characters from experiencing difficulties and suffering. Rather, for Conceição and those around her, suffering is par for the course. In fact, in this way, as does the *Cidade dos Homens*'s series as whole, Carvalho's microseries sheds light on a number of unacceptable situations that significant portions of the Brazilian population find themselves having to deal with on a daily basis: situations such as racism, police corruption, exploitation of child labor, sexual assault, and spaces controlled by drug traffickers, without a positive state presence. Moreover, as Soares notes, with the aesthetic sensibility and formal experimentation audiences and critics have come to expect, Carvalho portrays the periphery as a space that is home to a range of possibilities—from average working-class families to drug traffickers ("*Subúrbia*: A intensidade").

And yet, insofar as he allows "the intensity and the supremacy of form" to trump other more pressing concerns that are tied to real, lived realities, in *Subúrbia* Carvalho ultimately contributes to a long tradition on Brazilian television of misrepresenting people of color. As discussed throughout this book, for most of his career, Carvalho's emphasis on form over content has largely led to critical success, helping to distinguish him as one of, if not the most creative director working in Brazil today. However, as Carvalho branches out and begins to (co-)write original screenplays, especially ones like *Subúrbia* that attempt to realistically represent a space and group to which Carvalho himself does not belong and has historically been under- and misrepresented, if it is to be truly successful, his project of reimagining Brazilian television through the construction of an ethical-aesthetic will need to give equal weight to the formal *and* the narrative.

Conclusion

REIMAGINING THE
(ANTI-)TELENOVELA

During a 2001 roundtable interview centered on *Lavoura Arcaica*, Carvalho explained what led him to leave television in 1997. Despite having just directed *O Rei do Gado*, one of the most critically acclaimed and commercially successful telenovelas of all time, he felt trapped and dissatisfied with his work, no longer able to experiment with the audiovisual language in a way that was meaningful to him (*Luiz Fernando Carvalho* 30, 34). In short, as Carvalho puts it, TV Globo's overly commercial mode of production for television fiction had made him feel suffocated; unable to move beyond those few rules that had come to guide the process for a financially successful work (*Luiz Fernando Carvalho* 30, 34). That Carvalho left television at what was, in retrospect, the commercial apex of his career, speaks to the way the director conceives of himself as, first and foremost, an artist working in a structure driven by commercial imperatives that ultimately constrict his artistic capacity. When Carvalho returned to television in 2001, he slowly initiated a move toward focusing his creative efforts almost exclusively on shorter narrative formats, namely the microseries.

As I argue throughout this book, Carvalho made this decision in large part because the microseries—traditionally an experimental format in TV Globo's programming grid—almost always removes the powerful television writer from the equation, providing the director with a space and format over which she is able to exercise a greater degree of creative control. At the same time, Carvalho was only able to make this move and thereby secure a greater degree of creative control over his work because he had achieved significant commercial success and proved that he could work profitably within TV Globo's vertical production system (Schatz, "The Whole Equation" 653).

In 2014, however, Carvalho surprised many when he began production for *Meu Pedacinho de Chão*, his first telenovela in approximately twelve years. Just when it seemed as if he might never return to that genre, not only did he take on the project, but created a radicalized version of it, which represents the culmination of all of the preproduction and artistic experimentation Carvalho had elaborated in his film, specials, miniseries, and, most importantly, microseries over the seventeen years since *O Rei do Gado*. Indeed, since that moment of personal and professional dissatisfaction in 1997, Carvalho has experimented incessantly with narrative and form, discarding standardized television's rulebook to construct a singular *oeuvre* while solidifying himself as an auteur of Brazilian television. Perhaps more than any of his other works—insofar as it formally deconstructs Brazilian television's narrative vehicle par excellence—*Meu Pedacinho de Chão* cements Carvalho's unique place within the history of Brazilian television production. At the same time, however, it also lends support to the argument that, while much is changing at TV Globo—and within the field as a whole—the Rio de Janeiro network is still not ready for Carvalho's version of a prime-time telenovela, continuing instead to base its business model on outdated metrics, such as audience share.

THE (ANTI-)TELENOVELA

At its core, *Meu Pedacinho de Chão* is a traditional telenovela. From the perspective of Serelepe, the child protagonist and first-person narrator, the telenovela tells the story of life in the fictional village of Santa Fé. All the archetypal plotlines and characters of a traditional telenovela are present: there is Coronel Epaminondas Napoleão (Osmar Prado), the villain whose questionable moral compass will be transformed by the end; the ongoing familial conflict between the patriarch Epaminondas and his son Ferdinando (Johnny Massaro); the continuous business and power feuds between Epaminondas and Pedro Falcão (Rodrigo Lombardi) and between Epaminondas and the Prefeito das Antas (the mayor) (Ricardo Blat); the numerous love subplots surrounding the beautiful young professor Juliana (Bruna Linzmeyer), who has arrived to bring education to the backward village; and the narrator and orphan, Serelepe (Tomás Sampaio), who, in the end, reveals that Epaminondas was his biological father all along.

Written by Benedito Ruy Barbosa—with whom Carvalho also partnered for the telenovelas *Vida Nova* (1988), *Renascer* (1993), *O Rei do Gado* (1996), *Esperança* (2002), and *Velho Chico* (2016)—*Meu Pedacinho de Chão* is an adaptation of the telenovela of the same name that Barbosa wrote in 1971. As is the case with all of Carvalho's previously adapted screenplays, *Meu Pedacinho de Chão* is a literal adaptation of Barbosa's earlier work.[1] However, as far as the audiovisual treatment of the text is concerned, it bears no similarities with the 1971 version, which was a realist melodrama. While it radically differs in audiovisual terms from its hypotext, *Meu Pedacinho de Chão* shares a seemingly endless number of similarities with Carvalho's other works.

The most obvious of these—the telenovela's blatant artificiality—is also the one that, along with theatricality, most characterizes Carvalho's work in television. Like Carvalho's other works discussed in this book, *Meu Pedacinho de*

FIGURE 8.1. Coronel Epaminonda's home, *Meu Pedacinho de Chão* (2015). Right to reproduce granted by TV Globo.

Chão begins with an elaborate, attention-grabbing opening scene that strongly evokes the opening of *Hoje é Dia de Maria*. As is the case with most of Carvalho's works, *Meu Pedacinho de Chão*'s opening both alerts the audience to and invites it to take part in the playful and fantastical narrative that is about to unfold. *Meu Pedacinho de Chão* begins with a computer-generated rooster perched atop Coronel Empaminonda's home, which is itself set in a computer-generated landscape that evokes a Portinari painting (figure 8.1).

Following the rooster's crow, which repeats throughout the telenovela, clocklike mechanisms also used at different moments in *Hoje é Dia de Maria* turn on, setting the story in motion. The obvious suggestion here is that the narrative is itself a fabrication, a kind of man-made mechanism. While all television is a fabrication on some level, unlike the vast majority of TV Globo's telenovelas *Meu Pedacinho de Chao*'s opening makes no effort to mask its artificiality. Instead, it asks that the spectator to suspend expectations so as to enter the world of imagination that gives life to Serelepe's story.

The first time the spectator sees Serelepe, almost in the exact same manner as Maria, he is joyfully skipping along singing a lullaby with his best friend Pituquinha (Geytsa Garcia). When the two friends climb a nearby tree, Serelepe grabs his telescope to survey the space below. A crane shot pulls back to reveal the village of Santa Fé. At this point, Serelepe begins to narrate in voice-over for the first time, telling the audience his name, the name of the village, and the season, spring; he also notes that the year does not matter. Serelepe then introduces the main characters, each of whom is presented by a cut intended to mimic Serelepe's point of view as he examines his surroundings through the telescope. To complete his introductory narration, Serelepe provides the viewer with the conflict that drives the narrative—the antiprogressive Coronel Empaminondas does not want to allow a school to open in the village. As is typical in classical Hollywood cinema, this sets off an action/reaction or reaction/action process that will need to be resolved by the end of the telenovela (Bordwell 19).

As we have seen, all of Carvalho's microseries use voice-over narration at some point. However, in *Meu Pedacinho de Chão,* the narration serves a slightly different function. TV Globo has traditionally set aside their post–prime-time slot (approximately 10:30 p.m.) for more experimental programming. Those audience members familiar with TV Globo's programming grid understand this to be the case. Consequently, when watching a work of fiction in post–prime time, viewers are likely to be more patient and open to new forms. Those same viewers familiar with TV Globo's programming grid understand the 6:25 p.m. time slot—commonly known as the time when the *telenovela das 6* (the six o'clock telenovela) airs—to be designated (since the early 1980s) for works based in an aesthetics of realism. While these may sometimes be ludic comedies, they very rarely, if ever, reach the extreme degree of playfulness and artificiality that characterizes *Meu Pedacinho de Chão.* As a result, the network's decision to schedule *Meu Pedacinho de Chão* in the 6:25 p.m. time slot ran the risk of alienating a significant portion of the audience accustomed to the more traditional telenovelas usually aired during that slot. Thus, Serelepe's expository narration is an attempt to reassure audiences that *Meu Pedacinho de Chão*'s narrative is similar to the telenovelas to which they have grown accustomed, despite the fact that in visual terms the telenovela is unlike any ever seen on Brazilian television.

Central to the uniqueness of the visual makeup of *Meu Pedacinho de Chão* is the space in which the narrative is set. As he did with *Hoje é Dia de Maria, A Pedra do Reino,* and *Capitu,* Carvalho creates an elaborate physical space that serves as the audiovisual manifestation of Serelepe's imagination and emotional state. While this is hinted at in the telenovela's opening with Serelepe's vantage point framing each shot, it is confirmed in the telenovela's last scene, when the image cuts from the fictional universe of Santa Fé to Serelepe in his present-day bedroom in his parent's apartment located in some large Brazilian city. In the bedroom, the spectator sees that Serelepe has been playing with a train set that includes a model of the village of Santa Fé as well as cutouts of all of the story's characters. Thus, what is hinted at in the opening is revealed in this last scene, as the viewer learns that all ninety-six chapters of the telenovela represent the physical manifestation of the fictional universe as Serelepe imagines it to be.

Figure 8.2. Village of Santa Fé, *Meu Pedacinho de Chão* (2015). Right to reproduce granted by TV Globo.

Since as early as *Uma Mulher Vestida de Sol*, Carvalho has shown an interest in creating fictional worlds not anchored in reality. These allow Carvalho the freedom to experiment with sound and image in ways that would otherwise not be possible. From the toylike buildings to the character's costumes, from the plants to the cyclorama, *Meu Pedacinho de Chão*'s *mise-en-scène* pops with vibrant pinks, blues, reds, greens, oranges, and yellows (figure 8.2).

In large part this is due to the fact that, as in *Hoje é Dia de Maria*, in *Meu Pedacinho de Chão* Carvalho sought to create a world shaped by the wonder and imagination of children. In doing so, Carvalho not only eliminated the many rules of realism that would ultimately limit his artistic freedom and possibilities for experimentation, he also invited viewers to reconnect with their own playful, childlike imaginations. Along these lines, *Meu Pedacinho de Chão*'s fictional universe evokes the well-known board game *Candyland*. Of course, as the spectator learns at the end of the story, Serelepe is actually projecting this world from his own train set.

Like the space, the characters in *Meu Pedacinho de Chão* possess a cartoonish quality that is brought to life by their theatrical acting and their costumes.[2] For example, not unlike the strong presence of the *caipira* used by the characters in *Hoje é Dia de Maria*, all of the actors in *Meu Pedacinho de Chão* speak with different accents that function to call attention to their acting. Additionally, their costumes are elaborate manifestations of their personalities. As his name suggests, Epaminondas Napoleão, for example, is the area's

FIGURE 8.3. Col. Epaminondas, *Meu Pedacinho de Chão* (2015). Right to reproduce granted by TV Globo.

FIGURE 8.4. Catarina, *Meu Pedacinho de Chão* (2015). Right to reproduce granted by TV Globo.

FIGURE 8.5. Zelão as Lucky Luke, *Meu Pedacinho de Chão* (2015). Right to reproduce granted by TV Globo.

FIGURE 8.6. Gina as Princess Merida, *Meu Pedacinho de Chão* (2015). Right to reproduce granted by TV Globo.

FIGURE 8.7. Zelão as John Snow from *Game of Thrones, Meu Pedacinho de Chão* (2015). Right to reproduce granted by TV Globo.

powerful political leader who is capable of doing some very bad things. His costumes evoke late-eighteenth/early-nineteenth-century France, and they are always black or other dark colors to emphasize his status as the villain. Epaminondas's wife, Catarina (Juliana Paes), also wears elaborate costumes that reference late-eighteenth-century regal France—particularly images of Marie Antoinette. Most characters' costumes, however, do not simply reference this single historical time and place. Instead, as Serelepe makes clear in his opening narration, the story of *Meu Pedacinho de Chão* takes place at an undetermined time. As such, the visual sources and citations span vast historical periods and geographical territories. For example, Zelão (Irandhir Santos), Epaminondas's right-hand man, and Gina (Paula Barbosa), Pedro Falcão's daughter, wear costumes that are direct copies of Belgian cartoonist Maurice De Bevere's comic series *Lucky Luke* (1946–2001) and of Princess Merida, the protagonist of Pixar's 2012 film *Brave*, set in the Scottish Highlands (figures 8.3, 8.4, 8.5, and 8.6).

While *Candyland* may be the *Meu Pedacinho de Chão*'s primary visual reference, the telenovela contains a seemingly endless number of intertextual references and citations that range from those mentioned above to Hollywood westerns, Fellini, Tim Burton, and HBO's *Game of Thrones*. Though the objective here is not to examine all the telenovela's references, it is important to mention some examples where Carvalho cites his own work. *Meu Pedacinho de Chão* is not the first time Carvalho has done so; in fact, he cites himself in all his previous works, sometimes explicitly, other times more subtly. Of course, not all viewers recognize these citations. For those who do, Carvalho offers the extra pleasure of having followed his trajectory over the years. Thus, whereas some might find it odd or perhaps beautiful when Ferdinando, a recent graduate in agricultural engineering and a lover of all things related to the land, erotically immerses his feet in fertile soil while sitting below a large tree, others will recognize this scene as a direct reference to a similar scene from *Lavoura Arcaica*. Similarly, when in Chapter 83 Carvalho includes an elaborate snowstorm that covers the Village Santa Fé, some spectators will make the connection between this scene and the snowstorm that occurs in *Hoje é Dia de Maria*. In both these scenes seemingly lost loves are found—Maria uncovers Amado, who is frozen, and Zelão, dressed like John Snow from *Game of Thrones*, declares his love to Juliana, who had previously thought their relationship over (figure 8.7).

Another example is the song *Chuá Chuá*—a Brazilian classic written in 1926 by Pedro de Sá Pereira. In Chapter 8, Viramundo (Gabriel Sater) begins to sing the song for Milita (Cintia Dicker); however, as the music echoes through the village, the entire cast, each going about their business, begins to sing along. Together they sing the chorus "Chuá Chuá. . . ." This song extends a practice Carvalho first began in *Hoje é Dia de Maria*. As discussed in Chapter 5, in that microseries a number of songs are performed: Maria sings rounds at different moments throughout the *Primeira Jornada*; with Amado, Maria also sings a beautiful duet version of Villa-Lobos's *Melodia Sentimental* (1950); and in the *Segunda Jornada*, the entire cast sings while performing a choreographed dance as they move through the streets of the city. Similarly, in *Afinal, o que Querem as Mulheres?* there is a nine-minute scene during André's dream in which, in a coffin at his own funeral, he sings an original song accompanied by his myriad love interests. Whereas in these microseries the songs performed by the respective casts represent important emotional turning points for the protagonists, in *Meu Pedacinho de Chão*, song functions more like a lyrical pause to the narrative, further suggesting that anything can happen at any moment in this fictional universe.

In addition to the cast's choral performance, music almost constantly accompanies the narrative, reinforcing a particular scene's amorous, comic, tragic, or tense tone in *Meu Pedacinho de Chão*. Like parts of *Hoje é Dia de Maria, A Pedra do Reino*, and *Afinal, o que Querem as Mulheres?* and all of *Capitu*, the presence of the music at times gives the telenovela an operatic tone. As he did for *Hoje é Dia de Maria, A Pedra do Reino, Capitu*, and *Afinal, o que Querem as Mulheres?*, Carvalho collaborated with musician Tim Rescala, who composed 28 original songs for the telenovela, all recorded by the Orquestra Sinfônica Heliópolis (Heliópolis Symphony) and the Coral da Gente

(Chorus of the People). In addition, Carvalho and Rescala selected ten songs by the North American band *DeVotchKa*. As is typical of a Brazilian telenovela, the band's song "How It Ends," made famous in 2006 when it was featured on the *Little Miss Sunshine*'s soundtrack, was exclusively played in scenes featuring the young beau Ferdinando.

What is apparent, then, even with a cursory examination of *Meu Pedacinho de Chão,* is that the telenovela gives continuity to the aesthetic developed by Carvalho in his shorter-format work. That this is the case lends support to Jean Renoir's claim that a director makes only one movie—or television work in Carvalho's case—in his life before breaking it into pieces and making it again (British Film). Thus, although *Meu Pedacinho de Chão* embodies a number of elements that have come to characterize the traditional Brazilian telenovela, the ties it maintains to Carvalho's earlier work—namely its obvious artificiality, aesthetic hybridity, and its relatively shorter run (ninety-six chapters)—combine to make *Meu Pedacinho de Chão* an anti-telenovela.

When placed within the context of Carvalho's professional trajectory, *Meu Pedacinho de Chão* can be understood as having brought a circle of production to a close. The majority of Carvalho's work leading up to *Meu Pedacinho de Chão* was in the shorter mini- or microseries formats, aired in post–prime-time slots, was experimental in audiovisual terms, included elaborate preproduction processes, and took place outside the confines of TV Globo's Projac Studios. With *Meu Pedacinho de Chão,* Carvalho returned to the longer telenovela format, as well as to Projac Studios and a prime-time slot. Nonetheless, it is clear that, although Carvalho returned to a production space similar to that of his previous telenovelas, he brought with him the experimental, anthropophagic aesthetic hybridity he had been developing since the early 1990s. Finally, or so it seemed, Carvalho had brought his singular, defamiliarized aesthetic to one of TV Globo's most important time slots and, therefore, to a significantly larger audience than that which consumes post–prime-time programming, which is home to his specials and microseries.

However, even within the changing landscape of Brazilian television, TV Globo decided that it was not ready for such drastic innovation in and changes to its prime-time programming. Since 2005, Carvalho's works have been fairly consistent in terms of audience share. Clearly, among these, *Hoje é Dia de Maria* (2005) was an exception, achieving a 34-point audience share. Relative to the other works, *Capitu* (2008) also did fairly well, with an average of 15.4 points. *A Pedra do Reino* (2007), *Afinal, o que Querem as Mulheres?* (2010), and *Subúrbia* (2012) all registered between about 10 and 12 points. While these numbers are considered at least serviceable for a post–prime-time program that competes with the increasing presence of pay television and the

Internet, they are not acceptable for a prime-time telenovela. Nonetheless, the experimental *Meu Pedacinho de Chão* did not fare much better, registering an average audience share of 18 points, which at the time rated as the worst in the history of the "*novela* das 6" time slot. Interestingly, in 2015, Carvalho's more traditional telenovela, *O Rei do Gado,* in its third re-airing since 1997 (1999 and 2011), was outperforming *Meu Pedacinho de Chão* in terms of audience share (Xavier, "Sucesso de "*O Rei*").

Armed with such numbers, renowned telenovela writer and TV Globo's newly appointed general director of dramaturgy, Sílvio de Abreu, made it clear that the network intends to forgo experimental telenovelas in favor of the classic model, which has proved so successful over the years. Not surprisingly, *Meu Pedacinho de Chão* was at the center of Abreu's explanation: As Maurício Stycer reports, "When questioned about *Meu Pedacinho de Chão,* directed by Luiz Fernando Carvalho, Abreu threw a bucket of cold water on those that imagined that the innovative experience could bear fruit: 'I do not know if it worked. The telenovela was praised; was very well done, but it was not what the public expects of a telenovela, so it's just an experiment'" ("Em novo cargo"). So what does the public want, at least according to Abreu? In the same article, the TV Globo executive declares that: "A telenovela is a feuilletonistic story with romance, with comedy, with drama, that entices the spectator to tune in every day. It has a hook before every commercial break and a strong hook at the end of every chapter. This is what the telenovela is and this is how it has to be done. Anything that goes against these characteristics does not work. So if you do not like the telenovela, go make a miniseries, series, or do something else, because the telenovela is this" (Stycer). Although he does not cite his name, Abreu's conservative declarations seem directed at Carvalho as they both explicitly and implicitly marginalize the potential for the director's work to go mainstream, at least within the context of TV Globo's structure. What is more, Abreu's declarations make an implicit argument for the continued presence of the writer as the telenovela's primary creative figure.

In light of Abreu's position regarding what a telenovela is and is not, it is perhaps not surprising that after Carvalho finished the microseries *Dois Irmãos,* whose airing was pushed back to 2017, the director began working on TV Globo's next *novela das nove, Velho Chico.* Written again by Benedito Ruy Barbosa, starring the expected mix of Carvalho devotees and recently discovered not yet famous actors, and shot in part on-location in northeastern Brazil, the network hoped that *Velho Chico* could reproduce the success of *O Rei do Gado* (Oliveira). The network made it clear to Carvalho, however, that he would not have the creative freedom to experiment in the ways he did, say, in *Hoje é Dia de Maria* or *Meu Pedacinho de Chão* (Oliveira). Thus, in the mold of *O Rei do Gado,* particularly in narrative terms, *Velho Chico* is best understood as an updated version of that traditional telenovela, representing Carvalho's aesthetic growth over the decade and a half that separates the two telenovelas, albeit without the striking artificiality and experimentation of his more contemporary works.

However, to TV Globo's dismay, more than halfway through, *Velho Chico,* like its predecessors *Babilônia* (2015) and *A Regra do Jogo* (2015–2016), has had difficulty in securing an average audience share above 30 points (Feltrin). For now, then, it seems that Carvalho's reimagination of contemporary Brazilian television fiction will continue to be disseminated as post–prime-time, shorter-format works and the cooptation of select experimental characteristics from these works will work their way into prime-time programming. Nonetheless, as Brazilian television continues to experience significant changes, influenced by the increased competitiveness of pay television and the Internet, conservative views such as Abreu's will likely develop along with those emerging models for understanding television fiction's place within the broader field of cultural production. For example, Michael Wolff points out that in the United States—at least as it pertains to English-language television:

> [The] television industry has been steadily weaning itself *off* advertising—like an addict in recovery, starting a new life built on fees from cable providers and all those monthly credit-card debits from consumers. Today, half of broadcast and cable's income is non-advertising based. And since adult household members pay the cable bills, TV content has to be grown-up content: *The Sopranos, Mad Men, Breaking Bad, The Wire, The Good Wife.* Looking for irony? Television, once maniacally driven by Nielsen ratings, has gone upscale as online media becomes an absurd traffic game. TV figured out how to monetize stature and influence. Nobody knows how many people saw *House of Cards,* and nobody cares. Mass-market TV upgraded to class, while digital media—e.g., listicles, saccharine viral videos—chased lowbrow mass. ("How Television Won")

TV Globo, and Brazilian television in general, is clearly not quite there; nor does it need to be, considering its still relatively high audience. However, when and if TV Globo, or some other network, does decide to "monetize stature and influence" on a wider scale, Carvalho, the most creative director working in Brazil today, will be ready and waiting, it seems, to continue to reimagine contemporary Brazilian television fiction.

NOTES

INTRODUCTION

1. Though not the focus of Lotz's book, Spanish-language television in the United States still operates based largely on a more traditional network model. However, because the discussion in the first part of the introduction centers on English-language television and because Brazilian television, the central focus of this book, is close to being, if not actually, a monolithic whole, I adopt Lotz's outline characterizing English-language television in the United States to consider the ongoing transitions to contemporary Brazilian television.

2. All translations of Carvalho's works, with the exception of *Lavoura Arcaica,* are my own. Because most of the titles for Carvalho's television programs have not been translated for the Anglophone market, I provide their literal translations in English. When introducing a new work or term I give the translation in parentheses; subsequent references will be in the original Portuguese. For a complete list of Portuguese and English titles, consult the table at the end of this introduction. Regarding all other translations, unless noted otherwise, in the absence of an existing English translation I have attempted to provide fairly literal translations of the original Portuguese.

3. With regard to more recent film production in Brazil, one could argue that it has had to be more market-oriented in order to receive government financing mechanisms. For example, a report from Brazil's National Bank of Economic and Social Development notes that for production companies to be selected to receive financing from government-sponsored funding mechanisms, they now have to present a business plan that includes a projection of the film's target audience and profit, a description of its distribution plan, and an evaluation of potential revenue from subsequent commercial endeavors such as Video on Demand and sales to other new media (Mello et al. 303).

4. See, for example, the four-volume *Televisão: Formas Audiovisuais de Ficção e de Documentário* (2011).

5. While he never took up the study of television fiction per se, in 1998 Bourdieu did publish the translated version *On Television*, a vehement cri-

tique of television journalism and public intellectuals' complicity in producing problematic and often simplistic discourses surrounding pressing and important news topics.

6. The debate surrounding auteur theory and the role of the director as an auteur has a long and contentious history in film studies. For more on this debate and the seminal texts related to it, see David A. Gerstner and Janet Staiger, *Authorship and Film* (2003) and Barry Keith Grant, *Auteurs and Authorship: A Film Reader* (2008).

CHAPTER ONE: ASSERTING THE CREATIVE ROLE OF THE TELEVISION DIRECTOR IN A WRITER'S WORLD

1. Carvalho made this clear to me during an email exchange I had with him shortly before the microseries went to air.

2. It is worth noting that in *Historiografia clássica do cinema brasileiro*, film scholar and historian Jean-Claude Bernardet questions the validity of this date and the intentions behind those historians who helped secure its virtually unquestioned place within the history of Brazilian cinema: "To encounter the 'true' birth [of Brazilian cinema] would be a statement of authenticity that would oppose that birth 'granted' by the colonizers; it would oppose, to use the words of Darcy Ribeiro, 'these false birth certificates such Pero Vaz de Caminha's letter and its equivalents'" (22). In short, Bernardet concludes, "With a birthdate securely established and chosen by them, the elite try to face the uncertainties of their identity" (22).

3. In the same work cited above, Bernardet takes issue with the historical construction of this period, arguing that it privileges the production aspect of Brazilian cinema over exhibition and public reception: "the historian's object of concern is basically production, for which he has a particular affection (since this historic discourse is designed to dignify production), hence the impossibility in which he finds himself to question any potential internal factors to production that might have contributed to its end . . ." (*Historiografia* 47). In fact, Bernardet questions if it is even possible to consider a periodization of Brazilian cinema as a national whole. He argues that historians outlined the accepted periodization of the history of Brazilian cinema with the notion of a fall driving it—that is, periods end and lead into the next by way of some kind of decline. For Bernardet, this notion of the fall supports the positioning of the *Bela Época* as a lost paradise or a utopia (47, 52).

4. It is important to note that, unlike Carvalho who is a full-time employee of TV Globo, the aforementioned directors either run their own production companies or are closely associated with a particular production company. This is relevant because of current laws, namely the Lei do Audiovisual (8.685)

and the Lei da TV Paga (12.485), which encourage independent production companies to develop projects for both film *and* television.

5. Even if Carvalho did not himself write this particular line, which seems unlikely considering he is a cowriter and that the character uses words the director himself used previously in an interview, we know that Carvalho had final say over the text. Thus, at the very least, he allowed the line to be included in the final version.

CHAPTER TWO: CREATING THROUGH THE PREPRODUCTION PROCESS

1. For more on this disconnect, see the discussion in Chapter One or Bernardet's *Brasil em tempo de cinema* and Johnson's *The Film Industry in Brazil.*

2. Carvalho is not using naturalism in the literary or philosophical sense, but in the way film studies uses the term to imply the utilization of a realist aesthetic and narrative construction.

3. In "O Núcleo Guel Arraes sua 'pedagogia dos meios,'" Yvana Fechine argues that those works deriving from Guel Arraes's TV Globo production nucleus use different forms of experimentation and metalanguage as a means for teaching the television audience how to "make and watch TV" (21). While Fechine's point is well made, when compared to Carvalho's work, Arraes's fiction is decidedly more centered on the spoken word and thus tends to be more explicitly didactic in its attempt to communicate with TV Globo's audience ("O Núcleo" 7). Put simply, while interesting and often experimental and theatrical, Arraes's work lacks the audiovisual depth of the intricate theatricality and aesthetic hybridity that distinguishes Carvalho's televisual production from its peers.

4. About his long-standing relationship with Carvalho, Fagundes says, "We have worked together since *Renascer* (1993). I made a package deal with Luiz: *Meu pedacinho de chão, Dois Irmãos* and *A Aldeia* (a forthcoming adaptation of Dostoyevsky's 1859 novel *The Village of Stepanchikovo*)" (Kogut, "Luiz Fernando Carvalho Prepara"). Rather than working on the latter, which is still in the earliest phases of preproduction, Fagundes took on a lead role in *Velho Chico* (2016).

5. Carvalho's *Alexandre e Outros Heróis* starring Ney Latorraca is an adaptation of Graciliano Ramos's homonymous collection of three children's stories, published posthumously in 1962. Television critic Patrícia Kogut declared the one-hour year-end special a "small masterpiece" (*"Alexandre e outros"*).

CHAPTER THREE: SETTING THE STAGE

1. Though those familiar with Carvalho's work could certainly point out other aesthetic influences from theater—namely Bertold Brecht, Augusto

Boal, or even the theatrical or operatic elements found in some of Glauber Rocha's work—this chapter primarily focuses on Artaud because, as is demonstrated in the development of the argument, more than an aesthetic model, Carvalho finds in the Frenchman's work a theoretical model for understanding his own creative production and a point of departure for challenging standardized Brazilian television.

2. "A minissérie também assinada por Luiz Fernando Carvalho, teve média geral de 34 pontos, em 2005—época em que a TV aberta registrava maior audiência" ("Also directed by Luiz Fernando Carvalho, the miniseries registered an audience-share average of 34 points in 2005—a period in which network television amassed larger audiences") ("Capitu Estreia"). As a point of comparison, a fictional program airing in a similar time slot today, within the context of an increasingly competitive Brazilian television market, would be considered successful if it were to capture 15 to 20 points. Fernando Meirelles's excellent miniseries *Som e Fúria* (2009), for example, failed to impress with an average of 15 points over its twelve episodes ("ADO A ADO"). Indeed, all of Carvalho's work following *Hoje é Dia de Maria* has averaged around 12 to 15 points.

3. Like the already cited Hamburger and others such as Borelli, Caparelli, Mattos, and Straubhaar, Brandão notes that because of its cost and rarity, television sets quickly became a status symbol in mid-century Brazil (*TV Tupi* 26).

4. The radioteatro first appeared in Brazil in the early 1920s. Like the teleteatro, but obviously without the latter's visual component, the radioteatro produced plays and sketches for the radio. The genre was particularly strong up until the late 1930s, early 1940s, when the radionovela became the medium's dominant genre.

5. The work's title is taken from Revelations 12:1–2, which reads: "Now a great sign appeared in heaven: a woman clothed with the sun [*uma mulher vestida de sol*], with the moon under her feet, and on her head a garland of twelve stars. Then being with child, she cried out in labor and in pain to give birth" (*The Holy Bible*).

CHAPTER FOUR: ESTABLISHING THE AESTHETIC TONE

1. The identification of and emphasis on these two motifs is in no way meant to indicate that they are the only motifs that appear repeatedly in Carvalho's works. For example, other recurring motifs include: the *sertão*, journey, impossible love, incest, and the figures of the innocent young brunette girl, the *cangaceiro,* the mother, and *Nossa Senhora*. Rather than exhaust the numerous motifs present in Carvalho's work, I have selected the color red and

the theater due to their consistent presence and their strong connections, in both symbolic and formal terms, to each other and to the director's overarching aesthetic.

2. The use of a blacked-out space here is a precursor to a creative technique Carvalho uses in *Lavoura Arcaica*. In that film, the blacked-out image represents the unclear psychological and emotional state in which the protagonist finds himself and from which he struggles to free himself (*Luiz Fernando Carvalho* 102).

3. This type of introduction adheres to Vladimir Propp's analysis of the folktale, wherein he argues that a fairy tale usually begins with a "temporal-spatial determination ('in a certain kingdom')," which is followed by a description of the composition of the family: a tale generally begins with some sort of initial situation. Subsequently, "The members of a family are enumerated, or the future hero (e.g., a soldier) is simply introduced by mention of his name or indication of his status" (*Morphology* 25, 120).

4. Though not discussed here, Carvalho uses the color red in *Os Maias* to represent the relationship between Pedro da Maia and Maria Monforte, which is the root of Maria Eduarda's death and their children's tragic, incestuous relationship.

CHAPTER FIVE: REDISCOVERING AND REAPPROPRIATING ANCESTRAL ROOTS

1. Though Carvalho seems unaware of *ancestralidade's* importance in critical race theory in Brazil, his employment of the term to describe his creative search for a uniquely Brazilian audiovisual language picks up on some of this theory's defining characteristics. For example, Carvalho's use of the term *ancestralidade* evokes the ways in which the term in critical race theory signifies an ongoing interactive process through which "oral and expressive practices . . . cultural values, knowledge and cosmovisions (worldviews), which stem from ancestral memory," burst forth from the past and through time to "shape ways of understanding and acting in the world" (Costa, "Afro-Brazilian" 665).

2. It is worth mentioning that title, "Educação Pelos Sentidos," is strikingly similar to the title of João Cabral Melo Neto's 1965 collection of poems titled *Educação pela pedra*.

3. One might also note a similarity between *ancestralidade* and what Gabriel García Marquez, in *One Hundred Years of Solitude*, refers to as "that *hereditary memory* [which] had been transmitted from generation to generation . . . " (emphasis added, 184).

4. *A fala caipira* refers to an accent or dialect of Portuguese associated with inhabitants (often undereducated) of rural São Paulo, Mato Grosso do Sul,

Goiás, and parts of Minas Gerais and Paraná. As mentioned in Chapter Two, the accent was practiced and emphasized through prosody workshops during the preproduction process for *Hoje é Dia de Maria*.

5. In addition to *Hoje é Dia de Maria*, Prado played important roles in Carvalho's miniseries and telenovelas *Riacho Doce* (1990), *Renascer* (1993), *Os Maias* (2001), and *Esperança* (2002).

6. Fernanda Montenegro also played starring roles in *Riacho Doce*, *Renascer*, and *Esperança*.

7. Regarding the symbolism of the shadow in universal and Brazilian folklore, Cascudo explains "Por todo o mundo a sombra é entidade julgada quase independente do corpo que a projeta" ("In all of the world the shadow is judged to be independent of the body that projects it") (*Dicionário* 718).

8. Cassiano's poem is representative of the ufanist, conservative, and nationalist movement known as *verdeamarelismo*, which was an ideological literary movement of Brazilian modernism that directly contrasted with Oswald de Andrade's *antropofagia*.

9. The original Portuguese reads as: "Esse é um mundo que tá pra ser feito e, no fundo de tudo, um defeito é degrau importante na escada do perfeito. Torto, pobre, ou malfeito, todo vivente pode andar reto, porque humano não é ruim, nem bom, humano é ser incompleto" (*Hoje é Dia* DVD).

10. In the back and forth between naturalism and antinaturalism and *Hoje é Dia de Maria*'s "rupturas ostensivas" (ostensive ruptures), Renato Luiz Pucci Jr. sees the microseries as having a link to postmodern cinema (5).

11. According to *Memória Globo*, *Renascer* was originally supposed to be titled *Bumba-meu-boi*, but was changed to the former following public opinion research ("*Renascer*").

CHAPTER SIX: TAKING THE SHOW ON THE ROAD

1. In fact, a cursory examination of any of the country's best-seller lists for fiction reveals that canonical and critically acclaimed Brazilian authors are missing. The one possible recent exception is Chico Buarque's *O Irmão Alemão*, which sold over 24,000 copies in 2015 ("Lista de mais"). Nonetheless, Buarque's commercial success can be explained by his overwhelming fame as one of Brazil's most important composers and performers of popular music.

2. Interestingly, in a 2006 interview, while still shooting *A Pedra*, Carvalho revealed that the second installment of the project was originally supposed to be João Paulo Cuenca's *Corpo Presente*, also set in Rio ("Sertão é 'semente'"). Although there is no definitive documentation of this, it seems that TV Globo shelved the adaptation of Cuenca's work in favor of producing *Capitu* to celebrate the centennial of Machado de Assis's death. For his part, Cuenca was

one of the screenwriters, along with Carvalho, Cecelia Gianetti, and Michel Melamed, for *Afinal, o que Querem as Mulheres?*

3. Following the completion of *Capitu* in 2009, reports surfaced that the *Projeto Quadrante* had been suspended indefinitely, despite Carvalho's denial that the project was initially set to air with a predetermined regularity ("Projeto Quadrante"). Then in August 2010, the *Folha de São Paulo* reported the project to be back on track with the pending production of *Dois Irmãos*. In October of 2011 journalist Daniel Castro reported the project was on hold again due to the relatively high production costs of *Dois Irmãos*. Finally, in March 2013, with TV Globo's rights to Milton Hatoum's novel set to expire for the second time, multiple outlets confirmed the production of an eight-episode microseries ("Globo retoma planos"). As of January 2015, Carvalho was putting his cast and crew through his unique preproduction process on-site in Manaus, with shooting set to wrap up in June the same year. Though Carvalho completed the microseries in the latter half of 2015, the airdate of the project was pushed back to early 2017, due to Carvalho beginning production for the prime-time telenovela *Velho Chico*.

4. The website address was: www.passeadiantecapitu.com.br.

5. The website address was: www.milcasmurros.com.br.

6. For the definitions of hypertext and hypotext, Stam refers to Gérard Genette's five types of transtextuality—(1) intertextuality, or the copresence of two texts; (2) paratextuality, or the relation within the totality of a literary work between the text proper and its paratext—that is, titles, prefaces, postfaces, epigraphs, dedications, illustrations; (3) metatextuality, or the critical relation between one text and another; (4) architextuality, or the generic taxonomies suggested or refused by the titles or subtitles of a text; and finally, (5) hypertextuality, or the relation between one text, a "hypertext," to an anterior text or "hypotext," which the former transforms, modifies, elaborates, or extends ("Introduction" 26–31). Thus, a hypotext is the source-text, whereas the hypertext is the text that results from an adaptation.

7. Although Carvalho has never officially proclaimed to be a part of or adhere to the *Movimento Armorial*, he is certainly aware of it as evidenced by his personal recommendation that I read both Fonseca dos Santos's study on Suassuna's *Movimento Armorial* and Suassuna's *Aula Magna* as some key sources for understanding his own aesthetic project.

8. In 1578, during the Battle of Alcácer Quibir, Dom Sebastião, the then King of Portugal was likely killed. However, many in Portugal believed that he simply disappeared and could return at any moment. This belief, combined with the certainty that his return would restore Portugal as a great world power, came to be known as Sebastianism.

9. A journalist, politician, and writer, Plínio Salgado is most famous for his participation in the nationalist literary movement Verde-Amarelo and for the creation of the ultraconservative, fascist political party Ação Integralista Brasileira (1932).

10. Made famous in Euclides da Cunha's *Os Sertões* (1902), A Guerra de Canudos was a bloody dispute in northeastern Brazil between the Republic and a political and religious community led by Antônio Conselheiro.

11. Led by Luís Carlos Prestes, the Coluna Prestes (Prestes Column) was largely a group of middle-class military men dissatisfied with the Republic. As a demonstration of their dissatisfaction, the armed men marched more than 40,000 miles, traversing Brazil from the south to the north. The 1930 Revolution was a military *coup d'état,* marking the end of the Republic and the beginning of Getúlio Vargas's nearly twenty-five-year reign as Brazil's political leader.

12. Found in Chapter 20, titled "Uma Voz Misteriosa," the passage reads: "Não desconheço—disse Luís Batista quando concluiu a sua expansão amorosa—, não desconheço que uma aventura destas, em véspera de noivado, produz igual efeito ao de uma ária de Offenbach no meio de uma melodia de Weber. Mas, meu caro amigo, é lei da natureza humana que cada um trate do que lhe dá mais gosto. A vida é uma ópera bufa com intervalos de música séria" (Assis, *Ressurreição*).

13. Although Joplin's song was included in the microseries network airing, it was not included in the commercialized DVD due to copyright restrictions.

14. The original Portuguese reads as follows: "Era um encanto ir por ele; às vezes, inconscientemente, dobrava a folha como se estivesse lendo de verdade; creio que era quando os olhos me caíam na palavra do fim da página, e a mão, acostumada a ajuda-los, fazia o seu ofício. . . . Eis aqui outro seminarista. Chamava-se Ezequiel de Sousa Escobar. Era um rapaz esbelto, olhos claros, um pouco fugitivos, como as mãos, como os pés, como a fala, como tudo" (105).

15. The original Portuguese reads as follows: "A princípio, fui tímido, mas ele fez-se entrado na minha confiança. Aqueles modos fugitivos, cessavam quando ele queria, e o meio e o tempo os fizeram mais pousados. Escobar veio abrindo a alma toda, desde a porta da rua até o fundo do quintal. A alma da gente, como sabes, é uma casa assim disposta, não raro com janelas para todos os lados, muita luz e ar puro. Também as há fechadas e escuras, sem janelas ou com poucas e gradeadas, à semelhança de conventos e prisões. Outrossim, capelas e bazares, simples alpendres ou paços suntuosos.

Não sei o que era a minha. Eu não era ainda casmurro, nem Dom casmurro; o receio é que me tolhia a franqueza, mas como as portas não tinham chaves nem fechaduras, bastava empurrá-las, e Escobar empurrou-as e entrou. Cá o achei dentro, cá ficou, até que . . ." (106).

16. The original Portuguese reads as follows: "Oh! minha doce companheira da meninice, eu era puro, e puro fiquei, e puro entrei na aula de S. José, a buscar de aparência a investidura sacerdotal, e antes dela a vocação. Mas a vocação eras tu, a investidura eras tu" (97).

17. Included in a letter to Luís Câmara Cascudo in 1925 and later published in *O Clã do Jabuti* (1927), the poem reads: "Abancado à escrivaninha em São Paulo Na minha casa da rua Lopes Chaves De supetão senti uma friagem por dentro Fiquei tremendo muito comovido. Com o livro palerma olhando pra mim. Não vê que me lembrei que lá no Norte, meu Deus!, muito longe de mim, na escuridão ativa da noite que caiu Um homem alado, negro de cabelo nos olhos. Depois de fazer uma pele com a borracha do dia Faz pouco se deitou, está dormindo. Esse homem é brasileiro que nem eu" (*Poesias completas*).

CHAPTER SEVEN: CHANGING WITH A CHANGING LANDSCAPE

1. For the most up-to-date figures, consult the Agência Nacional de Telecomunicações website.

2. Law 12.485/11 defines a Brazilian independent production company as adhering to the following conditions: (a) not controlling, controlled by, or affiliated with programmers, packers, distributors or dealers of sound and image broadcasting services; (b) not bound by a contractual instrument that, directly or indirectly, confers or seeks to confer to minority shareholders—when these are programmers, packers, distributors or dealers of sound and image broadcasting services—commercial veto rights or any type of commercial interference regarding produced content; (c) not maintaining an exclusive relationship that would prevent it from producing or selling their audiovisual content to third-parties (Lei da TV Paga).

3. MP no. 2.228/01 of Article 39 of the Lei do Audiovisual (2001) (The Audiovisual Law) is one of the existing financing mechanisms of interest to international pay television programmers needing to comply with the Law 12.485. As long as they invest 3 percent of income tax in projects previously approved by ANCINE, Article 39 provides international pay television programmers an exemption from having to pay the Contribuição para o Desenvolvimento da Indústria Cinematográfica (CONDECINE) (Contribution for the Development of the Film Industry) levy, which is the equivalent of 11 percent of international remittances (Cesnik et al., "Brasil" 44–45). In other words, MP no. 2.228/01 of Article 39 provides pay television programmers a financial incentive to invest funds that would otherwise be lost to the government in local production.

4. Law 12.485 defines a Brazilian channel as a programming entity that executes its programming activities in Brazil; is incorporated under Brazilian law; and has its headquarters and management in the country. To qualify as a Brazilian channel, 70 percent of the total voting capital must be owned, directly or indirectly, by native Brazilians or those who have been naturalized for more than ten years; and whose management, editorial responsibility, and selection of channel programming must be reserved exclusively for native Brazilians or those who have been naturalized for a period of more than ten years (Lei da TV Paga).

5. Regarding the long-standing dominance of Brazilian produced content over that which is imported, see Joseph D. Straubhaar, "Brazilian Television: The Decline of American Influence," *Communication Research* 11.2 (1984): 221–40. Also along these lines, for a discussion of cultural proximity see Straubhaar, "Choosing National TV: Cultural Capital, Language, and Cultural Proximity in Brazil." *The Impact of International Television: A Paradigm Shift* (2003): 77–110.

6. As is the case with pay television, the Internet in Brazil is not equally accessible across the country's five different regions. Access is the highest in the southeastern and southern regions and lowest in the northern and northeastern regions. As stated previously with regard to the breakdown of the pay television numbers, these two broad geographical categories respectively represent the richest and poorest areas in Brazil.

7. The NeoTV association describes itself as being "responsible for negotiating content for independent operators in pay television and Internet, helping them in the format products. The organization also plays an important institutional role in the telecommunications industry, representing the interests of its members and fomenting competition and market competitiveness" ("História").

8. Carvalho's fifth microseries since 2005, *Subúrbia* (*Periphery*) premiered on TV Globo at 11:30 p.m. on Thursday, November 1, 2012. The remaining seven chapters of the microseries aired over the next seven Thursdays, coming to an end on December 20, 2012. The title *Subúrbia* is the generally nonexistent feminine of the more commonly used masculine word *subúrbio*. Despite its similarity to the English word suburb, *subúrbio* actually refers to the *redondezas* or outskirts of a city. Generally speaking, *subúrbio* denotes a marginalized space that is largely home to members of the C-Class. For this reason, I have translated the title to the English *Periphery*.

9. Written by João Emanuel Carneiro, *Avenida Brasil*'s 180 chapters cost approximately $45 million to produce. Estimates put the telenovela's total earnings at $1 billion (Antunes, "Brazilian Telenovela").

10. The figure of *Nossa Senhora da Conceição Aparecida* is another one of the motifs that runs throughout much of Carvalho's work, beginning with his 1994 special *Uma Mulher Vestida de Sol.*

11. For the better part of the 1960s, Cinema Novo directors focused on creating films that simultaneously *represented* and *aesthetically embodied* the country's poverty-stricken, unequal, and violent social reality. At the time, this meant low-budget, on-location shoots in marginalized spaces, and the frequent use of nonprofessional actors. The result was what the movement's figurehead Glauber Rocha referred to as "ugly, sad . . . screaming, desperate films" (Rocha, "The Aesthetics of Hunger" 70). Political engagement was a central consideration for determining content and the manner in which the filmmakers represented that content. For example, in his now famous theorization of the "aesthetics of hunger," Rocha aggressively argues that the filmmaker "ready to place his cinema and his profession at the service of the great causes of his time" represents "the correct definition which sets Cinema Novo apart from the commercial industry because the commitment of industrial cinema is to untruth and exploitation" (70–71). In no way do I intend to imply here that *Suburbia* (or *Cidade dos Homens,* discussed later in the chapter) shares the political and ideological engagement that characterized Cinema Novo. What is more, though they reappropriate certain production aspects of Cinema Novo, the two TV Globo produced series were decidedly more commercial and more aesthetically polished and technically refined than any typical film from the 1960s movement.

12. In another example of TV Globo's and Carvalho's interest in convergence media, he selected four actors out of 1,500 hundred applications submitted to TV Globo's Facebook page. The actors selected were: Renata Tavares, Vanessa Correa, André Dread, and Cássio Arbues ("*Suburbia*" *Memória Globo*).

13. The term *favela* was likely first used sometime around the end of the nineteenth century to refer to irregular hillside housing settlements in Rio de Janeiro. The word itself is believed to reference a hillside in northeastern Brazil known as Monte Favela; or possibly favela bushes from Canudos, a community that sat at the base of Monte Favela. Whatever its origin, the term has since taken on a negative connotation, signaling an impoverished, sometimes irregular, but always marginalized—albeit to different degrees—settlement, often home to drug trafficking and violence (Janice Perlman, *Favela: Four Decades of Living on the Edge in Rio de Janeiro* (Oxford: Oxford UP, 2010), 24–28.

14. *Brava Gente* was a TV Globo holiday special composed of eight independent thirty-minute specials. Each special was based on adaptations of national or international literature or plays that were set to air back to back

over a four-day period beginning on December 26, 2000 (Dicionário da TV Globo 543).

15. For more on the critique surrounding Mierelles's film see Ivana Bentes, "The Aesthetics of Violence in Brazilian Film," in *City of God in Several Voices: Brazilian Social Cinema as Action*, ed. Else R.P. Vieira (Nottingham: Critical, Cultural and Communications Press, 2005). 82–92.

16. To be clear, Ismail Xavier argues that Rocha's supposed criticism, both in formal and narrative terms, of the religious beliefs of the Brazilian people is more complex than it might otherwise appear at the surface level. Whatever the case, it is clear that religion is not the answer to this population's systemic problems, as it is in *Suburbia*. See "*Barravento*: Glauber Rocha 1962, alienação vs. identidade," *Discurso* 13 (1980): 53–86.

CONCLUSION: REIMAGINING THE (ANTI-)TELENOVELA

1. Barbosa is careful to emphasize that *Meu Pedacinho de Chão* was not a remake of his 1971 telenovela: "This *telenovela* has nothing to do with the other, only the names of the characters and locations. The present *telenovela* was an opportunity to say things that censorship would not allow me to say in 1971. This time I could talk about politics, health, and education" ("*Meu Pedacinho de Chão*"). Though Barbosa certainly altered and elaborated on his previous work, a summary of the earlier work's plot reveals that it is very similar to the current version.

2. For *Meu Pedacinho de Chão*, costume designer Thanara Schönardie replaced longtime Carvalho collaborator Luciana Buarque. Schönardie's elaborate costumes were such a success that there was a special three-month-long exposition at the Biblioteca Parque Estadual in Rio de Janeiro and a photo book, edited and released by TV Globo.

BIBLIOGRAPHY

"95% de novos clientes de TV por assinatura são classe C ou D." *Exame* (Apr. 23, 2013): n.pag. July 7, 2013.

"*A Pedra do Reino.*" *Memória Globo.* n.d. n.pag. Jan. 22, 2011.

"Acervo." *Projeto Portinari.* n.d. n.pag. Apr. 4, 2012.

"Ado Ado: *Som e Fúria* é Cancelado!" *TV Contacto* (Apr. 25, 2012): n.pag. June 12, 2012.

Adorno, Theodor W. "Television and the Mass Culture Patterns." *Quarterly of Film, Radio and Television* (U of California P) 8(1954): 213–35.

Allen, Woody, dir. *Manhattan.* 20th Century Fox, 2000. DVD.

Almeida, Candido José Mendes de, and Maria Elisa de Araújo. *As perspectivas da televisão brasileira ao vivo.* Rio de Janeiro: Imago Ed.: Centro Cultural Candido Mendes, 1995.

Altberg, Marco. "Brazilian Independent Television Production and the Multi-Platform Industry." *The Expanding Brazilian Film, Television, and Digital Industry / Cinema, televisão e mídia digital no Brasil: Uma indústria em expansão.* Edited by Steve Solot. Rio de Janeiro: LATC, 2016. 125–35.

Alzugaray, Paulo. "Os Maias: Superprodução da Rede Globo deve ser mais um *Titanic* para a emissora." *Isto É Gente.* n.d. n.pag. Web. Oct 1, 2009.

Anderson, Benedict. *Imagined Communities: Reflections on the Origin and Spread of Nationalism.* New York: Verso Books, 2006.

Andrade, Mário de. *Aspectos da literatura brasileira.* 5th ed. São Paulo: Martins, 1974.

Andrade, Mário de. *Macunaíma, o herói sem nenhum caráter.* Rio de Janeiro: Nova Fronteira, 2013.

Andrade, Mário de. *Poesias completas.* Edição crítica de Diléa Zanotto Manfio. Belo Horizonte: Itatiaia, 2005.

Andrade, Oswald. *Obras completas de Oswald de Andrade.* 2nd ed. Vol. VI. Rio de Janeiro: Civilização Brasileira, 1978.

Antunes, Anderson. "Brazilian Telenovela *Avenida Brasil* Makes Billions by Mirroring Its Viewers' Lives." *Forbes* (Oct. 19, 2012): n.pag. Apr. 20, 2014.

Appleby, David P. *The Music of Brazil.* Austin: U of Texas P, 1989.

Araújo, Joel Zito. *A negação do Brasil: o negro na telenovela brasileira.* São Paulo: Senac, 2000.

Artaud, Antonin. *The Theater and Its Double.* New York: Grove Press, 1958.

"Asmodeu." *Infopédia.* Porto: Porto Editora, 2003–2013. n.d. n.pag. Mar. 7, 2013.

Assis, Joaquim Maria Machado de. *Dom Casmurro.* São Paulo: Martin Claret, 2000.

Assis, Joaquim Maria Machado de. *Dom casmurro: A Novel.* Translated by John Gledson. New York: Oxford UP, 1998.

Assis, Joaquim Maria Machado de. *Ressurreição.* Rio de Janeiro: Civilização Brasileira, 1977.

"Ateliê." *Hoje é Dia de Maria.* n.d. n.pag. July 1, 2008.

Bakhtin, Mikhail Mikhailovich. *The Dialogic Imagination: Four Essays.* Vol. 1. Austin: U of Texas P, 2010.

Becker, Howard Saul. *Art Worlds.* Berkeley: U of California P, 1982.

Bentes, Ivana. "The Aesthetics of Violence in Brazilian Film," *City of God in Several Voices: Brazilian Social Cinema as Action.* Edited by Else R.P. Vieira. Nottingham: Critical, Cultural and Communications Press, 2005. 82–92.

Bergamo, Alexandre. "A reconfiguração do público." *História da televisão no Brasil: Do início aos dias de hoje.* Edited by Ana Paula Goulart Ribeiro, Igor Sacramento, and Marco Roxo. São Paulo: Contexto, 2010. 59–83.

Bernardet, Jean-Claude. *Brasil em tempo de cinema: Ensaio sobre o cinema brasileiro de 1958 a 1966.* São Paulo: Companhia das Letras, 2007.

Bernardet, Jean-Claude. *Historiografia clássica do cinema brasileiro.* São Paulo: Annablume, 2008.

Bernardo, Gustavo. *O problema do realismo de Machado de Assis.* São Paulo: Rocco, 2011.

Bordwell, David, et al. *The Classical Hollywood Cinema: Film Style & Mode of Production to 1960.* New York: Columbia UP, 1985.

Borelli, Silvia Helena Simões. *Ação, suspense, emoção: literatura e cultura de massa no Brasil.* São Paulo: FAPESP; EDUC, 1996.

Borelli, Silvia Helena Simões, and Gabriel Priolli. *A deusa ferida: por que a Rede Globo não é mais a campeã absoluta de audiência.* São Paulo: Summus Editorial, 2000.

Bourdieu, Pierre. *In Other Words: Essays Towards a Reflexive Sociology.* Translated by M. Adamson. Cambridge: Polity, 1994.

Bourdieu, Pierre. *On Television.* Translated by Priscilla Parkhurst Ferguson. New York: New Press, 1998.

Bourdieu, Pierre. *Sociology in Question.* Translated by Richard Nice. London: Sage, 1993.

Bourdieu, Pierre. *The Field of Cultural Production. Essays on Art and Literature.* Edited by Randal Johnson. New York: Columbia UP, 1993.

Bourdieu, Pierre. *The Outline of a Theory of Practice.* Translated by Richard Nice. Cambridge: Cambridge UP, 1977.

Brandão, Cristina. "As primeiras produções teleficcionais." *História da televisão no Brasil: Do início aos dias de hoje.* Edited by Ana Paula Goulart Ribeiro, Igor Sacramento, and Marco Roxo. São Paulo: Contexto, 2010. 37–56.

Brandão, Cristina. *O grande teatro Tupi do Rio de Janeiro: O teleteatro e suas múltiplas faces.* Juiz de Fora: Editora da UFJF, 2005.

British Film Institute (@BFI). "A director only makes one film in his life. Then he breaks it into pieces & makes it again." Sept. 15, 2015, 11:46 a.m. Tweet.

Brittos, Valério Cruz, and Denis Gerson Simões. "A reconfiguração do mercado de televisão pré-digitilização." *História da televisão no Brasil: Do início aos dias de hoje.* Edited by Ana Paula Goulart Ribeiro, Igor Sacramento, and Marco Roxo. São Paulo: Contexto, 2010. 219–38.

Bueno, Luís. "Nação, Nações: Os Modernistas e a Geração de 30." *Via Atlântica* 7 (2004): 83–97.

"Cadernos de anotações." *A Pedra do Reino.* n.d. n.pag. Mar. 5, 2010.

Caetano, Maria Rosário do. *Fernando Meirelles: Uma biografia prematura.* São Paulo: Imprensa Oficial, 2007.

Caldeira, Teresa Pires do Rio. *City of Walls: Crime, Segregation, and Citizenship in São Paulo.* Berkeley: U of California P, 2000.

Caldwell, John. *Televisuality: Style, Crisis, and Authority in American Television.* New Brunswick: Rutgers UP, 1995.

Canclini, Néstor García. *Imagined Globalization.* Durham: Duke UP, 2014.

Candido, Antônio. "Dialética da malandragem." *Revista do Instituto de Estudos Brasileiros* 8 (1970): 67–89.

Candido, Antônio. "Literatura e subdesenvolvimento." *A Educação pela noite e outros ensaios.* 3rd ed. São Paulo: Ática, 2000. 140–60.

"Candido Portinari." *Projeto Portinari.* n.d. n.pag. Apr. 4, 2012.

Caparelli, Sérgio. *Televisão e capitalismo no Brasil.* PA: LP&M, 1982.

"*Capitu.*" *Memória Globo.* n.d. n.pag. June 10, 2010.

"*Capitu'* estréia bem e lidera audiência no horário." *Estadão.com.* n.d. n.pag. Dec. 10, 2008.

"Caracterização." *Hoje é Dia de Maria.* n.d. n.pag. July 1, 2008.

Cardoso, Ronie Filho. "As minisséries nos processos da TV: O caso *Hoje é Dia de Maria.*" Dissertação de Doutorado em Ciências da Comunicação São Leopoldo: Universidade do Vale do Rio dos Sinos, 2009.

Cardwell, Sarah. "'Television Aesthetics' and Close Analysis: Style, Mood and Engagement in *Perfect Strangers.*" *Style and Meaning: Studies in the Detailed Analysis of Film.* Edited by John Gibbs and Douglas Pye. Manchester: Manchester UP, 2005. 179–94.

Carvalho, José Murilo de. "The Edenic Motif in the Brazilian Social Imaginary." *Revista brasileira de ciências sociais* SPE1 (2000): 111–28.

Carvalho, Luiz Fernando, dir. *A farsa da boa preguiça*. Globo Universidade DVD, 1995.

Carvalho, Luiz Fernando, dir. *A Pedra do Reino*. Globo Marcas DVD, 2007.

Carvalho, Luiz Fernando, dir. *Afinal, o que Querem as Mulheres?* Globo Universidade DVD, 2010.

Carvalho, Luiz Fernando, dir. *Capitu*. Globo Marcas DVD, 2009.

Carvalho, Luiz Fernando. *Diários de elenco de equipe: A Pedra do Reino*. São Paulo: Globo, 2007.

Carvalho, Luiz Fernando. "Educação Pelos Sentidos." *Caderno Rio Mídia III* 23 (2008): 23–27.

Carvalho, Luiz Fernando, dir. *Hoje é Dia de Maria*. Globo Marcas DVD, 2005.

Carvalho, Luiz Fernando. Interview by Alexandre Werneck. "Luiz Fernando Carvalho (não) está grávido." *Contracampo*. n.d. n.pag. Oct. 26, 2009.

Carvalho, Luiz Fernando. Interview by Carlos Helí de Almeida. "Luiz Fernando Carvalho: 'Não corro atrás de elogios.'" *JB Online*. n.d. n.pag. Mar. 15, 2010.

Carvalho, Luiz Fernando. Interview by Esther Hamburger. "Sertão é 'semente' de *A Pedra do Reino*." *Folha de São Paulo Ilustrada* (Dec. 17, 2006): n.pag. May 5, 2010.

Carvalho, Luiz Fernando. Interview by Geraldo Bessa. "Diretor de *Subúrbia* quer mostrar periferia sem caricaturas." *Terra* (Nov. 3, 2012): n.pag. Feb. 24, 2012.

Carvalho, Luiz Fernando. Interview by *O Estado de São Paulo*. "*Lavoura Arcaica* estréia sábado no Canadá." *O Estado de São Paulo* (Aug. 22, 2001): n.pag. Aug. 13, 2009.

Carvalho, Luiz Fernando. Interview by Patrícia Villalba. "Uma Comédia Filosófica." *Estado de São Paulo Caderno 2* (Oct. 13, 2010): n.pag. Oct. 19, 2010.

Carvalho, Luiz Fernando. Interview by Renato Félix. "Entrevistas: Luiz Fernando Carvalho." *Boulevard do crepúsculo* (Aug. 27, 2009): n.pag. Dec. 12, 2009.

Carvalho, Luiz Fernando. Interview by Rodrigo Grota. "A subversão: Entrevista com Luiz Fernando Carvalho." *Revista Taturana* (Nov. 3, 2009): n.pag. Feb. 2, 2012.

Carvalho, Luiz Fernando. Interview by Valmir Santos. "Carvalho invoca a cultura popular em microssérie." *Folha de São Paulo* (Jan. 9, 2005): n.pag. Mar. 12, 2009.

Carvalho, Luiz Fernando. *Luiz Fernando Carvalho: Sobre o filme Lavoura Arcaica*. Cotia: Ateliê Editorial, 2002.

Carvalho, Luiz Fernando, dir. *Uma mulher vestida de sol*. Globo Universidade DVD, 1994.

Cascudo, Luís da Câmara. *Antologia do folclore brasileiro*. São Paulo: Martins, 1971.

Cascudo, Luís da Câmara. *Dicionário do folclore brasileiro*. São Paulo: Melhoramentos, 1979.

Castro, Natália, and Thaís Britto. "A TV se rende à nova classe media: Mobilidade social no país influencia a programação dos canais de televisão" (May 20, 2012): n.pag. Aug. 5, 2013.

Castro Rocha, João Cezar de. "The 'Dialectic of Marginality': Preliminary Notes on Brazilian Contemporary Culture." *Centre for Brazilian Studies, University of Oxford, Working Paper Number* 62 (2005): 1–39.

"Celulares substituem telefones fixos em domicílios brasileiros." *Brazil.gov* (Mar. 13, 2013): n.pag. Jan. 13, 2016.

Cesnik, Fábio de Sá, and Jucá, Roberto Drago Pelosi. "Brasil." *Current Mechanisms for Financing Audiovisual Content in Latin America 2.* Edited by Steve Solot. Rio de Janeiro: Latin American Training Center, 2014. 39–48.

Clark, Walter, and Fernando Barbosa Lima. "Um pouco de história e de reflexão sobre a televisão brasileira." *TV ao vivo: Depoimentos.* Edited by Cláudi Macedo, Angela Falcão, and Candido José Mendes de Almeida. São Paulo: Brasiliense, 1988. 25–44.

"Classe C elimina gastos, mas preserva internet e TV paga: Serviços são vistos como forma de manter filhos seguros em casa." *O Tempo* (May 3, 2015): n.pag. June 20, 2015.

"Classe C já é maioria da população do País." *Portal Brasil* (Mar. 22, 2012): n.pag. Feb. 18, 2015.

Costa, Alexandre Emboaba Da. "Afro-Brazilian *Ancestralidade*: Critical Perspectives on Knowledge and Development." *Third World Quarterly* 31.4 (2010): 655–74. May 12, 2014.

Crook, Larry, and Randal Johnson. "Introduction." *Black Brazil: Culture, Identity, and Social Mobilization.* Edited by Larry Crook and Randal Johnson. Los Angeles: UCLA Latin American Center Publications, 1999. 1–13.

Cruz, Breno de Paula Andrade. "O fenômeno 'social TV' na Classe C e as mudanças na programação da Rede Globo." *Academia.edu.* n.d. n.pag. Apr. 15, 2014.

Debord, Guy-Ernest. *The Society of the Spectacle.* New York: Zone Books, 1994.

Dicionário da TV Globo, vol. 1: *Programas de dramaturgia & entretenimento.* Rio de Janeiro: Jorge Zahar, 2003.

"Dúvidas freqüentes." *Ibope.* n.d. n.pag. Apr. 9, 2012.

Epstein, Adam. "Television Is Being Taken over by Filmmakers, and That's a Beautiful Thing." *Quartz* (Sept. 30, 2014): n.pag. Mar. 12, 2015.

"Exposição de arte marca o lançamento do seriado "*Afinal, o que Querem as Mulheres?*" *Área vip.* (Nov. 5, 2010): n.pag. Apr. 25, 2012.

Fechine, Yvana. "O Núcleo Guel Arraes e sua 'pedagogia dos meios.'" *Revista da associação nacional* 8 (2007): 1–22. Aug. 17, 2009.

Feldman, Ilana. "A Pedra do Reino: A *opera mundi* de Luiz Fernando Carvalho." *Cinética.* n.d. n.pag. May 15, 2009.

Feltrin, Ricardo. "Ibope instável de *Velho Chico* acende alerta vermelho na Globo." *UOL TV e Famosos* (June 13, 2016): n.pag. June 20, 2016.

"Figurno." *Hoje é Dia de Maria.* n.d. n.pag. July 1, 2008.

"Filmes brasileiros com mais de 500 mil espectadores entre 1970–2011." *ANCINE.* n.d. n.pag. Nov. 15, 2012.

Fonseca, Rodrigo. "Luiz Fernando Carvalho desbrava a periferia no seriado, *Subúr-bia*." *O Globo* (Sept. 8, 2012): n.pag. June 12, 2015.

Freedman, Des. *The Contradictions of Media Power*. London: Bloomsbury, 2014.

Freire Filho, João. "O debate sobre a qualidade da TV no Brasil: da trama dos discur-sos à tessitura das práticas." *Discursos e Práticas de Qualidade na Televisão da Eu-ropa e América Latina*. Edited by Gabriela Borges, Vitor Baptista, and Vítor Reia. Lisbon: Livros Horizonte, 2008.

Freire Filho, João. "Por uma nova agenda de investigação da história da TV no Brasil." *Contracampo* 10.11 (2004): 201–17. Aug. 12, 2008.

Freire Filho, João. "TV de qualidade: Uma contradição em termos?" *Líbero* 4.7–8 (2001): 86–95. Aug. 12, 2008.

Freyre, Gilberto, and Samuel Putnam. *The Masters and the Slaves (Casa-Grande & Senzala): A Study in the Development of Brazilian Civilization*. New York: Knopf, 1946.

Gallagher, Mark. *Another Steven Soderbergh Experience: Authorship and Contempo-rary Hollywood*. Austin: U of Texas P, 2013.

García, Márquez Gabriel, and Gregory Rabassa. *One Hundred Years of Solitude*. New York: Harper Perennial Modern Classics, 2006.

Gerstner, David A., and Janet Staiger. *Authorship and Film*. New York: Routledge, 2003.

"Giramundo." *Hoje é Dia de Maria*. n.d. n.pag. July 1, 2008.

"Globo lança minissérie com dois personagens de *Cidade de Deus*." *Folha de São Paulo* (Oct . 4, 2002): n.pag. Dec. 2, 2009.

Goes, Tony. "Novela da Globo dar menos audiência é o 'novo normal.'" *Folha.Uol* (Mar. 31, 2015): n.pag. June 11, 2015.

Grant, Barry K. *Auteurs and Authorship: A Film Reader*. Malden, MA: Blackwell, 2008.

Grijó, Wesley Pereira, and Adam Henrique Freire Sousa. "O negro na telenovela bra-sileira: A atualidade das representações." *Estudos em Comunicação* 11 (2012): 185–204.

Grossberg, Lawrence. *Cultural Studies in the Future Tense*. Durham: Duke UP, 2010.

"Grupo Teatro Mambembe." *Enciclopedia Itaú Cultural: Teatro* (Oct. 16, 2007): n.pag. Feb. 25, 2012.

Guia ilustrado TV Globo: Novelas e miniséries. Rio de Janeiro: Jorge Zahar Ed., 2010.

Guimarães, Ana Beatriz Wiltgen da Costa. "Itinerância teatral no Brasil do século XX: História & desdobramentos no processo atorial." *Cadernos virtuais de pesquisa em artes cênicas* 1 (2010): 1–10.

Guimarães, Hélio. "Literatura em televisão: Uma história das adaptações de textos literários para programas de TV." Diss. Unicamp, 1995.

Haberly, David T. "The Brazilian Novel from 1850 to 1900." *The Cambridge History of Latin American Literature*. Edited by Roberto González Echevarría. Vol. 3. New York: Cambridge UP, 1996. 137–56.

Haberly, David T. *Three Sad Races: Racial Identity and National Consciousness in Brazilian Literature*. New York: Cambridge UP, 1983.

Hamburger, Esther, et al. *A TV aos 50: Criticando a televisão brasileira no seu cinqüentenário*. São Paulo: Editora Fundação Perseu Abramo, 2000.

Hamburger, Esther. *O Brasil antenado: A sociedade da novela*. Rio de Janeiro: Jorge Zahar Editor, 2005.

Hamburger, Esther. "Violência e pobreza no cinema brasileiro recente: Reflexões sobre a ideia de espetáculo." *Novos Estudos* 78 (2007): 113–28.

Havens, Timothy, Amanda D. Lotz, and Serra Tinic. "Critical Media Industry Studies: A Research Approach." *Communication, Culture & Critique* 2 (2, 2009): 234–53.

Helmore, Edward. "Silver Screen to Small Screen: Why Film Directors Are Taking over TV." *The Guardian* (Mar. 15, 2014): n.pag. Mar. 12, 2015.

"História." *Associação NeoTV*. n.d. n.pag. June 20, 2015.

Hogan, Patrick Colm. "Auteurs and Their Brains: Cognition and Creativity in the Cinema." *Visual Authorship: Creativity and Intentionality in Media*. Edited by Torben Grodal, Bente Larsen, and Iben Thorving Laursen. Copenhagen: U of Copenhagen P, 2005. 67–86.

"Hoje é Dia de Maria." *Memória Globo*. n.d. n.pag. Dec. 18, 2011.

Holanda, Sérgio Buarque de. *Roots of Brazil*. Translated by G. Harvey Summ. South Bend: U of Notre Dame P, 2012.

Houaiss, Antônio, and Mauro de Salles Villar. *Minidicionário Houaiss da língua portuguesa*. Rio de Janeiro: Objetiva, 2004.

"Ibope: Audiência de todos os episódios de *Suburbia*." *Telemaniacos*. n.d. n.pag. Feb. 9, 2013.

"Ibope de *A Pedra do Reino* faz Globo reavaliar series." *Estadão* (Aug. 22, 2007): n.pag. Mar. 14, 2009.

Jacob de Souza, Maria Carmem. *Telenovela e representação social Benedito Ruy Barbosa e a representação do popular na Telenovela Renascer*. São Paulo: E-Papers, 2000.

Jacobs, Jason. "Issues of Judgement and Value in Television Studies." *International Journal of Cultural Studies* 4.4 (2001): 427–47.

Jenkins, Henry. *Convergence Culture: Where Old and New Media Collide*. New York: New York UP, 2006.

Jimenez, Keila. "TV paga quer manter em 2015 crescimento de 11%." *Folha de São Paulo* (Oct. 15, 2014): n.pag. Oct. 17, 2014.

Johnson, Randal. "Brazilian Modernism: An Idea out of Place?" *Modernism and Its Margins*. Edited by A.L. Geist and J.B. Monleón. New York: Garland Publishing, 1999. 186–214.

Johnson, Randal. "The Dynamics of the Brazilian Literary Field, 1930–1945." *Luso-Brazilian Review* (1994): 5–22.

Johnson, Randal. *The Film Industry in Brazil*. Pittsburgh: U of Pittsburgh P, 1987.

Johnson, Randal. "Pierre Bourdieu on Art, Literature and Culture." *The Field of Cultural Production*. Edited by Randal Johnson. New York: Columbia UP, 1993. 1–25.

Johnson, Randal, and Robert Stam. *Brazilian Cinema: Expanded Edition*. New York: Columbia UP, 1995.

Joyce, Samantha Nogueira. *Brazilian Telenovelas and the Myth of Racial Democracy*. Lanham: Lexington Books, 2012.

Jung, Carl. *The Archetypes and the Collective Unconscious*. Princeton: Princeton UP, 1981.

Jung, Carl. *Mandala Symbolism*. Princeton: Princeton UP, 1972.

Kehl, Maria Rita, et al. *Um país no ar: História da TV brasileira em 3 canais*. São Paulo: Brasiliense/FUNARTE, 1986.

Kogut, Patrícia. "*Alexandre e outros heróis*: uma pequena obra-prima na Globo." *O Globo: Patrícia Kogut* (Dec. 20, 2013): n.pag. Dec. 22, 2013.

Kogut, Patrícia. "Luiz Fernando Carvalho mergulha no mundo dos ciganos da Rússia, Sérvia e Polônia para construir sua nova série de TV, *A Aldeia*." *O Globo* (Aug.30, 2011): n.pag. Dec. 6, 2011.

Kogut, Patrícia. "Luiz Fernando Carvalho prepara a minissérie *Dois Irmãos*." *O Globo: Revista da TV* (Feb.15, 2015): n.pag. Feb. 25, 2015.

Lafetá, João Luiz. *1930: A Crítica e o Modernismo*. Sao Paulo: Duas Cidades, 1974.

La Pastina, Antonio C., Joseph D. Straubhaar, and Lirian Sifuentes. "Why Do I Feel I Don't Belong to the Brazil on TV?" *Popular Communication* 12 (2014): 104–16.

Leal, Ondina Fachel. *A Leitura Social da Novela das Oito*. Petrópolis: Vozes, 1986.

Lei da TV Paga 12.485, de 11.09.2011.

Lima, Fabio. "Digital Distribution and VOD in Brazil." *The Expanding Brazilian Film, Television, and Digital Industry / Cinema, televisão e mídia digital no Brasil: Uma indústria em expansão*. Edited by Steve Solot. Rio de Janeiro: LATC, 2016. 153–64.

Lima, Heverton Souza. "A lei da TV paga: impactos no mercado audiovisual." Master's thesis. Universidade de São Paulo, 2015.

"Lista de mais vendidos de 2015: Ficção." *Publishnews.com* (Mar. 17, 2015): n.pag. Mar. 17, 2015.

Lotz, Amanda D. *The Television Will Be Revolutionized*. 2nd ed. New York: New York UP, 2014.

Machado, Arlindo. *A televisão levada a sério*. São Paulo: Editora Senac, 2005.

Maerz, Melissa, and Nicole Sperling. "Film Directors Are Embracing TV." *LA Times* (June 5, 2011): n.pag. Mar. 12, 2015.

Martín-Barbero, Jesús. *Communications, Culture, and Hegemony*. Translated by E. Fox and R. White. London: Sage, 1993.

Maton, Karl. "Habitus." *Pierre Bourdieu: Key Concepts*. Edited by Michael Greenfell. Durham: Acumen, 2008. 49–66.

Mattos, Sérgio. *Um perfil da TV brasileira*. Salvador: A Tarde, 1990.

Meirelles, Fernando, dir. "Uólace e João Victor." *Cidade dos Homens.* TV Globo, 2002–2005. DVD.

Mello, Gustavo Afonso Taboas de, Marcelo Goldenstein, and Rafael Ferraz. "O audio-visual brasileiro em um novo cenário." *BNDES setorial, Rio de Janeiro* 38 (2013): 291–327.

"*Meu Pedacinho de Chão.*" *Memória Globo.* n.d. n.pag. Feb. 15, 2015.

Mello e Souza, Gilda de. *O tupi e o alaúde: uma interpretação de Macunaíma.* São Paulo: Editora 34, 2003.

Meyer, Marlyse. *Folhetim: Uma história.* São Paulo: Companhia das Letras, 1996.

Miller, Toby. *Television Studies: The Basics.* New York: Routledge, 2009.

Miranda, André. "Aprovada após cinco anos de polêmica, lei da TV por assinatura cria cotas para o conteúdo nacional." *O Globo* (Sept. 22, 2011): n.pag. 8 9 15.

Mitchell, Jasmine. "Popular Culture Imaginings of the Mulatta: Constructing Race, Gender, Sexuality, and Nation in the United States and Brazil." Diss., University of Minnesota, 2013.

Mittell, Jason. "Best Stuff of 2014." *Just TV: Random Thoughts from Media Scholar Jason Mittell.* n.pag. Dec. 30, 2014.

Mittell, Jason. *Complex TV: The Poetics of Contemporary Television Storytelling.* New York: New York UP, 2015.

Moreira, Roberto. "Vendo a televisão a partir do cinema." *A TV aos 50: Criticando a televisão brasileira no seu cinqüentário.* Org. Esther Hamburger e Eugênio Bucci. São Paulo: Editora Fundação Perseu Abramo, 2000. 49–64.

Nakagawa, Fábio Sadao. "As espacialidades em montagem no cinema e na televisão." Diss. Universidade de São Paulo, 2008.

Ndalianis, Angela. "Neo-Baroque to Neo-Baroques?" *Revista Canadiense de Estúdios Hispânicos* 33.1 (2008): 265–80. Mar. 1, 2013.

"O *Ver TV* analisa os programas voltados para a chamada 'nova classe C.'" *Ver TV* (May 6, 2012): n.pag. Jan. 12, 2013.

"Oficinas." *Capitu.* n.d. n.pag. Dec. 18, 2011.

Oliveira, Fernando. "Globo veta 'ousadias' em próxima novela das 21h, de Benedito Ruy Barbosa." *Folha de São Paulo* (Oct. 18, 2015): n.pag. June 20, 2016.

Ortiz, Renato. *Moderna tradição brasileira.* 5th ed. São Paulo: Brasiliense, 2006.

"Papéis avulsos." *Capitu.* n.d. n.pag. Dec. 18, 2011.

Passos, José Luiz. *Romance com pessoas: A imaginação em Machado de Assis.* Rio de Janeiro: Editora Objetiva, 2014.

Passos, José Luiz. *Ruínas de linhas puras: quatro ensaios em torno a Macunaíma.* São Paulo: Annablume, 1998.

Peacock, Steven, and Jason Jacobs, eds. *Television Aesthetics and Style.* New York: Bloomsbury Publishing USA, 2013.

Perlman, Janice. *Favela: Four Decades of Living on the Edge in Rio de Janeiro.* Oxford: Oxford UP, 2010.

Porto, Mauro. *Media Power and Democratization in Brazil: TV Globo and the Dilemmas of Political Accountability*. New York: Routledge, 2012.

Proença, Manuel Calvacanti. *Roteiro de Macunaíma*. 4th ed. Rio de Janeiro: Civilização Brasileira, 1977.

"*Projeto Quadrante* suspenso na Globo." *O Diário* (June 26, 2009): n.pag. Feb. 16, 2010.

Propp, Vladimir. *Morphology of the Folktale*. Austin: U of Texas P, 2000.

Pucci, Reanto Luiz Jr. "A televisão brasileira em nova etapa?: *Hoje é Dia de Maria* e o cinema pós-moderno." Trabalho apresentado ao Grupo de Trabalho "Fotografia, cinema e vídeo," do XIX Encontro da Compós, na PUC-RJ, Rio de Janeiro. Dec. 2, 2010. 1–17.

"Qual a faixa de renda familiar das classes?" *Fundação Getúlio Vargas—Centro de Políticas Sociais* (Jan 1, 2014): n.pag. Nov. 13, 2014.

Queiroz, Maria Isaura Pereira de. "Sociologia e folclore—O bumba-meu-boi, manifestação de teatro popular no Brasil." *Revista do instituto de estudos brasileiros* 2 (1967): 87–97.

Rajewsky, Irina O. "Intermediality, Intertextuality, and Remediation: A Literary Perspective on Intermediality." *Intermédialités: Histoire et théorie des arts, des lettres et des techniques/Intermediality: History and Theory of the Arts, Literature and Technologies* 6 (2005): 43–64.

Ramos, Fernão, et al. *História do cinema brasileiro*. São Paulo: Art Editora, 1987.

Ramos, José Mario Ortiz. *Televisão, publicidade e cultura de massa*. Petrópolis: Vozes, 1995.

Rangel, Manoel. Interview by *Ver TV*. "*Ver TV*—Entrevista com Manoel Rangel, diretor da ANCINE." Online video clip. *YouTube* (Nov. 7, 2014): n.pag. Nov. 15, 2014.

Rêgo, Cacilda. "Centering the Margins: The Modern Favela in the Brazilian Telenovela." *Brazil in Twenty-First Century Popular Media: Culture, Politics, and Nationalism on the World Stage*. Edited by Naomi Pueo Wood. Lanham: Lexington, 2014. 91–111.

"Renascer." *Memória Globo*. n.d. n.pag. Dec. 18, 2011.

Ribeiro, Ana Paula Goulart, and Igor Sacramento. "A renovação estética da TV." *História da televisão no Brasil: Do início aos dias de hoje*. Edited by Ana Paula Goulart Ribeiro, Igor Sacramento, and Marco Roxo. São Paulo: Contexto, 2010. 109–35.

Rocha, Glauber, dir. *Deus e o diabo na terra do sol*. Rio de Janeiro: Civilização Brasileira, 1965.

Rocha, Glauber. "The Aesthetics of Hunger." *Brazilian Cinema: Expanded Edition*. Edited by Randal Johnson and Robert Stam. New York: Columbia UP, 1995. 69–71.

Rosas-Moreno, Tania Cantrell. *New and Novela in Brazilian Media: Fact, Fiction, and National Identity*. Lanham: Lexington, 2014.

Sacramento, Igor. "Depois da revolução, a televisão: Cineastas de esquerda no jornalismo televisivo dos anos 1970." Diss. UFRJ, 2008.

Said, Edward. *Orientalism*. London: Penguin, 2003.

Sales, Jaqueline. *Hoje é Dia de Maria: Livreto-Brinde junto ao DVD*. Rio de Janeiro: Globo/Som Livre, 2006.

Salles, João Moreira. "Imagens em conflito." *O cinema do real*. Edited by Maria Dora Mourão e Amir Labaki. São Paulo: Cosac Naify, 2005. 82–95.

Santos, Idelette Muzart Fonseca dos. *Em demanda da poética Popular: Ariano Suassuna e o Movimento Armorial*. Campinas: Editora da Unicamp, 1999.

Schatz, Thomas. "The Whole Equation of Pictures." *Film Theory and Criticism*. 6th ed. Edited by Leo Braudy and Marshall Cohen. New York: Oxford UP, 2004. 653–56.

Schepelern, Peter. "The Making of an Auteur: Notes on the Auteur Theory and Lars Von Trier." *Visual Authorship: Creativity and Intentionality in Media*. Edited by Torben Grodal, Bente Larsen, and Iben Thorving Laursen. Copenhagen: U of Copenhagen P, 2005. 103–27.

Sevcenko, Nicolau. *Literatura como missão: Tensões sociais e criação cultural na primeira república*. São Paulo: Brasiliense, 1983.

Shklovsky, Viktor. "Art as Technique." *Literary Theory: An Anthology*. Edited by Julie Rivkin and Michael Ryan. Malden: Blackwell, 2004. 15–21.

"*Segunda Jornada*." *Memória Globo*. n.d. n.pag. Dec. 18, 2011.

Setoodeh, Ramin, and Todd Spangler. "Filmmakers Moving Where the Money Is: Digital TV Series." *Variety* (Apr 30, 2014): n.pag. Mar. 12, 2015.

Silva, Denise Ferreira da. "The Drama of Modernity: Color and Symbolic Exclusion in the Brazilian Telenovela." *Black Brazil: Culture, Identity, and Social Mobilization*. Edited by Larry Crook and Randal Johnson. Los Angeles: UCLA Latin American Center Publications, 1999. 339–61.

Simpson, Amelia. *Xuxa: The Mega-Marketing of Gender, Race, and Modernity*. Philadelphia: Temple UP, 1993.

Singleton, Brian. *Le Théâtre et son Double*. London: Grant & Cutler, 1998.

Smith, Anthony D. *Ethno-Symbolism and Nationalism: A Cultural Approach*. New York: Routledge, 2009.

Smith, Anthony D. *The Antiquity of Nations*. Cambridge: Polity, 2004.

Smith, Anthony, and Richard Patterson, eds. *Television: An International History*. Oxford: Oxford UP, 1998.

Smith, Christen A. *Afro-Paradise: Blackness, Violence, and Performance in Brazil*. Urbana: U of Illinois P, 2016.

Soares, Luiz Eduardo. "*Suburbia*: A intensidade e a supremacia da forma." *O Globo* (Nov. 15, 2012): n.pag. Sept. 17, 2014.

"Social Mission." *Rede Globo*. n.d. n.pag. Jan. 2, 2014.

Soffredini, Carlos Alberto. *Hoje é Dia de Maria*. Roteiro Original. Santos: Mimeo, 1995.

Sovik, Liv. "We Are Family: Whiteness in the Brazilian Media." *Journal of Latin American Cultural Studies* 13.3 (2004): 315–25.

Stam, Robert. *Film Theory: An Introduction.* Oxford: Blackwell, 2000.

Stam, Robert. "Hybridity and the Aesthetics of Garbage: The Case of Brazilian Cinema." *Estudios Interdisciplinarios de América Latina y El Caribe* n.pag. 9.1 (1998). E.I.A.L. Nov. 25, 2006.

Stam, Robert. "Introduction: The Theory and Practice of Adaptation." *Literature and Film: A Guide to the Theory and Practice of Film Adaptation.* Edited by Robert Stam and Alessandra Raengo. Oxford: Blackwell, 2005. 1–52.

Straubhaar, Joseph D. "Brazilian Television: The Decline of American Influence." *Communication Research* 11.2 (1984): 221–40.

Straubhaar, Joseph D. "Choosing National TV: Cultural Capital, Language, and Cultural Proximity in Brazil." *The Impact of International Television: A Paradigm Shift* (2003): 77–110.

Straubhaar, Joseph D. "The Dominant Markets—Brazil." *Latin American Television Industries.* London: Palgrave, 2013.

Straubhaar, Joseph D. "Telenovelas in Brazil: From Travelling Scripts to a Genre and Proto-Format Both National and Transnational." *Global Television Formats: Understanding Television across Borders* (2012): 148–77.

Stycer, Maurício. "Em novo cargo, Sílvio de Abreu decreta o fim das inovações em novela." *UOL TV e Famosos* (Nov. 19, 2014): n.pag. July 3, 2015.

Suassuna, Ariano. *Farsa da boa preguiça.* Rio de Janeiro: José Olympio, 1974.

Suassuna, Ariano. *Romance d' A Pedra do Reino e o Príncipe do Sangue do Vai-e-Volta.* Rio de Janeiro: José Olympio, 1971.

Suassuna, Ariano. *Uma mulher vestida de sol.* Recife: Universidade do Recife, 1964.

"Subúrbia." *Memória Globo.* n.d. n.pag. Feb. 15, 2011.

"Superávit." *Porta dos Fundos.* Online video clip. YouTube, Aug. 20, 2012. Sept. 9, 2015.

Susman, Gary. "Why Are Top Movie Directors Defecting to TV?" *Moviefone* (June 8, 2011): n.pag. Mar. 12, 2015.

Szalai, George. "Study: U.S. Posted First Full-Year Pay TV Subscriber Drop in 2013." *The Hollywood Reporter* (Mar. 19, 2014): n.pag. Oct. 20, 2014.

Tacey, David. *The Jung Reader.* New York: Routledge, 2012.

"Taperoá." *A Pedra do Reino.* n.d. n.pag. Apr. 9, 2012.

Tardivo, Renato. *Porvir que vem antes de tudo: Literatura e cinema em Lavoura Arcaica.* São Paulo: Ateliê Editorial, 2012.

Televisão: Formas Audiovisuais de Ficção e de Documentário. Faro e São Paulo. Volume I-IV (2011–2015).

Telles, Edward E. *Race in Another America: The Significance of Skin Color in Brazil.* Princeton: Princeton UP, 2004.

The Holy Bible, King James Version. New York: Oxford Edition, 1769.

"The World Factbook: Brazil." *Central Intelligence Agency* (June 23, 2014): Nov. 11, 2014.

Thompson, Ethan, and Jason Mittell. *How to Watch Television*. New York: New York UP, 2013.

Thompson, John B. *Ideology and Modern Culture*. Stanford: Stanford UP, 1990.

Thompson, John B. *The Media and Modernity: A Social Theory of the Media*. Palo Alto: Stanford UP, 1995.

Thorburn, David. "Television as an Aesthetic Medium." *Critical Studies in Media Communication* 4.2 (1987): 161–73.

Travers, Ben. "10 Best TV Shows Created by Filmmakers." *IndieWire* (May 9, 2014): n.pag. Web. Mar 12, 2015.

"TV paga registra 18,9 milhões de assinantes em maio de 2016." *Agência Nacional de Telecomunicações* (June 14, 2016): n.pag. Web. July 21, 2016.

"TV por assinatura cresce 9,53% nos dois bimestres de 2012." *Agência Nacional de Telecomunicações* May 28, 2012): n.pag. Web. June 23, 2015.

Vaidhyanathan, Siva. "'Big Bird and Big Media': What *Sesame Street* on HBO Means." *Time* (Aug. 21, 2015): n.pag. Web. Aug. 30, 2015.

Waugh, Patricia. *Metafiction: The Theory and Practice of Self-Conscious Fiction*. Florence: Routledge, 1984.

Wheatley, Jonathan. "Brazil's Winning Game Plan." *The Financial Times* (June 5, 2008): n.pag. Web. Apr. 4, 2015.

Wolff, Michael. "How Television Won the Internet." *New York Times* (June 29, 2015): n.pag. Web. June 29, 2015.

Xavier, Ismail. *Alegorias do subdesenvolvimento: Cinema Novo, Tropicalismo, Cinema Marginal*. São Paulo: Cosac Naify, 2012.

Xavier, Ismail. "*Barravento*: Glauber Rocha 1962, alienação vs. identidade." *Discurso* 13 (1980): 53–86.

Xavier, Ismail. "Brazilian Cinema in the 1990s: The Unexpected Encounter and the Resentful Character." *The New Brazilian Cinema*. Edited by Lúcia Nagib. London: I.B. Tauris, 2003. 39–64.

Xavier, Ismail. "Do texto ao filme: A trama, a cena e a construção do olhar no Cinema." *Literatura, cinema e televisão*. Edited by Tânia Pellegrini. São Paulo: Editora Senac, 2003. 61–90.

Xavier, Ismail. "Ismail Xavier: Sobre a Globo Filmes." Online video clip. *YouTube* (Nov. 5, 2009): n.pag. Dec. 31, 2009.

Xavier, Nilson. "Sucesso de *O Rei do Gado* aponta opção do público por novelões clássicos." (Feb. 22, 2015): n.pag. Web. June 27, 2015.

INDEX

Note: Page numbers in *italics* refer to figures.

Abreu, Luis Alberto de, 176
Abreu, Silvio de, 246
actors/casts, 15, 43, 47; Carvalho's goals
 for, 61, 63–64, 182–83; Carvalho
 using non-famous, 181–82, 225–26;
 in *Lavoura Arcaica,* 182; nonprofessional, 226; of *A Pedra do Reino,*
 178–79; in preproduction process,
 50–52, 56; selection based on
 location, 181–83, 259n12; sharing
 Brazilian-ness, 61–62; working with
 Carvalho, 52, 60; workshops and
 seminars for, 15, 58–64
adaptations, 49; Carvalho's *aproximação*
 vs., 8, 185; changing media in,
 184–85
Adorno, Theodor, 50
advertising, 184; audience interaction
 with television and, 69–70; large audiences attracting, 25, 44; television
 funding from, 9–10, 247
aesthetic hybridity, Carvalho's, 89, 183,
 185, 225; *ancestralidade* and, 136–37,
 139, 147; as characteristic, 246,
 251n3; effects of, 112, 118; goals of,
 67, 132, 168–73, 202–4; in opening
 scenes, 91–93, 118
A Farsa da Boa Preguiça, 70–71, *102,*
 109, *110*
Afinal, o que Querem as Mulheres?, 21,
 245, 254n2; aesthetic experimentation in, 75–76; Carvalho's critiques
 of television fiction in, 51, 87, 165;

clapperboards in, *40–41;* compared
 to other Carvalho works, 223, 244;
 confusion of past and present in,
 120–22; director character in, 38–42;
 Livia in, *37,* 38–39; as metafiction,
 29–44; *mise-en-scène* in, *119,* 244;
 narration in, 112–13; objectification
 of women in, 121–22; opening scene
 of, *31, 32,* 98, 120; red motif in, *129,*
 130; space in, 87–89, *88,* 121–22;
 theatricality of, *129,* 130; writer *vs.*
 director in, 15, 28
Afro-Brazilians, 221–23, 226, 230, 233
Alexandre e Outros Heróis, 59, 251n5
Allen, Woody, 32, 36
Almeida, Manuel Antônio de, 232–33
Altberg, Marco, 214
Amado, in *Hoje é Dia de Maria,* 83,
 127–28, 144–45
A Moderna Tradição Brasileira (Ortiz),
 174
ancestralidade (ancestrality), 135–39,
 138, 173, 253n3; Carvalho's use of,
 142, 253n1; ethics and, 146–48;
 influences outside Brazil in, 168–69;
 Projeto Quadrante as exchange of,
 180–81; shared content of, 146–47,
 151, 156, 192
ANCINE, 214–15
Andrade, Mário de, 140–41, 146, 210
Andrade, Oswald de, 136
André Newmann, in *Afinal, o que Quer-*
 em as Mulheres?, 29, 38–39, 43–44;